W9-ACY-562

Compassionate Cuisine

125 PLANT-BASED RECIPES FROM OUR VEGAN KITCHEN

LINDA SOPER-KOLTON AND SARA BOAN

STORIES BY KATHY STEVENS

PHOTOGRAPHY BY ALEXANDRA SHYTSMAN

A COOKBOOK FROM CATSKILL ANIMAL SANCTUARY

Skyhorse Publishing

CATSKILL
ANIMAL SANCTUARY

Skyhorse Publishing books may be purchased in bulk at special discounts for sales promotion, corporate gifts, fund-raising, or educational purposes. Special editions can also be created to specifications. For details, contact the Special Sales Department, Skyhorse Publishing, 307 West 36th Street, 11th Floor, New York, NY 10018 or info@skyhorsepublishing.com.

Skyhorse® and Skyhorse Publishing® are registered trademarks of Skyhorse Publishing, Inc.®, a Delaware corporation.

Visit our website at www.skyhorsepublishing.com.

10 9 8 7 6 5 4 3 2 1

Library of Congress Cataloging-in-Publication Data is available on file.

Cover design by Sean M. Smith/Echo66
Cover photo credit by Alexandra Shytsman

Print ISBN: 978-1-5107-4437-0
Ebook ISBN: 978-1-5107-4438-7

Printed in China

Contents

Kelly Mullins, Animal Care Director, and rescued goat Leo who was blind and deaf from birth

Dedication

To the animals. All of them, everywhere. For the ones who have called this place home, who have been given names, who are known to us, and who have quietly changed the hearts, minds, and appetites of thousands upon thousands of people. And for the ones who still suffer, who are exploited, who are neglected, who are nameless—we know you, too, and we are coming for you. With every breath and with each bite, with hope in our hearts and fire in our bellies, we are coming for you.

May you know what love feels like one day.

To the people. For the compassionate choices you make each day and for the ones we hope you are inspired to make tomorrow, thank you.

To the staff and volunteers at Catskill Animal Sanctuary, past, present, and future. For choosing work that serves and defends the defenseless. For every keystroke, task, project, letter, post, report, and appeal that makes this sanctuary hum. For every day you work—with joyful or broken hearts—undeterred by blistering heat or bone-chilling cold, to tend to each and every animal with tenderness and respect. For all the loving kindness each one of you pours into the lives of our friends. For emptying your hearts into your work each and every day. For teaching, inspiring . . . and hoping. You are true heroes.

To Kathy. For encouraging . . . and demanding the urgency that pulses through our veins. For your pain-filled tears and raucous laughter, for your wide-open heart, and for creating this unique and magical place. Your love lives on in every two-legged and four-legged creature fortunate enough to have been touched by your spirit.

With awe and gratitude,
Linda

Welcome to Our World

It's there when I walk in the barn:
a love so palpable I often feel my heart will explode.
—from "Introduction," *Where the Blind Horse Sings* by Kathy Stevens

These words are as true today as they were when I wrote them thirteen years ago. As Catskill Animal Sanctuary nears its twentieth anniversary, we've had our fair share of challenges . . . and yet, as an organization, we still insist on love. Our tagline, "Love Spoken Here," embodies a philosophy that informs all that we do, from how we engage with each other to every public interaction, from how we welcome broken beings to this place of profound peace to how we say our final goodbyes to those same beloveds, often many years later. "With love" is *how* we do our work. We wouldn't have it any other way.

Let's be clear, however, that Catskill Animal Sanctuary also wants the world to go vegan, and *vegan* is not always a term that's synonymous with love. Nor do we want this change to happen *someday.* Nope—we want it right now. This vision of a world free from suffering is why over five thousand rescued farmed animals have called Catskill home since we opened our doors in 2001, but it's also why we welcome thousands of visitors from around the globe each year. They come to learn about the impact of their diet on the animals, their health, and our ailing planet; but they come, primarily, to meet the animals. And friends, that's when the magic happens. It's in the disarming moments between a human heart and an animal heart that the marriage of love

and urgency lives out its promise. *Vegan* really is synonymous with *love*—at least it surely is at Catskill Animal Sanctuary.

You see, when a first-time visitor sits quietly among the turkeys, immersed in the grace and forgiveness and wholeheartedness of these remarkable beings; or when Zeke the sheep walks up, his only agenda to connect, soul to soul, in the way that he does; or when a herd of cows accompanies us back to the gate after we've visited their pasture, there's often a profound shift inside that human heart. These moments and others like them disarm us. They invite us to understand that in the ways that truly matter, whether child or chicken, dog or duck, we *really are* very much the same. We are all delightfully individual. We all have rich, nuanced emotional lives that inform how we engage in the world. We all want our lives, and we want them filled with joy. Just because our culture discourages us from understanding this obvious truth doesn't make it untrue, and no human can share this truth as powerfully as the animals.

At Catskill Animal Sanctuary, we know full well the impact of these moments: we witness the tears that often accompany them or hear words like the ones from a recent visitor, who, overcome, took my forearms in his hands and, with tears streaming down his face, said simply, "I get it now. Please tell me what to do."

Love and urgency: our special sauce, rooted in the belief that people are good.

For sure, a narrower mission would have been an easier choice. To rescue and provide a safe haven for animals—or, alternatively, to run a center for vegan programming—either of these choices would have been simpler and more straightforward. But would they have been as effective? I dare say no. Absolutely not. The fact that 93 percent of our non-vegan visitors say they intend to reduce or eliminate animal products from their diet is proof that what we're doing—that unique combination of love and urgency, of connecting people with animals and supporting them in their vegan journey—is working.

And of course, the animals are just one of several compelling reasons for humanity to embrace vegan living. We've known for many years that animal agriculture—the raising or catching of *trillions* of animals (including sea animals) annually to feed humans—is the single leading cause of today's most urgent environmental challenges: global warming, water pollution, ocean dead zones the size of entire states, topsoil erosion, species extinction, and sea level rise, with oceans already encroaching on many coastal regions. It takes exponentially more land, water, and air to feed a meat- and dairy-eater than to feed a vegan, and with the human population projected to reach ten billion by mid-century, and Earth incapable of expanding to accommodate that growth, we're on an insane and self-destructive collision course that can only be halted if one by one— *and quickly*—humanity says, "I get it. I'm done. I will not participate."

And, oh, the personal benefits of making that choice! Despite what we've been taught about the necessity of animal protein for optimum health, the truth about the health costs of the Standard American Diet are well-established, with dramatically increased risks of heart disease, stroke, high blood pressure, type 2 diabetes, many forms of cancer, Alzheimer's disease, Parkinson's disease, gastrointestinal troubles, acne, and many other ailments linked to—you got it—our consumption of meat and dairy products.

Catskill Animal Sanctuary chooses to believe in the goodness in all of us. Healing broken beings and offering a joyous, expansive, peaceful space for people to be with and among animals whose "who-ness" they've never considered: these are some of the ways we change hearts, minds, and behavior. Another way is through food, hence the reason for this cookbook.

Inside these pages you'll also find stories of our animals: raucous chickens and fragile blind horses, a wise old cow and some sheep who'll work their way into your heart and stay there, singing. We are an animal sanctuary, after all, so here they are, saying hello through these pages, reminding you of why the choice to go vegan matters.

These are our friends. This is our food. Welcome to Catskill Animal Sanctuary.

—Kathy Stevens, founder and executive director

WHAT WE DO

Catskill Animal Sanctuary rescues farmed animals and champions veganism. The Sanctuary serves as a safe haven to these animals and offers educational programs to help people experience farm animals as the unique individuals they are and to educate people about their institutionalized suffering.

The Homestead

Located at the top of our 148-acre property, where it has stood since 1813, The Homestead is a home away from home for visitors. We converted this farmhouse into a guest house so that people could come to linger over breakfast, deeply connect with our animals, and learn about why we do what we do.

Tours

Through individual stories of our animal residents, trained tour guides teach visitors about what farmed animals endure and what we can do to help them. A day at the Sanctuary allows you to see chickens, pigs, horses, and other feathered or four-legged friends in a new way.

New Leaf Vegan Mentor Program

Whether you're committed to the ethics of vegan living or seeking a healthier, more ecologically friendly lifestyle, our New Leaf Vegan Mentor Program connects trained mentors with individuals for one-on-one support, answering questions, sharing information, discussing challenges, and celebrating successes. They'll help with shopping, meal creation, dining out, nutritional advice, networking, and more.

Camp Kindness

Camp Kindness, a summer day program, is one of several youth programs offered at the Sanctuary. Interactions with the rescued farmed animals connect children with their inner sense of kindness, compassion, and justice, and encourages them to see animals for who

they are, not what they can do for humans. A day at camp might include visiting the cows, taste-testing different vegan milks, learning about the links between animal agriculture and the environment, enjoying a vegan lunch, and feeding willow leaves to the goats!

Welcome to Our Kitchen

Compassionate Cuisine is the name of our vegan culinary program—and it's also our philosophy about food. We chose this name for our program, and for this book, because we believe that eating can be kind to animals, to our bodies, and to our planet. Our goal is to inspire, educate, and empower people to make meals using plant-based food—and to love doing it.

Over the years, Compassionate Cuisine has evolved to include a wide variety of activities. Our public cooking classes are more popular than ever: in fact, we are proud to have been recognized by *Hudson Valley Magazine* for having the best vegan cooking classes of 2018! Through our food blog, we share new recipes with eager readers and answer questions about cooking and nutrition. Curious visitors to the Sanctuary learn about new foods and gobble up samples at our cooking demonstrations. We cater meaningful and exciting events—from casual picnics to elegant cocktail parties—for all kinds of eaters. In the summer, we teach excited young campers a thing or two about making fun, creative, delicious food. And we create the recipes that make for memorable breakfasts at our on-site guest house, The Homestead.

As chefs, we are passionate and enthusiastic educators and ambassadors for our mission. We both completed our chef's training at the Natural Gourmet Institute in New York City and found our way to the Sanctuary because of our love of animals and desire to inspire others to find joy in cooking compassionately. Over the years, we've fed and taught thousands of people, and our recipes have been savored and made in homes around the world. We couldn't be happier—but there is still work to do.

Maybe one day you'll find yourself bellied up to a prep table in a cooking class or enjoying an unforgettable meal made with love and plants. Until then, this book is an invitation to take a peek into the heart and kitchen behind our mission. In these pages, we hope you feel the magic that is Catskill Animal Sanctuary. Nothing would make us happier than knowing we inspired you to think about why it matters what you eat.

With love, from our kitchen to yours,
Chef Linda, Director Culinary Arts,
Vegan Chef and Instructor
Chef Sara, Vegan Chef and Instructor

ABOUT THIS BOOK

All the recipes here are vegan. References to things like sausages, butter, milk, or meatballs are also vegan in the context of this book, so don't be alarmed when we use those words without quotations or qualifiers. These words belong to us, too. Our butter does the same thing as dairy-based butter—it melts on our pancakes, makes our cakes tender, and gives us silky, salty sauces. Our milk, our mayonnaise, our cream cheese—they check all the boxes, except one: they don't contain animal ingredients. We didn't create cute names or make up new words to describe our ingredients and recipes because we feel that means they are somehow "less than" the animal-based version. Vegan food can be exciting, flavorful, and comforting in its own right. We want you to make these recipes not just because they're vegan, but because they're darned delicious! If we can help you realize that you don't need animal ingredients to make things taste terrific, then we're happy. Very happy.

Did we mention also that we want you to enjoy cooking? If we don't inspire you to get into the kitchen, we haven't done our job. Cooking doesn't have to be tedious or intimidating. It's just food, folks! We also hope to support you by providing information about ingredients, techniques, transitioning to a plant-based diet, and nutrition to get you started.

It all begins with a desire to prepare your own food. Eating prepared foods or dining out may have their places, but making your own food is where the magic happens. If you're reluctant, remember that when you cook, you're the boss! You control the ingredients you use. You decide how your food tastes. And you choose how to spend your money. Cooking is a valuable life skill, and one that doesn't need to be learned in culinary school. A relaxed approach and sense of curiosity in the kitchen means looking forward to being there. Creating food that

you can't wait to eat and that makes you feel good means you'll *want* to cook.

Someone once said, cooking is like jazz music: There should be lots of room for improvisation. We encourage you to try our recipes as we created them, but make them your own by swapping out ingredients, amplifying certain flavors, or toning down others. Baking, on the other hand, is like classical music—precise and accurate—so we encourage you to make the recipes as written.

You might like to know that when we cook (not bake), we often don't measure as precisely as the directions in our recipes. Over time, you'll realize that whether you use a cup of chopped carrots in a stew or a cup and a half usually doesn't matter. In this book, we've used weights and measures because specificity provides comfort for some people. Choose the approach that works for you.

ABOUT THE INGREDIENTS

A plant-based diet should support your healthiest self. Our goal is to thrive, not just survive, which is why we use fresh fruits and vegetables, whole foods, and organics whenever possible.

Most of our recipes include common ingredients that are available in well-stocked grocery stores. We hope this dispels the myth that vegan ingredients are unusual and hard to find. There's something amazing and empowering about creating creamy cheese sauce from carrots, potatoes, and chickpeas; or hearty meatballs from eggplant and beans; or luscious key lime pie from avocados. Before long, you'll be looking at everyday foods in fresh and exciting ways. Did you ever imagine you could fill cannoli with baked potato? We did—and you've got to try it!

We kept the use of hard-to-find ingredients to a minimum, but there are a few items on our pantry list (see pg. 1) that are important to have on hand on your journey through this book and beyond.

While our recipes call for fresh ingredients and whole foods, we absolutely acknowledge that decadence and convenience have their rightful places in our lives! So, some recipes use ingredients like vegan meat alternatives, puff pastry, white flour, and sugar. We're human, too! If you choose to find healthier substitutes, by all means, do so.

When recipes call for store-bought foods, like sausage, cheese, milk, or mayo, we, of course, recommend vegan brands. The plant-based food market continues to grow, and there are always new things to try. Go ahead and experiment, then decide which are your favorites. We don't make specific brand recommendations, with the exception of the vegan butter we use in some of our baked goods and sweets—Earth Balance Buttery Sticks is our preferred brand because of the consistent results we achieved.

We chose not to be overly prescriptive about our ingredient selection. For example, we don't specify what kind of oil to use unless we feel it is important to the taste or technique, though we generally use olive oil. We don't specifically call for organics, but be aware that certain fruits and vegetables can retain more residues from pesticides and fungicides than others, so to the extent that you can make your choices organic, the better off you'll be (refer to the Environmental Working Group's annual lists, "Dirty Dozen" and "Clean 15." Learn more at EWG.org).

We'd like to point out that sugar and wine are not necessarily vegan. Both products may be *refined* using animal ingredients. When we call for sugar, we encourage you to buy organic, which the USDA certifies as using no animal ingredients in its processing. As far as wine and beer, use the Internet or apps like Barnivore to check if your favorite brands are vegan.

In general, flexibility and freedom are at the root of our philosophy—we'd rather you try a recipe than not because you don't have a particular type of onion, sugar, or oil. Choose the healthy options you're familiar with or research online to become a more informed shopper—and eater.

Allergens

All of our recipes are dairy- and egg-free. Additionally, we've made special note of the other common allergens—gluten, nuts, peanuts, and soy—so you can find substitutes or avoid them completely. If you have severe allergies or sensitivities to any foods, please read the recipes and ingredient labels carefully. We offer this information to help, but you are ultimately responsible for taking care to avoid your own allergens.

ABOUT THE RECIPES

Although these recipes were developed by chefs, the inspiration for this book came from home cooks and regular people who enjoy delicious food. Participants in our Compassionate Cuisine cooking classes, guests at our events, visitors to the Sanctuary, hungry staff—these were the people who ate our food and said "Wow, you guys should write a cookbook!"

These recipes have been tested by a merry band of volunteer testers who come from a wide range of backgrounds and who have a variety of skill levels in the kitchen. Some were vegans, many were not. During testing, they shared the food with family and friends and provided feedback about the cooking process, what they thought of the food, and whether ingredients were difficult to find. We took that information seriously so these recipes would reflect real-life results.

And because we know that cravings and schedules are always in flux, these recipes are intended to strike a balance between simple and challenging, familiar and exciting, comforting and health-supportive. We hope there's something for everyone and that you find them to be as fun and delicious as the people who inspired them did.

A FEW WORDS ABOUT NUTRITION

Eating well is one of the most important things you can do to ensure a long and healthy life. A well-balanced diet includes a wide variety of foods like vegetables, fruits, whole grains, legumes (beans, peas, lentils), nuts, and seeds—and only a limited intake of highly processed foods. If you're making the move to reduce or eliminate animal foods from your diet, the good news is those foods make up only a small percentage of all the many things there are to eat.

If you're concerned about getting everything you need from a vegan diet, rest assured that all the nutrients your body needs are found easily in everyday plant foods. We encourage you to do your own research so you feel informed and empowered when making changes to your diet. Some books we recommend are *The China Study* by T. Colin Campbell, *How Not to Die* by Michael Greger and Gene Stone, and *Vegan for Her* by Virginia Messina. Documentaries like *Forks over Knives* and *What the Health* are available on video and Netflix. Finally, organizations like Physicians Committee for Responsible Medicine provide educational web-based information.

We did not calculate the nutritional makeup of our recipes because we do not fret over our nutrients. There is too much proof, from doctors and nutritionists, and from listening to our own bodies, to worry at every meal if we are consuming enough protein or calcium or iron . . . A balanced diet, made up of a variety of whole foods, nourishes and sustains us. Talk to your doctor if you're unsure, read the research that's widely available, and give your body a

chance to adjust and adapt to new flavors and foods. Our expectation is that you, too, will thrive.

Having said that, we would be remiss not to mention the key nutrients that many people are concerned about when considering a vegan diet—protein, iron, and calcium.

Protein

How much do you really need? The current recommended daily allowance for adults is 8 grams of protein for every 20 pounds of body weight. For a woman over the age of nineteen, that's about 46 grams per day; and about 56 grams for a male over nineteen. That equates to roughly 10 to 35 percent of your daily calories. So, despite the fact that protein is a critical part of a healthy diet, it's not where most of your calories should come from. Do some research to calculate your individual protein needs. If you're thinking about eliminating animal foods from your diet, there's no reason to panic about protein. Plants have protein! A well-balanced diet that includes a variety of whole foods will allow you to meet your protein needs.

You might ask, "But are they *complete* proteins?" In order to discuss complete proteins, we need to mention amino acids, the building blocks of protein. Our bodies make many amino acids, but there are some that our body can't produce on our own that we need—essential amino acids. The good news is that our bodies are designed to grab essential amino acids from the foods we eat, taking some from one food and picking up more from others. Our bodies are so smart that they combine these amino acids for us, so we don't have to worry about combining foods on our plate to make complete proteins. The well-intended belief that you need to combine foods to make complete proteins at every meal was dispelled by scientists some years ago. Some foods that are particularly high in protein include quinoa, soy (including tempeh, tofu, and edamame), hemp and chia seeds, lentils, beans, seeds, nuts, seitan, grains, and sea vegetables, just to name a few!

And remember: the biggest, strongest animals on the planet (think elephants, gorillas, and cows) eat plants, not other animals. They are plant-strong, and you can be, too!

Calcium

Calcium is an important mineral that strengthens our bones and supports muscle and nerve function. Most of us learned that dairy was the best place to find calcium. You'll be happy to know that many plant-based foods are reliable sources of calcium and are often better for your bones than milk. Some of the best nondairy sources of calcium are dark leafy greens, tofu, sesame/poppy/chia/flaxseed, beans, almonds, oranges, many grains, and sea vegetables.

Iron

Iron is an important mineral that supports many critical bodily functions. There are two types of dietary iron—heme and non-heme. Heme iron comes from animals; non-heme iron comes from plants. It's widely known that our bodies absorb less plant-based, non-heme iron, so we should eat not only foods that are rich in iron, but also those that increase our absorption.

Fortunately, it's easy to increase the absorption of plant-based iron: just add a vitamin C source at your meal. For instance, add sliced red pepper or orange segments for vitamin C in a spinach salad to increase the amount of iron your body absorbs from this leafy green. The vitamin C source doesn't need to be in the same dish, so don't stress. Note that the tannins in coffee and tea can interfere with iron absorption, so it's best not to have them immediately before or after your meals.

You don't have to look hard to find foods that are high in iron. Lentils, spinach, soy, chickpeas, Swiss chard, kidney beans, black beans, sea vegetables, and even blackstrap molasses are just a few good sources of non-heme iron.

Remember, when investigating your own nutritional needs, we recommend you do your own research and consult with your physician, holistic doctor, or nutritionist, as every individual's needs vary.

CHAPTER 1

Getting Started

If you're interested in transitioning to a plant-based diet, you might be wondering where and how to start. Luckily, changing the way you eat—and live—has never been easier! Today's markets are bursting with vegan options for everything, from burgers, roasts, and sausages to cheese, butter, mayonnaise, and milk. In fact, vegan food products are at the forefront of innovation and technology as we search for healthy and ethical alternatives to animal products. Plus, many restaurants now offer vegan options on their menus. There has never been a better time to explore a plant-based diet. And we've got a few tips and resources to help you get started.

PART ONE: YOUR KITCHEN AND PANTRY

Whether you're a seasoned vegan or beginning to add more plant-based recipes to your repertoire, maintaining a well-stocked pantry and refrigerator is a great help. Below, we'll outline some of our favorite ingredients to keep on hand. We'll also cover a few potentially unusual ingredients that may seem mysterious, but that add wonderful flavor and texture.

Agar

Also known as kanten or vegetarian gelatin, agar is a healthy thickening agent derived from red algae. Agar is tasteless and odorless, making it the perfect ingredient to use in desserts, including our Coconut Cream Pie (pg. 203). You can find it in health food stores or online, in powder form or flakes.

Beans

Whether dried or canned, beans are an economical, fiber-rich source of plant protein. We use commonly found beans like black, white, and chickpeas in many of our recipes, but we encourage you to experiment with the wide variety of beans available. Always drain and rinse canned beans before adding—you can reduce the sodium by almost 50 percent with a good rinse. Learn more about how to prepare dried beans in "Techniques, Tips, and Tricks" (pg. 5).

Black Salt

Also known as kala namak, black salt (which is actually pinkish in color) adds an egg- and sulphur-like taste and aroma to food. It's the not-so-secret ingredient in our Ultimate Tofu Scramble (pg. 34) and Deviled Potatoes (pg. 41). You can find black salt online, in health food stores, and in Indian grocery stores. Just like regular salt, it keeps indefinitely.

Grains

From tiny amaranth to chewy barley and fragrant long-grain rice, there are many interesting grains to add to your recipes. Again, feel free to experiment by swapping different types of grains in and out of your recipes. We used some of the more familiar ones, like rice, oats, and quinoa, as well as a couple that may not be familiar to you:

- Farro is an ancient form of wheat that has a nutty, pleasantly chewy texture, and it tastes great in our Farro and Wild Mushroom Pilaf (pg. 109). If you can't find farro, pearl barley makes a nice substitute.

- Forbidden black rice: looking for a grain that packs some serious drama? These gorgeous, glossy black grains cook to yield a deep-purple dish that's beautiful to behold. Try it in our Forbidden Rice and Edamame Salad (pg. 99). If you can't find black rice, try short-grained brown rice instead.

Jackfruit

Jackfruit is an enormous tropical fruit that can weigh up to 80 pounds! Thankfully, you can purchase it cut, cleaned, and canned from well-stocked grocery stores, Asian markets, or online outlets. Packed with essential vitamins, iron, and potassium, it's a healthy, versatile food used to create familiar dishes, like BBQ Jackfruit Sandwiches (pg. 123) and Compassionate "Crab" Cakes (pg. 125).

Miso

A secret ingredient in many recipes, miso is a fermented paste traditionally made from soybeans. Today miso is made from a variety of ingredients like farro, lima beans, adzuki beans, and chickpeas, which is a plus if you're avoiding soy in your diet. There is also a wide variety of colors and textures to choose from. Generally speaking, the darker the miso, the stronger the taste.

Miso is used in different ways to add complexity, richness, or balance to food. We've all heard of miso soup, but did you know you can add it to salad dressings, like our Cashew Caesar Salad Dressing (pg. 188), or use it to roast vegetables, like we do in our Miso Mushroom Squash Bowl (pg. 152)? Experiment by adding it to recipes where you feel a little extra "oomph" is needed!

Nondairy Milks

From almond and hemp to oat and cashew (and beyond!), nondairy milks are widely available and simple to use: just substitute it for dairy milk. For a lighter, less creamy milk, try rice milk; for a richer, thicker milk, try cashew or coconut. Most brands come in sweetened, unsweetened, and flavored varieties.

Nutritional Yeast

Known affectionately as *nooch* in vegan circles, this tasty seasoning is an inactive form of yeast that lends a savory, cheesy flavor to foods. It works wonders in vegan cheese sauces and adds richness to gravies. Once you try it, you may wonder how you lived without it! Look for brands that are fortified with the vitamin B_{12}. For a quick, satisfying snack, sprinkle nutritional yeast on freshly popped popcorn.

Nuts and Seeds

Nuts and seeds play an important role in many recipes by adding taste, texture, and nutrients. They can even stand in for dairy products with the right treatment! We especially love raw, unsalted cashews, the magical ingredient that makes vegan milks, sauces, and cheeses so wonderfully creamy. We soak our cashews for up to 30 minutes before using, which softens them and helps them blend into a smooth, luscious texture. Soaking also makes nuts and seeds more digestible. Store raw nuts and seeds in a cool and dry place, refrigerator, or freezer, which will keep the volatile oils in the nuts from going rancid. These nutrient-dense ingredients go a long way.

Oils

It's nice to have a few different oils on hand so you're always ready to make a salad dressing, sauté food on the stovetop, or bake a cake. When we call for oil in a recipe, we often don't specify which kind unless a particular type of oil is important to the taste or cooking technique. We recommend using oils that are minimally processed and derived from healthy ingredients whenever possible.

A note about oil selection: the term *smoke point* is used to indicate the temperature at which an oil begins to break down or smoke. When oils break down, not only do tastes change, but the oil also becomes damaged and potentially unhealthy. Generally, oils with a high smoke point are used for stir-frying, deep-frying, or other high-heat cooking methods. Low-heat oils, those that smoke at a lower temperature, are best used in dressings, for light sautéing, and in some baking. High-heat oils are more refined, while low-heat oils tend to be less processed. Do your own research so you can be confident about your choices.

We used these oils in this book:

- Extra virgin olive oil works great for salad dressings, gentle cooking, and even baking.
- Regular olive oil is more refined and can be used at higher temperatures. It works well in stovetop cooking as well as baking.
- Unrefined coconut oil lends a gentle coconut flavor to your baked goods. We often use it in place of butter. It has a subtle coconut flavor.
- Refined coconut oil is treated to remove the coconut scent and flavor. It can be used at higher temperatures than unrefined coconut oil and can substitute for butter in baking.
- Grapeseed, sunflower, safflower, and canola oils have high smoke points, which means they can handle higher temperatures before degrading. These oils are more highly processed than olive oil and coconut oil, so do some research on their health benefits and risks.
- Toasted sesame oil has a distinct flavor and dark brown color. It is used to season dressings, sauces, grains, and vegetables and is not intended as a cooking oil.

Sea Vegetables

Sea vegetables are just what the name implies: vegetables from the sea. High in many vitamins and minerals, we use a few varieties in our recipes where a briny flavor is welcome. Sold dry, they are often found in the ethnic aisle in well-stocked grocery stores. We used these in this book:

- Kelp Flakes might be the easiest sea vegetables to work with—just open the shaker container, measure out the ground kelp flakes, and you're good to go! They add great flavor to our Compassionate "Crab" Cakes (pg. 125) and Caesar dressing (pg. 188).
- Kombu is a thick, dense sea vegetable that is sold in dry pieces. It adds great flavor to stocks and broths and is usually removed before eating. Try it in our Tempeh, Shiitake, and Green Tea Noodle Bowls (pg. 155). We also recommend using it occasionally to cook dried beans or grains—just add a piece to the water. Kombu contains a significant amount of iodine, so use moderation if you have a history of thyroid problems.
- Wakame is a tender, leafy seaweed that adds a briny, ocean-like flavor to recipes like our Moqueca (Brazilian Stew) (pg. 71).

Seitan

Seitan, also known as *wheat meat*, is a plant-based protein made from wheat gluten. It's actually a minimally processed food and very safe to use in your diet. Its dense, chewy texture allows it to hold its shape extremely well when chopped, sliced, or rolled. You can find prepared seitan in well-stocked stores, but you can also make your own with just a few simple ingredients (see recipe on pg. 138).

Tamari, Soy Sauce, and Coconut Aminos

Tamari is a traditionally brewed and fermented soy sauce that adds not only a mellow saltiness, but also a wonderfully rich flavor and color to soups, stews, and other recipes. In general, tamari has a more complex taste and may seem less salty than soy sauce. Many brands are gluten-free, but check the label to see if it was fermented using wheat. Choose what works best for you. If you're sensitive to soy you can achieve the same results by substituting coconut aminos for tamari or soy sauce.

Tempeh

Tempeh is made by fermenting soybeans with active cultures, yielding a dense, protein-rich cake. Tempeh needs to be refrigerated and can generally be found near the tofu in your grocery or natural foods store. Tempeh's firm texture holds up well during cooking, and it can be sliced, cubed, or ground. See "Techniques, Tips, and Tricks" on how to prepare tempeh (p. 5).

Tofu

Tofu is made by coagulating soy milk, then pressing the curds into a cake—much like making cheese from dairy-based milk. You can generally find it in the refrigerated section at your grocery store. Tofu is distinguished by its firmness, which relates to its water content. Soft tofu has a higher water content than firm. Soft and silken tofu are great for sauces and fillings. Firm and extra-firm hold up well to baking, stir-frying, and pan-frying.

Vegan Butter

Move over margarine—there are so many delicious vegan butters on the market today! The difference between margarine and vegan butter generally has to do with how they are made. Many margarines are highly processed using strong chemicals and are hydrogenated (read: unhealthy)—learn the difference by reading the labels. If you have dietary restrictions to soy or coconut, you can find brands that offer allergen-free options like olive and avocado oils. Try all brands and see what you like. Note that in our recipes for baked goods, we used Earth Balance Buttery Sticks specifically.

PART TWO: TOOLS

Having a handful of kitchen tools will ensure you're prepared to make almost any recipe. But that doesn't mean you have to buy a huge assortment of kitchen gadgets; we believe that, in the kitchen, less is more and simple is best. Here's a few that will make your time in the kitchen enjoyable and more efficient.

Blender

A high-speed blender is the trick for getting lusciously creamy sauces, soups, and smoothies without a hint of gritty texture. Vitamix, a reliable brand that's built to last, is a favorite in both home and commercial kitchens and a worthwhile investment. Affordable models can be purchased on the Vitamix website in the refurbished section and come with a warranty. Not ready for a Vitamix? There are plenty of good blenders out there that will still fit your budget.

Food Processor

If there's one affordable tool that will make kitchen prep more efficient, it's a food processor. It's great for chopping vegetables, making hummus, grinding nuts, making nut-cheese, pulsing pie crusts, and finely chopping the ingredients for recipes like our Scarlet Black Bean Burgers (pg. 127). You can find a good one for under $150.

Knives

A good 7- or 8-inch chef's knife is a kitchen must-have. Not just for professionals, the chef's knife is a multi-purpose tool that will perform different tasks, such as mincing, slicing, and chopping—almost all of your prep work. A paring knife is a small knife that gives you greater control for detail work, like paring, trimming, or slicing small foods. A serrated knife makes quick work of slicing bread, and it won't smash tomatoes when slicing. Good knives don't have to break the bank, and investing in a few can mean the difference between slogging away or breezing through prep work quickly. A perfectly acceptable chef's knife can start at no more than $15 or $20. New to using a chef's knife? There are great tutorial videos on YouTube.

Parchment Paper

We recommend lining your baking trays with parchment paper. It's a healthier alternative to aluminum foil (which means no aluminum will leach into your food), and it makes clean-up a snap. Note that parchment paper and wax paper are not the same things—wax paper will melt and potentially burn in the oven. For a reusable alternative, silicone baking mats are a great choice that last for years.

Swiss Peeler

These Y-shaped peelers are inexpensive, comfortable to hold, and sharp enough to zip through even the tough skin on butternut squash. You won't be efficient using a rusty old peeler!

Zester (or Rasp)

This inexpensive tool makes it easy to remove the outermost skin of lemons, limes, and oranges for wonderful flavor and brightness. If you love to bake, use it to grind whole nutmeg. You can even use it to grate garlic and ginger instead of mincing it.

Baking Pans, Cake Pans, Pie Plates, etc.

In our recipes, we specify the ideal shape and size of baking pans to yield the best results. If you don't have the exact baking vessel specified, use one closest in size and adjust the baking time as needed—a smaller dish generally means longer baking; a larger requires shorter time. Here's a list of the pans we use in this book:

- Two 5¾-by-3¼-inch mini loaf pans
- 9-by-5-inch loaf pan
- 9-inch round cake pan
- 8-inch square baking pan or casserole
- 9-by-13-inch baking pan or casserole
- 9-inch pie plate (glass or stoneware work especially well)
- 9-inch springform pan
- 10-inch tart pan with removable bottom

PART THREE: TECHNIQUES, TIPS, AND TRICKS

We love to share the tips and tricks we've learned in professional kitchens and from years of cooking to make cooking more enjoyable and fun. Some of these are techniques we use several times in our recipes, and we'll refer you back to this section. We also use these in our own homes and at the Sanctuary to save time, improve flavors, add nutrients, and work smarter or more safely.

Cooking Dried Beans

The taste and texture of dried beans is so much more superior to canned beans that we recommend you learn how to make them. We promise that it's simple and cost-effective.

Buy dried beans in bags or in the bulk section of your grocery store. Store them in your pantry in bags or glass containers so you can easily see what you have and how much. Dried beans are best when soaked before cooking. Soaking not only improves texture and reduces cooking time, but it also helps to remove some indigestible sugars that cause flatulence. P.S. Research says that adding a small amount of baking soda (about 1/16 teaspoon per quart) to the soaking water will help reduce that pesky side effect.

Soak dried beans in salted water for several hours or overnight (renowned food scientist Harold McGee recommends 1½ tablespoons salt for every 8 cups of water). Beans can be left to soak on the counter, no need to refrigerate. Drain the water and put the beans in a pot. Add fresh water to cover them by at least an inch and add 1 teaspoon of salt (unless you are cooking them with something salty, then reduce salt to ½ teaspoon). Bring to a boil, partially cover, and simmer until tender, between 30 to 90 minutes, depending on the type of bean and how old it is (older beans take longer to cook). One cup of dried beans yields about 3 cups cooked. Freeze extra beans in one-cup portions for up to six months. Forgot to soak your beans? No worries. A quick-soak alternative is to bring the beans and water to a boil and let them stand, covered in the pot, for 1 hour or so, before cooking. Quick-soak water should be discarded and replaced with fresh when cooking.

Pressing Tofu

Pressing tofu removes excess water, yields a firmer, denser texture, and allows it to absorb more flavor. Unless we specifically call for it, you don't need to press your tofu. Rinse tofu and wrap it in a clean kitchen towel or several layers of paper towels. Place it on a cutting board or flat surface. Then, place another cutting board or something else flat on top and balance something heavy on top (we like using a full tea kettle or a cast iron pan). Leave it to sit for about 15 to 30 minutes. You can also buy a tofu press for about $30. You'll be amazed at how much water is released!

Flavoring Tempeh

We've heard people say they don't like tempeh because of the texture or its bitter taste. Right out of the package, we would agree, but tempeh is such a versatile, delicious food if you take an extra step to prep it—and we don't want you to miss out!

To get your tempeh is recipe-ready, cut it into the desired shape or texture (cubes, slices, cutlets, or ground, like in our Tempeh Oven Hash [pg. 31]). Use about 1¼ cup water plus 3 tablespoons of tamari or soy sauce for every 8 ounces of tempeh and place everything in a pot. Simmer for about 10 minutes. You'll notice that the tempeh expands, softens, and absorbs flavor. Drain the water, then use the tempeh in your recipe.

Making Substitutions

When you're trying to make a more compassionate version of a non-vegan recipe, consider why the non-vegan ingredients are used. Is the ingredient a prominent feature of the dish—like the chicken or steak in fajitas? If so, use store-bought "chicken" strips or cut portobello strips for a healthy, tasty alternative. Does the ingredient play a supporting role, like helping to make a cake to rise? You can usually achieve the same results with simple substitutions.

This list is by no means exhaustive, but it should help you get started.

IF YOUR RECIPE CALLS FOR . . .	. . . TRY ONE OF THESE SUBSTITUTIONS!
Ground beef or turkey (as in chili, tacos, spaghetti and meat sauce, or sloppy joes)	Crumbled or ground extra-firm tofu, tempeh, or seitan Cooked brown lentils Store-bought meatless crumbles
Sliced or diced beef, chicken, pork, or turkey (as in stir-fry or fajitas)	Pressed, marinated tofu Tempeh, simmered in water and tamari (pg. 31), and marinated Seitan Sliced portobello mushrooms Store-bought meatless substitutes
Bacon	Shiitake crisps (pg. 99) Store-bought bacon alternatives Look for recipes for carrot, eggplant, and coconut bacon
Milk	Unsweetened or sweetened versions made with soy, almond, cashew, hemp, coconut, oat, flax, or rice
Heavy cream	Make cashew cream: ½ cup soaked and drained cashews blended with 1 cup water and a pinch of salt (great in savory dishes) Canned full-fat coconut milk (best in sweet dishes, curries, or soups)
Buttermilk	For each cup of buttermilk: use a scant 1 cup unsweetened nondairy milk mixed with 2 tsps apple cider vinegar
Sour cream	Store-bought or make your own by blending silken tofu with a squeeze of fresh lemon juice and a pinch of salt Try our Cashew Sour Cream (pg. 188) Plain, unsweetened nondairy yogurt
Yogurt	Nondairy yogurts come in all varieties and flavors from almond, cashew, coconut, and soy
Butter	Solid refined and unrefined coconut oil Store-bought brands—many are soy-free For baking and sweets, we use coconut oil or Earth Balance Buttery Sticks
Cheese	Store-bought options are plentiful and come in a variety of flavors and textures, from shredded to sliced and spreadable options
Mayonnaise	Vegan mayonnaise is made with everything from soybean, canola, avocado oil, and even aquafaba—and most are absolutely indistinguishable from traditional mayonnaise

A Special Word about Eggs

Eggs can play a very specific role in cooking and baking. They may be used for their binding (helping to hold ingredients together) or leavening (helping ingredients to rise) properties. They can also add moisture to make the result tender. Luckily, there are lots of easy, and often nutritious, substitutes.

In many baked recipes we've simply replaced the volume of liquid in an egg (generally 3 tablespoons) with the same quantity of another liquid (think non-dairy milk, coconut cream, or juice). This works best in recipes that use wheat-based flours containing gluten, like all-purpose or whole wheat. The gluten holds the ingredients together, and the addition of a leavener, like baking soda or baking powder provides the necessary rise. Some of our recipes recommend one of the substitutions below, and others do not, so experiment and see what works best for you.

SUBSTITUTION FOR EACH EGG:	FUNCTION:	WORKS BEST FOR:
1 Tbsp ground flaxseed mixed with 3 Tbsps water, left to thicken for a few minutes	Binding; for additional leavening action, add ¼ tsp baking powder to recipe	Cookies, muffins, quick breads, cakes (with added leavening), waffles, pancakes
1 Tbsp chia seeds, mixed with 3 Tbsps water, left to thicken for a few minutes	Binding; for additional leavening action, add ¼ tsp baking powder to recipe	Cookies, muffins (especially poppy seed muffins, where the texture isn't noticeable)
¼ cup well-blended soft silken tofu	Binding; adds moisture	Muffins, quick breads
¼ cup unsweetened vegan yogurt	Binding; adds moisture	Cookies, muffins, quick breads
2 Tbsps garbanzo bean flour mixed with 2 Tbsps water or nondairy milk	Binding; for additional leavening action, add ¼ tsp baking powder to recipe	Cookies, cakes
3 Tbsps peanut butter, almond butter, cashew butter, tahini, or sunflower seed butter	Binding; adds moisture	Cookies, quick breads, muffins
¼ cup unsweetened applesauce, puréed pumpkin, or mashed banana	Binding; adds moisture	Quick breads, muffins, cookies (lends a more tender, cake-like texture; avoid if you prefer chewy cookies)
2 Tbsps organic cornstarch mixed with 2 Tbsps water or nondairy milk	Binding	Bread pudding, cakes, cookies, waffles, pancakes
1½ tsps agar flakes mixed with ¼ cup water, simmered for 5 minutes	Binding (strong)	Chilled puddings and pie fillings

Working Safely

It goes without saying that no one wants to get hurt in the kitchen. Yet, it's easy to make mistakes if you don't take a few simple precautions. Here are a few top tips:

To ensure your cutting board stays in place when you're slicing and dicing, take a piece of spongy shelf liner and cut it to a smaller size than your board. Keep it in your drawer with your knives as a reminder to place it under your board every time you use it. A damp paper towel also does the trick. This is a game changer—your board will stay in place and not slide around.

Keep your work area and cutting board clean and free from debris. Many a finger has been sliced because the cutting board is wet and sloppy or because there's too much clutter to position your knife and food properly. Please, clean as you go. It makes a difference.

This kitchen safety rule is broken all the time at home, but we'll repeat it again (for you and ourselves!): wear close-toed shoes when cooking. A dropped pot, plate, or knife even from counter-height can cause serious damage when you're wearing flip flops. Who needs that?

And wash your hands. 'Nuff said.

PART FOUR: MAKING CHANGES

It's important to extend compassion to yourself as you begin important lifestyle changes. Consider the transition to a plant-based diet or to being a better home cook a personal journey, one that will take some time, patience, and desire. Your reward will show up in the way you feel about yourself and how you think about food. To assist you, consider these helpful suggestions:

Ease into it. New habits are sometimes more likely to stick if you take a gradual approach and employ them consistently. While some people go vegan all at once, many find that a slow and steady approach allows them to gather information, learn new recipes and techniques, and make changes that will last. Easing into it also helps your friends and family understand your goals and provide the encouragement and support you'll need for long-term success. Build on and celebrate your successes.

Plan to keep changing. Some people cut out red meat as the first step and never move beyond that. Have a plan to keep your goal in sight and continue to learn and move forward. What changes will you make after giving up meat? Will you eliminate chicken . . . fish . . . dairy . . . eggs? Be open to the possibility that once you start, you will continue making changes, and realize that there are resources for each step of your journey. As far as cooking goes, master a few easy recipes first. Feel comfortable making them without directions, then add to your repertoire by introducing recipes that use a new technique or ingredient. Before long, you'll have lots to draw on and the ability to improvise and create your own dishes.

Don't judge or punish. Reward yourself for the important changes you make and for each meal that aligns with your goals. If you (knowingly or unknowingly) eat something that came from an animal, acknowledge the reasons and move on. Extend a compassionate approach to yourself and others on this journey. If you make something that doesn't come out quite right, it's probably still worth eating! If not, that's okay, too. The best chefs and home cooks have experienced epic failures! It's all part of learning.

Get familiar with new ingredients, and experiment. Being vegan isn't simply about eliminating certain foods; it's also about including new ones and looking at your meals in a different way. There's an exciting world of food out there that you may never have considered simply because you're accustomed to eating meals centered on animal protein or dairy. Get creative. Ask questions at the store. Research online. Explore unfamiliar foods. Read cookbooks. Visit farmers' markets. It won't be long before you get comfortable identifying and using new foods.

Read labels. When the time is right, start reading labels more closely. The more you familiarize yourself with a vegan lifestyle, the easier it will be to spot "hidden" ingredients that come from animals. Casein and whey, for example, are both derived from dairy. Gelatin, which is made from the bones, cartilage, tendons, and skin of animals, is found in marshmallows, some yogurts, and some frosted cereals. Some vegetable fats and oils are derived from animal tallow (fat). Don't get overwhelmed; just be aware and learn as you go.

Make extra! Many of our recipes are easy to double. Batch cooking means you cook once and eat twice— what could be better?

Don't forget what you know and look for simple substitutions. Many recipes and foods are already vegan; other recipes are very simple to veganize by swapping out an ingredient or two. For example, swap out ground beef for an equal quantity of crumbled tempeh, tofu, seitan, or cooked lentils in your favorite recipe. Sauté vegetables in vegan butter or oil instead of dairy butter. Make your sandwich with vegan mayonnaise. Use nondairy milk in your cereal. It's easier than you might think, and it often only requires a few changes. Refer to our substitution guide to help (pg. 7).

Ask for help. Whether you are surrounded by people on the same journey or starting out solo, take advantage of helpful resources and people who can encourage and support you. Look into local vegan meet-ups in your community. Search online for answers to questions on nutrition, cooking, and lifestyle. Watch cooking videos. Let us connect you with a vegan mentor from our New Leaf Vegan Mentor Program who can guide you (NewLeafVegans.org). And you can always contact Chef Linda and Chef Sara through our website at Casanctuary.org.

CHAPTER 2

Recipes and Sanctuary Stories

Kindness is a language all beings understand.
Let us speak it with the food we choose.

Add love and stir. It's the main ingredient in every recipe we develop. Whether intended for cooking classes, cocktail parties, or camp, our recipes are designed to meet people wherever they are in their journey. If our goal is to help others understand that eating without the use of animals is not only possible, but also delicious, then our food must be scrumptious and approachable while still gently challenging the ideas many people have about vegan food. Food should taste good. It should leave you feeling happy and satisfied. It's that simple, and these recipes will do just that. Some recipes are riffs on familiar dishes—meatballs, macaroni and cheese, pulled pork, beef stew—all of which we wholeheartedly believe can be made better with plant-based ingredients. Other dishes were created to highlight the versatility or simplicity of an ingredient or technique. These recipes, which cover a wide spectrum of tastes, textures, colors, and skill levels, have delighted and amazed our guests. We hope they'll do the same for you.

A note about allergens: We've noted the most common allergens in our recipes to the best of our ability; gluten, nuts, peanuts, and soy. If dairy or eggs are problematic, the good news is all our recipes are vegan and do not include those ingredients, directly or indirectly. We also indicate where there may be ingredients that, depending on the version or brand you choose, contain certain allergens. Please read your labels carefully. We leave it to you to be ultimately responsible for taking care to avoid your own allergens.

Sanctuary Story

THANK YOU

It's 6:30 a.m., and everyone's talking about breakfast. Everyone but the cows, that is. Relative to the others—the roosters calling nonstop from all over the sanctuary, the incessantly chatting ducks, and the pigs, who've begun the prelude to what will become a full-scale ear-splitting cacophony—cows are the patient ones. They start their day slowly, mooing only when they see the breakfast truck leave the barn.

In the senior pig barn, the pigs' chorus reaches a pitch and frenzy that would surely terrify the uninitiated. I sit on a bale of straw to take it all in: the sweet smell of the barn. The cool morning air. And especially the pigs. Impatient Lucy is growling, as are barn mates Ginger and Moses. The deep bass decibels bounce off the barn walls. Amelia and Reggie (who's trucking along at age fourteen, thanks to outstanding care, his own joie de vivre, and a daily regimen of anti-inflammatories, nerve pain relief, and CBD oil), are slightly more restrained. Unlike the rest, who are pacing in anticipation of breakfast, these two are motionless, staring out the open front door, waiting for breakfast delivery. All pigs love to eat and do so with unmatched gusto and exuberance. In fact, I think it's fair to say that all that they do, pigs do with gusto.

"Good morning, ladies," I call to caretakers Hannah and Rachel as they walk past leading thirty-seven-year-old Ashley, a blind Appaloosa, and Pliers, her thirty-five-year-old son. Both horses have serious health issues and will likely not make it through the winter, but we're grateful to have had the chance to help two once-desperate animals know what love and comfort feel like.

"Kathy, Leo is feeling *so much better*," Hannah says as she passes, referring to our blind and mostly deaf baby goat. "He drank his bottle in a split second."

"SO-OOOO glad to hear this, Hannah. Thanks for telling me!" I yell back.

A car pulls up. It's Kellie, head of our healthcare team, who is making her rounds and delivering not food but Maloxicam (an anti-inflammatory) disguised in Reggie's peanut butter and jelly sandwich. It's the only way he'll take his medicine. Kellie chats with him as he eagerly chomps down on the sandwich, before climbing the fence and moving to her next task.

Moments later, the food arrives and the pigs scream so loudly that staying put literally hurts my ears. The moment their bowls touch the barn floor, I think of the cliché because I really could have heard it: the pin dropping, that is.

"Have a good day, sweet ones," I say to them, then head toward the main barn.

The "main barn," one of nine large barns on Sanctuary grounds, is the only original building that remains from the days when Catskill Animal Sanctuary was Fortune Valley Farm, a Standardbred racehorse training facility. A wide aisle runs down the middle, with ten box stalls on both sides. We store alfalfa hay, a calorie-dense sweet-smelling hay used to support weight maintenance in elderly animals, in a stall closest to the barn entrance. I step into the aisle, pause, inhale. Alfalfa. Wood shavings. Animals. "Barn smell" is my favorite smell on Earth.

"Mullins!" I greet Kelly Mullins, our Animal Care Director, who is six stalls down, opening a stall door to let the mayhem begin.

"Stevens!" she responds. The Underfoots—a free-ranging cast of characters comprised of many goats and sheep, a few chickens, two special needs ducks, and Sister Mary Frances, a spotted potbelly pig with a tail set on "permanent wag," are being let out to begin their day. Is this arrangement convenient? Hell no! Does it make us more efficient? Uh, *you try* driving the tractor through a free-roaming flock of sheep convinced that they're invincible and then answer that question. But we continue to honor this long-standing tradition, this Underfoot Family, because it's the best way we've figured out to maximize the happiness of these lucky ones.

And, of course, we—the staff, volunteers, and visitors—benefit, too. Right now, for instance, I'm sitting in the aisle surrounded by goats saying good morning. Bartleby and Tigger, Lonnie and Loretta. Hermione, a large Nubian with ears that feel like silk, is six inches in front of me.

"Good morning, beautiful," I say to her, and she greets me by placing her forehead on mine.

As I make my way back to the house, seven sheep are grazing on the hill. Once again, I sit: being eye-level matters, for them and for me.

"Zeke! Scout! Atticus!" I call, naming them one by one.

Zeke turns toward me first. He walks, but then runs over, followed by Mika, Atticus, Christopher, Scout, Stewart, and Davy. In a moment, Zeke is pressing his head into my chest, Scout and I are cheek to cheek, and I am in the middle of a pile of sheep, all of whom are offering love. And while today, my heart *doesn't* burst, one day, decades from now, maybe it will . . . and it would not be a bad way to go.

"Good morning, beautiful ones," I whisper to them. "I love you." And as they surround me, pushing in ever closer, they say it back.

Eventually I stand, so grateful for this life, inhaling the breath and promise of this new day.

After rising at 5 a.m., writing, and communing with Zeke and friends, I'm hungry! But whether it's Breakfast Burritos (pg. 33) or Banana Bread (pg. 16), when it's made with love and compassion, it nourishes the soul.

Breakfasts and Morning Meals

Is there no greater prospect than a new day and breakfast? Some days we linger and indulge. Others we can hardly get out the door without trampling over something . . . or someone! Whether your mornings are crazy or sane, we've got recipes to help start your day—deliciously and compassionately.

Best Banana Bread

MAKES 1 LOAF, ABOUT 8 TO 10 SLICES

Chef Linda: *Best* is a term reserved for things of the highest quality and excellence. It is not to be taken lightly, which is exactly why we use it to describe our banana bread. Conjure up the cozy scent of cinnamon and banana. Close your eyes and imagine biting into a thick, warm piece of bread that's moist, not too sweet, gently spiced, and studded with nuts and chocolate chips. Our banana bread is a regular on the breakfast menu at The Homestead; now, make it a regular in your home.

Allergens: Contains gluten, nuts, and ingredients that may contain soy
Tip: Use heavily-speckled, brown bananas for the most banana flavor. Set aside a few to ripen up just for this recipe.

Ingredients

1 cup whole wheat flour
½ cup almond flour or almond meal
    (or ¾ cup raw almonds, finely ground)
½ cup old-fashioned oats
¼ cup ground flaxseed
1 tsp ground cinnamon
1 tsp baking powder
½ tsp baking soda
½ tsp salt
3 very ripe bananas, peeled
¼ cup unrefined coconut oil, melted, plus more for
    the pan (or your favorite oil)
½ cup maple syrup, room temperature
¼ cup unsweetened applesauce, room temperature
1 tsp vanilla extract
1 tsp fresh lemon juice
½ cup chopped walnuts
½ cup vegan chocolate chips or blueberries (optional)

Directions

1. Preheat oven to 350°F. Lightly oil a 9- by-5-inch loaf pan.
2. In a large bowl, whisk together the whole wheat flour, almond flour, oats, flaxseed, cinnamon, baking powder, baking soda, and salt.
3. In a medium bowl, mash bananas very well with a fork. Add in melted coconut oil, maple syrup, applesauce, vanilla, and lemon juice. Alternatively, blend bananas and wet ingredients together in a food processor for a smoother result. Pour the wet ingredients into the dry ingredients and mix gently. Gently stir in nuts and chocolate chips. Be careful not to overmix as you will create a tough, not tender, bread.
4. Pour the batter into prepared pan and bake for 50 to 55 minutes. You'll start to really smell the bread when it is close to being done. Bread is done when the edges are nicely browned, the bread is just firm to the touch, and a toothpick or knife inserted into the middle comes out clean. Cool for about 20 minutes. Insert a knife along the edge of the pan and invert onto a cutting board or plate. Let cool another 10 minutes before cutting, or gently slice while warm.

Nutty Breakfast Bars

MAKES 16 (2-INCH) SQUARES

Chef Linda: Delightful and delicious—a little sweet, a little salty—these easy breakfast bars feel like a treat no matter what time of day you enjoy them. In just one bite, you'll taste crunchy nuts, sweet and chewy dried fruit, and just enough chocolate chips to make you wonder if you should be eating these for breakfast or dessert! These breakfast bars have graced the table of our board meetings, Homestead breakfasts, and staff lunches. Any morning that starts with one of these is bound to be a good one.

Allergens: Contains nuts and ingredients that may contain soy
Special Equipment: Food processor

Ingredients

1 cup raw cashews
¾ cup vegan chocolate chips
½ cup raw walnuts
½ cup hemp seeds
½ cup unsweetened, shredded coconut
½ tsp coarse salt
1½ cups pitted, chopped dates (about 11–13 dates)
½ cup dried cranberries
2 Tbsps raw or roasted unsalted almond butter
1 Tbsp melted coconut oil

Directions

1. Place the cashews, chocolate chips, walnuts, hemp seeds, coconut, and salt in a food processor. Pulse until nuts and chocolate chips are ground to a medium texture. You want very small pieces, but not the consistency of nut flour. Empty the mixture into a bowl and set aside.

2. Place dates, cranberries, almond butter, and coconut oil in the food processor and process until the dates and cranberries are broken down and everything is combined, but it still has a bit of texture. Add the nuts back into the processor and pulse a few times to combine. Mixture should be moist enough to hold together when pinched.

3. Line an 8-inch square baking pan or casserole with parchment, allowing two ends to hang over the sides of the pan slightly so you can lift the contents out after chilling. Empty contents of food processor into the lined baking pan and firmly press down. Chill in the refrigerator for about 1 hour. Remove from refrigerator, carefully lift out parchment paper, and cut into squares. Serve chilled.

Blueberry-Banana and Praline French Toast Casserole

SERVES 6 TO 8 PEOPLE

Chef Linda: There you are on a lazy Saturday morning, sitting curbside at an intimate French café. Nearby, steam swirls upward from rich mahogany coffee. A sweet scent ignites your appetite as you wait with anticipation for a forkful of decadent French toast. Wait—France is not in your future, you say? Then let this buttery, praline-adorned breakfast delight take you there. Without relying on unkind standbys like eggs, cream, and butter, this French toast casserole, a Homestead specialty, gets its luscious custard filling from bananas and nondairy milk. A lovely addition to special brunches and holiday mornings, this simple dish will pamper your spirit.

Allergens: Contains gluten, nuts, and ingredients that may contain soy
Make Ahead: Bake and cool the dish 1 or 2 days in advance, then cover with foil and refrigerate overnight. Reheat in the oven at 350°F for about 20 minutes while the coffee is brewing.

Ingredients

Praline Topping
¼ cup vegan butter
1 cup brown sugar, packed
½ cup maple syrup
1 cup finely chopped pecans

French Toast
1 large (14- to 16-ounce) French baguette, cut into ½-inch thick slices
2 large, ripe bananas, peeled and sliced into ¼-inch thick rounds
2 cups fresh or frozen and thawed blueberries
2 cups unsweetened nondairy milk (if using sweetened, reduce maple syrup by 1–2 tsps)
½ cup maple syrup
1 Tbsp vanilla extract
1 tsp ground cinnamon

Directions

1. Preheat oven to 375°F. Lightly oil a 9-inch square casserole dish.
2. To make the praline topping, melt the butter in a small pot over medium heat. Add brown sugar and syrup. Stir and bring to a simmer. Continue to cook, stirring occasionally, for about 5 minutes or until the sugar is dissolved. Stir in the pecans and turn off the heat. Leave the pot on the stove to keep warm or else the mixture will harden. If the praline mixture hardens, reheat for a few minutes, stirring occasionally.
3. To assemble the French toast casserole, arrange one layer of baguette slices on the bottom of the casserole dish. Top the bread with a single layer of banana slices. Sprinkle half of the blueberries over the bananas and drop spoonfuls of the praline topping over the blueberries, using about half of it. Add another layer of bread and bananas, and top with remaining blueberries. Set aside.
4. In a medium bowl, whisk together milk, syrup, vanilla, and cinnamon. Pour over the bread in the casserole, saturating the top pieces. Spoon on the remaining half of the praline topping.
5. Cover the dish with foil and place on a baking tray. Bake for 35 to 40 minutes. Remove the foil for the last 10 minutes of baking. There should be liquid bubbling around the sides and corners when it's done. Remove from the oven and let sit for a few minutes before serving.

Pecan Chocolate Chip Coffee Cake

MAKES 8 (2-INCH) SQUARES

Chef Linda: There's nothing sweeter than the promise of a day that begins with cake. A favorite at The Homestead, our Pecan Chocolate Chip Coffee Cake has been rousing sleepy guests for years. Some equip themselves with forks and others with bare hands, but all of them end up wiping crumbs and traces of melted chocolate from their satisfied smiles. Tender, moist, vanilla cake, liberally studded with chocolate chips and topped with a nutty, sweet crumble, it's a cake you'll covet—but please consider sharing with friends and family.

Allergens: Contains gluten, nuts, and ingredients that may contain soy

Ingredients

Crumble Topping

1 cup whole wheat flour
¼ cup brown sugar, packed
6 Tbsps melted coconut oil (or your favorite oil)
¾ cup finely chopped pecans
¼ tsp salt

Cake

1 cup unsweetened nondairy milk
1 tsp apple cider vinegar
1 cup all-purpose flour
½ cup whole wheat flour
½ cup granulated sugar
2 tsps ground cinnamon
1 tsp baking powder
1 tsp baking soda
½ tsp salt
⅓ cup melted coconut oil (or your favorite oil)
2 tsps vanilla extract
¾ cup vegan chocolate chips

Glaze

⅔ cup powdered sugar
1 Tbsp nondairy milk
¼ tsp vanilla extract

Directions

1. Preheat oven to 350°F and lightly oil an 8-inch square baking pan.
2. To make the crumble topping, combine the flour, sugar, oil, pecans, and salt in a small bowl. Mix together until everything is moist and crumbly. Set aside and make the cake.
3. To make the cake, mix the milk and vinegar together in a small bowl. Set aside while preparing the dry ingredients. In large bowl, whisk together the flours, sugar, cinnamon, baking powder, baking soda, and salt. Add the oil and vanilla to the bowl with the milk and stir. Pour the wet mixture into the bowl with the dry ingredients and mix well to form a thick batter. Gently stir in the chocolate chips.
4. Empty the batter into the prepared baking pan. Spoon the crumble topping evenly over the batter and press down gently. Bake for 35 to 40 minutes, or until a toothpick inserted into the middle of the cake comes out clean. The cake should feel just firm to the touch. Set aside to cool.
5. To make the glaze, mix together powdered sugar, milk, and vanilla in a small bowl. When the cake has cooled, drizzle the frosting over the top of the cake. Let sit for about 10 minutes to set before cutting and serving.

Homestead Granola
with Vanilla Cashew Cream

MAKES ABOUT 4 CUPS

Chef Linda: Making homemade granola is like casting a cozy, cinnamon-and-vanilla-scented spell. People will wander into your kitchen, asking, "What's that smell?" A glorious assortment of oats, nuts, seeds, and a touch of sweetness will make this granola a healthy and delicious household staple. A beloved breakfast favorite at The Homestead, our granola is heaped into bowls and splashed with freshly made vanilla cashew cream. This recipe is forgiving and made for substitutions, so feel free to mix and match nuts and seeds to suit your tastes.

Allergens: Contains nuts
Special Equipment: Blender, for the vanilla cashew cream
Tip: Substitute the same quantity of seeds for a nut-free version.

Ingredients

Granola
½ cup maple syrup
½ cup olive oil (or your favorite oil)
2 tsps vanilla
3 cups old-fashioned rolled oats
½ cup raw nuts of your choice, like almonds, walnuts, or cashews
½ cup raw seeds of your choice, like pumpkin, sunflower, or hemp
¼ cup shredded, unsweetened coconut
2 tsps ground cinnamon
½ tsp salt
1 cup dried fruit, like cranberries, cherries, or raisins

Vanilla Cashew Cream
1 cup raw cashews, soaked for 15–30 minutes, drained
3 cups water, plus more to thin if necessary
4–6 pitted dates (or 2 Tbsps maple syrup), increase for more sweetness
2 tsps vanilla extract
½ tsp ground cinnamon (optional)
Pinch of salt

Toppings (Optional)
Chopped apples, pears, bananas, or seasonal berries

Directions

1. Preheat oven to 350°F. Line a rimmed baking tray with parchment. Using a rimmed tray will prevent granola from spilling when you stir it.

2. In a large bowl, whisk together the maple syrup, oil, and vanilla. Stir in the oats, nuts, seeds, coconut, cinnamon, and salt.

3. Pour the granola onto the prepared baking tray. Bake for about 15 minutes. Remove tray from the oven and stir to ensure all granola gets toasted. Return to the oven and bake for another 10 to 15 minutes, or until lightly browned and fragrant. Watch carefully so as not to burn. Remove tray from oven and let cool slightly, then mix in the dried fruit. Serve with vanilla cashew cream or store in sealed plastic bag or container.

4. To make the vanilla cashew cream, place all the ingredients in a blender and blend on high speed for 1 minute. Cashew cream should be completely smooth and have the consistency of thick milk; you should be able to pour and drink it. Serve immediately or pour into mason jars and chill in the refrigerator before serving. The cream will keep for three to four days. Cashew cream will separate as it sits, so shake well before each use.

Lemon-Blueberry Polenta Griddle Cakes with Lemon-Butter Syrup

MAKES 8 (4-INCH) GRIDDLE CAKES

Chef Linda: If ever there was a reason to spring from your bed in the morning and greet the day with delight, these griddle cakes are it. Delicate and crispy on the outside, creamy and bursting with tart-sweet blueberries on the inside, these little beauties come together in a flash and are eaten just as quickly. You'll need quick-cooking instant polenta here, not the regular kind, so that the result is tender, not gritty. Pine nuts are buttery and soft and add just the right texture. And as if these weren't good enough on their own, a lovely lemon-butter syrup adds a salty-sweetness in each mouthful. One person can easily gobble up most of these, so you might need to make more than you planned!

Allergens: Contains gluten, nuts, and ingredients that may contain soy

Ingredients

Griddle Cakes

1¼ cup unsweetened nondairy milk

2 Tbsps olive oil, plus more for frying

1 Tbsp lemon zest, from 2 large lemons

½ tsp vanilla extract

¾ cup instant polenta

½ cup all-purpose flour

¼ cup almond meal

2 Tbsps granulated sugar

2 tsps baking powder

½ tsp salt

½ cup fresh blueberries (or frozen and thawed)

⅓ cup pine nuts

Lemon-Butter Syrup

⅓ cup maple syrup

2 Tbsps vegan butter

¼ tsp vanilla extract

¼ tsp lemon extract

Directions

1. To make the griddle cakes, start by heating the milk in a small pot just until it simmers. Remove from heat and add in oil, lemon zest, and vanilla.
2. Mix together the polenta, flour, almond meal, sugar, baking powder, and salt in a large bowl. Pour the warmed milk into the polenta mixture and stir to combine. Fold in the blueberries and pine nuts. Let the mixture sit for a few minutes so that the polenta softens and absorbs the liquid. Rinse out the pot.
3. To make the lemon-butter syrup, heat the syrup and butter in the pot until the butter melts. Remove from heat and stir in the vanilla and lemon extract.
4. Heat about 1 teaspoon of oil in a large pan over medium heat. Use a ¼ cup measure or large spoon to spoon the batter onto the hot pan. (Pancakes should measure 3½ to 4 inches.) Cook until the bottoms are golden brown, 3 to 4 minutes. Flip and cook for another 3 minutes until bottoms are golden brown. Serve immediately with the warm syrup.

Spiced Zucchini Carrot Bread

MAKES 1 LOAF, ABOUT 8 TO 10 SLICES

Chef Linda: Even a summer blight would not deny the zucchini its inalienable right to multiply and barge out of the garden in search of the spotlight: subtlety and humility are not its strongest virtues. To tame it is to strip it of its most notable attribute: abundance. A friendlier approach yields one of the season's most comforting treats—zucchini bread. This midsummer headliner has no use for eggs or dairy, demonstrating how liberating a compassionate approach to baking can be. Hearty and humble, speckled with shredded carrots, studded with nuts, and moistened with applesauce, this bread is heady with warming spices. Sadly, summer's bounty will leave no trace in the garden when the seasons change, but an extra loaf of this zucchini carrot bread, tucked away in the freezer, serves as a delightful reminder on winter's darkest days.

Allergens: Contains gluten and nuts
Special Equipment: Food processor or box grater
Tip: Serve with a "schmear" of artisan vegan cream cheese for a real treat.

Ingredients

1½ cups whole wheat flour
½ cup old-fashioned oats
2 tsps baking powder
2 tsps ground cinnamon
1 tsp salt
1 tsp ground allspice
1 tsp baking soda
1 medium zucchini, grated, about 1 cup packed
2 large carrots, peeled and grated, about 1 cup
½ cup maple syrup
⅓ cup apple or orange juice
¼ cup unsweetened applesauce
2 Tbsps oil
2 tsps vanilla extract
2 tsps fresh lemon juice
½ cup chopped walnuts or pecans

Directions

1. Preheat oven to 350°F. Lightly oil a 9-by-5-inch loaf pan. In a large bowl, combine flour, oats, baking powder, cinnamon, salt, allspice, and baking soda.

2. Squeeze excess moisture from zucchini and carrots with your hands or wring them out in a clean dish towel. Add zucchini and carrots to the bowl with the dry ingredients. Toss to combine, coating them with flour and breaking up any clumps.

3. In a small bowl, combine the syrup, juice, applesauce, oil, vanilla, and lemon juice. Pour the wet ingredients into the bowl with the dry ingredients. Gently mix until ingredients are almost completely incorporated. Gently stir in nuts.

4. Pour the batter into the prepared loaf pan. Bake for 55 to 60 minutes. The bread is ready when the top is golden brown, the sides have begun to pull away from the loaf pan, it's just firm to the touch, and an inserted toothpick comes out clean. Leave to cool in the pan for 20 minutes. Slide a knife around the edges and invert on a cutting board or plate to remove the bread. Let cool another 5 to 10 minutes before slicing and serving.

Simple, Sweet Chocolate Chip Scones

MAKES 8 SCONES

Chef Linda: Who doesn't love a nice scone? Whether sweet or savory, this lovely treat is crispy on the outside while delicate and light on the inside. Some say scones originated in Scotland; others believe England's fashionable habit of high tea included these biscuit-like cakes from the outset. Then there's the Irish who call dibs on the original scone. Scones needn't instigate another war of the three kingdoms; the kitchen is neutral territory for making these simple treats. Chocolate chips are an indulgent add-in, but try your own favorites, such as dried cranberries and pistachios, currants and walnuts, or sun-dried tomatoes and chives (omit the sugar for this savory version). These scones should be savored slowly and lovingly on a lazy Saturday morning—in your pajamas, of course.

Allergens: Contains gluten and ingredients that may contain soy
Tip: Replace chocolate chips with add-ins like dried cranberries and pistachios, currants and walnuts, or sun-dried tomatoes and chives (omit sugar for this savory version).

Ingredients

2 cups all-purpose flour
2 Tbsps granulated sugar
1 Tbsp baking powder
1 tsp salt
¼ cup refined coconut oil
1 cup vegan chocolate chips
¾ cup + 2 Tbsps nondairy milk, plus more for
    brushing scones
Coarse sugar for finishing

To Serve

Vegan butter
Jam
Coconut Whipped Cream (pg. 223)

Directions

1. Preheat oven to 375°F. Line a baking tray with parchment. Mix together the flour, sugar, baking powder, and salt in a large mixing bowl. Using your fingers, work the coconut oil into the dry ingredients until the particles are the size of small peas. Mix in the chocolate chips. Add the milk and use your hands to gently mix until the dough is slightly sticky and soft. Add a little more milk if necessary. Don't overwork the dough or scones will be tough, not tender.

2. Place the dough on a lightly floured work surface and form it into an 8-inch circle. Cut the circle into 8 equal triangles with a floured knife or use a biscuit cutter to cut out round scones. Re-roll scraps and make as many scones as you can. Arrange scones on the prepared baking tray, leaving 2 inches between each one. Brush with milk and sprinkle the coarse sugar on top.

3. Bake for 18 to 20 minutes, until the bottoms are lightly browned. Remove from the oven and serve the scones warm with vegan butter, jam, or coconut whipped cream. You probably won't have any to store, but if you do, place extras in a sealed container or zip-top plastic bag. Freshen them up by popping them into the oven for a few minutes. Baked scones freeze well for up to three months.

Weekend Waffles with Fudge Sauce

MAKES 4 BELGIAN-STYLE OR 8 REGULAR-SIZED WAFFLES

Chef Linda: Waffles shouldn't come out of a box. They should come right off of a hot waffle iron to be devoured with giddy delight. The subtle scent of homemade waffles can coax even the most reluctant risers to the breakfast table. Without eggs and milk, this batter still holds together perfectly, and the leavening power of baking powder helps the waffles rise to any occasion. They're crisp on the outside, tender on the inside, and full of nooks and crannies for all your favorite toppings—like this decadent fudge sauce.

Allergens: Contains gluten and ingredients that may contain soy
Special Equipment: Waffle iron (Note: waffle irons vary greatly and will impact the final product.)

Ingredients

Chocolate Fudge Sauce
½ cup canned regular coconut milk
¾ cup brown sugar, packed
½ cup unsweetened cocoa powder
¼ tsp salt
1 Tbsp vegan butter
1 tsp vanilla extract

Waffles
2½ cups all-purpose flour
3 Tbsps granulated sugar
1 Tbsp baking powder
1 tsp ground cinnamon
¼ tsp salt
2 cups + 2 Tbsps unsweetened nondairy milk, plus
    more to thin if necessary
3 Tbsps oil
2 tsps vanilla extract

Other Toppings
Maple syrup
Vegan chocolate chips
Vegan butter and powdered sugar
Fresh fruit such as chopped apples, bananas, or berries

Directions

1. Preheat oven to 250°F to keep waffles warm, if desired.

2. To make the chocolate fudge sauce, whisk together the coconut milk, brown sugar, cocoa powder, and salt in a medium pot over medium heat. Cook, stirring occasionally, until the brown sugar has dissolved, about 6 minutes. Add the butter and stir to melt. Remove pot from heat and stir in vanilla. Set aside to cool slightly before serving. Store extra in a sealed container in the refrigerator and heat desired portion in a microwave-safe bowl for 15 seconds to serve.

3. To make the waffles, mix together, in a medium bowl, the all-purpose flour, sugar, baking powder, cinnamon, and salt. In a small bowl, whisk together the milk, oil, and vanilla. Pour the wet ingredients into the dry ingredients and stir gently until a thick batter is formed. The batter should be thick enough that you can scoop up a heaping spoonful. If it's too thick, add another 1 tablespoon of milk.

4. Read and follow manufacturer's instructions for your waffle iron. When the waffle iron is hot, spoon the batter so that the surface isn't entirely covered, allowing room for the batter to spread. Close the lid and wait for the indicator to alert you that the waffle is done. Do not open lid prematurely. Use a fork or toothpick to gently loosen the waffle from the iron. Serve immediately, drizzled with chocolate fudge sauce, or keep warm in the oven.

Superfood Smoothie Bowls

MAKES 1 GENEROUS SERVING

Chef Sara: Created for a winter cleanse cooking class at the Sanctuary, this nutrient-dense, antioxidant-rich smoothie bowl makes a delicious, nourishing breakfast year-round. In the colder months, tart and juicy pomegranate seeds add a crunchy burst of flavor that's sure to brighten up the dreariest winter morning. And if pomegranates are out of season? Top your smoothie bowl with sliced strawberries, blackberries, raspberries, or any favorite fruit—the sky's the limit! Regardless of which toppings you choose, use a generous hand and give yourself permission to have fun and be creative. This may be a simple recipe, but it certainly doesn't have to be boring.

Allergens: Contains nuts and ingredients that may contain soy
Special Equipment: Blender

Ingredients

Smoothie

½ ripe banana
2 Tbsps old-fashioned oats
1 Tbsp goji berries
2 Brazil nuts or 1–2 Tbsps raw cashews
　　(or 2 Tbsps pumpkin seeds)
1 cup frozen blueberries
1 scoop vegan protein powder (or 2 Tbsps hemp
　　seeds)
Small handful baby spinach or 2–3 leaves kale,
　　leaves only
1–1½ cups nondairy milk

Topping Suggestions

Sliced strawberries
Seasonal berries
Sliced banana
Pomegranate seeds
Unsweetened coconut flakes
Hemp seeds
Chia seeds
Granola

Directions

1. To make the smoothie, combine all the smoothie ingredients in a blender and blend on high speed until smooth and creamy. Depending on the power of your machine, this may take a couple of minutes.

2. Pour into a wide, shallow bowl and sprinkle with toppings (or any of your choice). Enjoy immediately.

Chunky Monkey Pancakes

MAKES ABOUT 6 (4-INCH) PANCAKES

Chef Linda: Making pancakes is an act of love. Without thinking about it, we pour our affection and nurturing energies into every spoonful of batter. Without eggs and milk, these pancakes are still gloriously light and fluffy, with just enough crisp on the outside to bring tears to your eyes. While we like the addition of banana, chocolate chips, and peanut butter syrup, you can omit them and simply stack plain pancakes high on your plate and dress with a pat of (vegan) butter and maple syrup. The simple pleasure of home-made pancakes will make you wonder why boxed was ever good enough . . . and why you thought you needed eggs to make them!

Allergens: Contains gluten, peanuts, and ingredients that may contain soy
Tip: For a seasonal spin, add 1 tablespoon of canned pumpkin (reduce the milk by the same amount) and add a bit of cinnamon. For added protein and texture, use ¼ cup hemp seeds or cooked quinoa.

Ingredients

Peanut Butter Syrup
1 cup maple syrup
½ cup smooth, salted peanut butter
½ tsp vanilla extract

Pancakes
1¼ cup unsweetened nondairy milk
1 tsp apple cider vinegar
½ cup all-purpose flour
½ cup whole wheat flour
1 tsp baking powder
¼ tsp baking soda
¼ tsp salt
2 Tbsps maple syrup
1 Tbsp olive oil, plus more for cooking pancakes
1 tsp vanilla extract
1 large very ripe banana, chopped into small pieces, about 1 cup
½ cup vegan chocolate chips

Directions

1. To make the peanut butter syrup, mix the syrup and peanut butter together in a small pot over medium heat until smooth, about 2 minutes. Remove from heat, add vanilla, and stir. Cover and set aside.

2. To make the pancakes, whisk together milk and apple cider vinegar in a small bowl. Set aside while preparing the dry ingredients. In a medium bowl, mix together the all-purpose and whole wheat flours, baking powder, baking soda, and salt. Stir the syrup, oil, and vanilla into the milk mixture and pour this into the bowl with dry ingredients. Stir to combine, being careful not to overmix. Gently stir in the banana.

3. Warm a large nonstick pan over medium heat. Add 1 teaspoon of oil to the pan and carefully spread with a paper towel. Test the temperature by cooking one small pancake first. If the batter sizzles when it hits the pan and forms bubbles on the top after 1 to 2 minutes without burning, your temperature is right. If it doesn't sizzle, wait 1 or 2 minutes longer, or increase the heat slightly. If the batter burns quickly, turn down the heat and wait for the pan to cool down.

4. Use a ¼ cup measure to create 4-inch pancakes. Pour batter onto the pan and wait until bubbles form on the surface, 2 to 3 minutes. Sprinkle on a few chocolate chips. Use a spatula to flip pancakes and cook for another 1 or 2 minutes or until bottoms are lightly browned. Continue until the batter is gone. To serve pancakes, top with warm peanut butter syrup. Store extra syrup in a covered container for up to 1 week.

Tempeh Oven Hash

SERVES 8 AS A SIDE DISH

Chef Linda: A common description of a "hash" generally involves two words you won't find here—meat and eggs. Instead, ground tempeh and a winning combination of fresh vegetables make for a savory breakfast dish that is just as good. Hash is often made on the stovetop, but we roast ours, not only to reduce the amount of oil used in frying, but also to deepen and lock in the flavors. Enjoy this hash alone, as a side dish to our quiche (pg. 37) or Tofu Scramble (pg. 34), or stuffed and roasted in a bell pepper or acorn squash.

Allergens: Contains soy and ingredients that may contain gluten
Special Equipment: Food processor or box grater
Tip: This hash loves a splash of hot sauce.

Ingredients

1 (8-ounce) package of tempeh
1¼ cup water
3 tsps tamari or soy sauce
½ pound waxy potatoes (Yukon Gold, red, or yellow), cut into ¼-inch cubes, about 2 cups
½ medium onion, finely chopped, about ½ cup
1 red or green bell pepper, chopped in ¼-inch pieces, about 1 cup
1 jalapeño pepper, minced (optional)
2 large cloves garlic, minced, about 2 tsps
2 Tbsps olive oil
1 Tbsp maple syrup
2 tsps paprika
1 tsp dried oregano
¼ tsp cayenne pepper (optional)
¾ tsp salt
Ground black pepper, to taste

Directions

1. Use a large-holed box grater or food processor to grate/grind tempeh. Alternatively, use your hands to crumble the tempeh into very small pieces. Place ground in a small pot with the water and tamari. Bring to a simmer and cook for about 10 minutes, until the tempeh has softened. Drain remaining liquid and transfer tempeh to a large bowl.

2. Preheat oven to 400°F. Line a baking trays with parchment. To the bowl with the tempeh, add the potatoes, onion, bell pepper, jalapeño, garlic, oil, syrup, paprika, oregano, cayenne pepper, salt, and pepper. Toss to combine. Empty contents of the bowl onto prepared baking tray and spread evenly. Roast in the oven for 25 to 30 minutes, stirring occasionally. The hash is done when the vegetables are soft and tempeh has browned nicely. Serve immediately.

Freezer-Friendly Breakfast Burritos

MAKES 8 BURRITOS

Chef Sara: These breakfast burritos are easy, hearty, and fun, packing a walloping 20 grams of protein each, which will help you power through your busy mornings. They're also economical. Not a fan of tofu? Substitute crumbled tempeh. Need a soy-free option? Substitute crumbled seitan.

Allergens: Contains gluten and soy

Tip: Make the spice blend in advance to save time—double the recipe to keep extra on hand for spicing up a basic tofu scramble or roasted potatoes. It's seriously delicious!

Ingredients

Spice Blend

2 Tbsps nutritional yeast
1 Tbsp ground cumin
1 tsp ground coriander
1 tsp ground turmeric
1 tsp salt
½ tsp dried oregano
½ tsp chili powder
½ tsp smoked paprika
½ tsp granulated garlic
Ground black pepper, to taste

Burritos

1 Tbsp olive oil
1 medium red onion, chopped in ¼-inch pieces, about 1 cup
1 large red bell pepper, chopped in ¼-inch pieces, about 1 cup
1 (10-ounce) package frozen chopped spinach, thawed, excess water squeezed out
1 (14- to 16-ounce) package extra-firm tofu, rinsed and crumbled
2 (15-ounce) cans black beans, drained and rinsed
Hot sauce, to taste (optional)
8 large (approximately 10-inch) wraps or flour tortillas

Directions

1. To make the spice blend, mix together all the ingredients in a small bowl.

2. To make the burritos, heat the olive oil in a large pan over medium-high heat. Add onion and bell pepper. Cook, stirring occasionally, until the onions are softened and translucent, 8 to 10 minutes. Add spinach, tofu, and black beans. Cook for about 5 minutes, stirring frequently. Add the spice mix and stir. Add hot sauce, taste, and adjust seasonings as necessary. Cool for 10 to 15 minutes before assembly to keep your burritos from getting soggy.

3. Divide the mixture into 8 equal portions. Place filling on the bottom third of a wrap and roll while tucking the ends in. Place seam-side down on a cutting board or plate. To freeze, place all of the burritos on a large plate, freeze until solid, and then place in a freezer bag or wrap individually in plastic. The burritos will keep in the freezer for three to six months. Store unused spice blend in a covered container.

4. To heat in the microwave: remove a burrito from the bag or plastic wrap, place on a microwave-safe plate, and tent with a paper towel. Microwave on high for 1 minute, flip the burrito, then microwave for an additional 1 minute, until the burrito is heated through. To heat in the oven: preheat the oven to 350°F. Remove a burrito from the bag or plastic wrap, wrap in foil, and bake for 50 to 60 minutes, or until heated through, turning over once during baking. Serve immediately.

Ultimate Tofu Scramble

SERVES 4

Chef Linda: If you're discouraged at the thought of life without eggs, this recipe is for you! With the right seasonings and add-ins, tofu can be transformed into a scrumptious, compassionate, and healthy alternative to scrambled eggs, with all the comfort and promise of a hot, savory scramble to start the day. Turmeric gives a sunny, yellow color to the tofu and sulphur-scented black salt lends the familiar "eggy" taste: Tofu scrambles are also good for substitutions. Use black beans, avocado, and salsa if you feel like wearing your sombrero to breakfast, or try spicy harissa, black olives, and peppers if the Middle East is teasing your taste buds.

Allergens: Contains soy

Ingredients

2 Tbsps olive oil

½ medium onion, finely chopped, about a ½ cup

1 red bell pepper, seeded and chopped in ¼-inch pieces, about 1 cup

½ cup sliced mushrooms

2 large cloves garlic, minced, about 2 tsps

1 tsp ground cumin

¾ tsp black salt (or regular salt)

½ tsp ground turmeric

1 (14- to 16-ounce) package of firm tofu, drained and rinsed

¼ cup nutritional yeast

Large handful of fresh, baby spinach, chopped, about 1 cup packed

1 medium avocado, pitted and diced

Ground black pepper, to taste

Directions

1. Heat oil in a large pan over medium heat. Cook onion, stirring occasionally, for 8 to 10 minutes until they start to soften and become translucent. Add bell pepper, mushrooms, garlic, cumin, black salt, and turmeric. Cook for another 8 to 10 minutes, or until vegetables are tender.

2. Using your hands, crumble the tofu into the pan and stir. Stir in nutritional yeast and spinach. Cook for another several minutes, or until all the ingredients are combined, any excess liquid has cooked off, and flavors have begun to mingle. Remove from heat, gently stir in avocado, and season with salt and pepper, to taste. Serve immediately.

Avocado, Edamame, and Kale Tartines

MAKES 4 TARTINES

Chef Linda: *Tartines* are just a fancy way to say *open-faced sandwiches*—and the ingredients in this recipe certainly call for a fancier name than *avocado toast*. If you're looking for a way to rejuvenate this popular breakfast, look no further. Fresh, curly kale gets a shower of bright lemon juice and is combined with creamy avocado and tender edamame beans to meet in a verdant mashup. Sweet seasonal fruit tops it all off to balance out the flavors. Enjoy this dish in the morning to start your day, or in the evening to end it (alongside a bowl of Rustic Summer Gazpacho [pg. 67]).

Allergens: Contains soy
Special Equipment: Food processor (optional)
TIP: Turn this into a creative and colorful crostini for your next party by using toasted baguette slices.

Ingredients

3 large kale leaves, stemmed and finely chopped, about 1 cup packed
2 tsps fresh lemon juice
2 tsps extra-virgin olive oil, divided
½ tsp coarse salt, divided
½ avocado, pitted
¼ cup frozen edamame cooked according to package instructions or thawed
4 slices hearty multigrain or gluten-free bread
½ cup chopped seasonal fruit, like strawberries, peaches, nectarines, apples, or pears

Directions

1. Place kale in a medium bowl and add lemon, olive oil, and ¼ teaspoon of the salt. Use your hands to massage for 1 or 2 minutes, until the kale softens.

2. Scoop avocado flesh into the bowl of a food processor. Add edamame and the remaining ¼ teaspoon of salt. Pulse several times to combine, creating a chunky-smooth mixture. Alternatively, mash the avocado and edamame in a bowl with a fork.

3. Toast the bread. Spread about 2 tablespoons of avocado-edamame mash on each piece of toast. Top with kale mixture and 1 tablespoon of chopped fruit. Serve immediately.

Spinach, Asparagus, and Sausage Quiche

MAKES ONE (9-INCH DEEP-DISH QUICHE), 8 TO 12 SERVINGS

Chef Sara: Quiche has endured because of its great taste, festive appearance (it's a savory breakfast in a pie shell!), and chameleon-like ability to adapt to a variety of delicious seasonings. It can easily be made vegan by substituting tofu and cashews for the eggs typically used in this dish, without losing any of the familiar texture. This favorite quiche incarnation was inspired by a recipe by Isa Chandra Moskowitz. It gets a seasonal springtime twist with spinach, asparagus, and vegan sausage.

Allergens: Contains gluten, nuts, and soy
Special Equipment: Food processor
Tip: Scoop extra filling into a lightly oiled ramekin and bake alongside the pie for about 15 to 20 minutes. To convert this to a vegan frittata, skip the pie crust and spread the filling into an oiled 8-inch square baking dish and bake.

Ingredients

1 unbaked vegan pie crust (store-bought or homemade [pg. 209]), fitted into a 9-inch pie plate

Tofu-Cashew Custard

½ cup raw cashews, soaked in water for 4–8 hours, drained (or soaked sunflower seeds)
1 pound extra-firm tofu, drained and rinsed
2 Tbsps nutritional yeast
2 tsps Dijon or yellow mustard
½ tsp ground turmeric
1 Tbsp cornstarch or arrowroot

Vegetables

1 Tbsp olive oil
2 large shallots, finely chopped, about ½ cup
½ pound fresh asparagus, ends trimmed, thinly sliced
3 medium garlic cloves, minced, about 1 Tbsp
1 (10-ounce) package frozen chopped spinach, defrosted and water squeezed out
2 large vegan sausages, crumbled
2 tsps fresh thyme, leaves only, finely chopped (or 1 tsp dried thyme, crumbled)
1 tsp salt
Ground black pepper, to taste

Directions

1. Preheat the oven to 350°F. Use a fork to prick the unbaked pie crust several times (both on the bottom and the sides) and place on a baking tray. Bake for 10 to 12 minutes, until the crust is partially baked and just starting to brown. Remove from the oven and set aside.

2. To make the tofu-cashew custard, combine the cashews, tofu, nutritional yeast, mustard, turmeric, and cornstarch in the bowl of a food processor. Process until smooth. Set aside while you prepare the sautéed vegetables.

3. To make the vegetables, heat the oil in a large pan over medium-high heat. Add the shallots and a pinch of salt, and cook until mostly translucent, about 5 minutes. Add the sliced asparagus and cook for an additional 5 to 7 minutes, until the asparagus is bright green and just tender when pierced with a fork. Add the garlic, cook for 1 minute or so, until fragrant. Stir in the spinach, crumbled sausage, thyme, salt, and pepper, and cook until heated through. Remove from the heat.

(continued on next page)

4. Stir the tofu-cashew custard into the vegetable-sausage mixture, until everything is well-incorporated. Pour the mixture into the par-baked pie shell, smoothing the top with the back of a spoon or spatula, and transfer the quiche to the oven.
5. Bake the quiche for 40 to 50 minutes, until the custard is set and the crust is golden brown. If the crust browns before the filling is ready, cover the edges with strips of foil to prevent burning. Remove from the oven, allow to cool for 10 minutes, then slice and serve.

Appetizers and Nibbles

Tonight, we dine! That is the promise of the pre-meal morsel. Intended to arouse and appease, these appetizers will show you how even classic recipes can be redesigned with kindness in mind. Kick off the Super Bowl with buffalo cauliflower instead of wings. Begin your baby shower with deviled potatoes, not eggs. You get the idea. Whether you make these for yourself or for a crowd, with each nibble you'll affirm that compassionate choices are delicious choices.

Deviled Potatoes

MAKES 28 POTATO HALVES

Chef Linda: Working as a chef at Catskill Animal Sanctuary can often feel like an episode of *Dinner: Impossible*. Whether we're feeding five hundred people on a scorching summer day or catering an upscale vegan cocktail party—in a barn, without a kitchen—we are always up for the challenge! Hearts swelled and tongues wagged when we served our deviled potatoes at a cocktail party for our beloved animal sponsors. Using common ingredients like potatoes and chickpeas to create a familiar party staple assured folks that we can make food we love while respecting all beings. With such simple changes, you'll find how liberating living egg-free can be.

Allergens: Contains ingredients that may contain soy
Special Equipment: Blender

Ingredients

2 Tbsps olive oil

¼ tsp salt

14 small (about 2-inches in diameter) Yukon gold, red, or yellow potatoes

1 (15.5-ounce) can chickpeas, drained and rinsed

2 large garlic cloves, roughly chopped, about 2 tsps

3 Tbsps vegan mayonnaise

2 Tbsps yellow mustard

1 Tbsp fresh lemon juice

1 tsp black salt or regular salt

½ tsp ground turmeric

⅛ tsp ground cayenne pepper

Ground black pepper, to taste

¼ cup chives, finely chopped, for garnish

Paprika, for garnish

Directions

1. Preheat oven to 350°F. Line a baking tray with parchment. Drizzle the lined baking tray with the olive oil and sprinkle with the salt. Cut potatoes in half, then place them, cut-side down, on the baking tray. Bake for about 20 to 25 minutes, or until potatoes are soft and can be pierced with a sharp knife. Check the face-down sides for a very light golden color. The potatoes should not be allowed to brown otherwise the bite will have resistance.

2. Place chickpeas, garlic, mayonnaise, mustard, lemon juice, black salt, turmeric, cayenne, and black pepper in a blender. Blend until completely creamy and smooth and the chickpea skins are no longer noticeable. This will take several minutes and require the sides to be scraped down intermittently. Taste and adjust flavors, if desired. This will taste strong, but when paired with the potato, it will mellow.

3. When the potatoes are tender, remove from oven and allow to cool for a few minutes. Using a teaspoon or melon baller, scoop out the center of each potato, leaving about ¼-inch border inside so that the potato is stable enough to be filled. Place about one quarter of the scooped-out potato centers into the blender with the chickpea mixture. This will add stability to the filling. (Reserve remaining potato centers for use in another recipe, such as thickening a soup.) Blend everything again, scraping down the sides, until smooth. If necessary, add 1 or 2 teaspoons of water. This should have a very thick consistency.

4. Spoon 1 heaping teaspoon of mixture into the center of each potato. Place the potatoes on a serving platter and garnish with chives and paprika. Serve warm or at room temperature.

Creamy White Bean and Cashew Fondue

MAKES 6 TO 8 GENEROUS APPETIZER SERVINGS

Chef Sara: Being vegan doesn't mean you have to miss out on fondue! This dairy-free fondue achieves its rich and creamy texture from cashews, butter beans, and waxy yellow potatoes. Potatoes may seem like an odd addition to a vegan cheese sauce, but trust us: they have an almost magical ability to turn a humble purée into a luscious, glossy cheese sauce. For an appetizer that's sure to please, serve the warm fondue with bread cubes (gluten-free, if desired), steamed broccoli, and sliced Granny Smith apples. And if you really want to pull out all the stops, serve the fondue over pasta for a decadent take on vegan mac 'n' cheese.

Allergens: Contains nuts and soy
Special Equipment: Blender

Ingredients

2 Tbsps olive oil
2 large shallots, roughly chopped, about ½ cup
3 cloves garlic, peeled
3 cups vegetable stock
2 large yellow potatoes, peeled and diced, about 2 cups
1 (13.5- to 15.5-ounce) can butter beans, drained and rinsed
½ cup nutritional yeast
¾ cup raw cashews
½ cup dry white wine (for a nonalcoholic alternative, use a scant ½ cup apple juice and 2 tsps apple cider vinegar)
2 Tbsps cornstarch
2 Tbsps white wine vinegar
2 Tbsps mellow white miso
1 Tbsp Dijon mustard
1 tsp salt, plus more to taste
Pinch of nutmeg, preferably freshly ground

To Serve

Cubed bread
Lightly steamed vegetables, like broccoli, cauliflower, carrots, green beans, potatoes, or asparagus tips
Fresh fruit, like sliced apples, pears, figs

Directions

1. Heat the olive oil in a large pot over medium-high heat. Add the shallots and cook for 5 minutes, until translucent. Add the garlic and cook, while stirring, for 1 to 2 minutes more, until fragrant.

2. Add the vegetable stock, potatoes, butter beans, nutritional yeast, and cashews, and bring to a boil. Reduce the heat, cover, and simmer until the potatoes are soft, approximately 25 to 30 minutes. Allow to cool slightly.

3. Carefully transfer to a blender and add the wine, cornstarch, vinegar, miso, mustard, and salt. Use a towel to cover the blender lid to protect your hands from steam, and blend until completely smooth. Rinse out the pot and transfer the fondue mixture back to it.

4. Cook over medium heat, stirring frequently to prevent scorching, until the fondue is bubbling and slightly thickened. Stir in the nutmeg. Taste, adding additional salt if necessary. Serve immediately by using a fondue pot or by placing the warm pot on a cutting board and surrounding it with your "dippers."

Roasted Mushroom and Walnut Pâté

MAKES ABOUT 2 CUPS

Chef Linda: Like moths to a light, guests will gather round when you put this silky, rich spread on the table at your next party. When ordinary mushrooms and walnuts meet the complex flavors of miso and tamari, the result is indescribably addictive and decadent. Fresh rosemary teases the palate with its subtle, piney fragrance. Reinvented with compassion, this simple but elegant pâté makes a lovely winter or holiday appetizer and should grace your table often.

Allergens: Contains nuts, soy, and ingredients that may contain gluten
Special Equipment: Food processor

Ingredients

1 pound button mushrooms, quartered (or mix of exotic mushrooms)
2 medium shallots, peeled and sliced, about ½ cup
2 large garlic cloves, peeled and chopped
2 Tbsps tamari or soy sauce
2 Tbsps extra-virgin olive oil
1 Tbsp nutritional yeast
1 tsp fresh rosemary, minced
½ cup walnuts, chopped, plus 2 Tbsps for garnish
1 Tbsp miso (white, yellow, or red; the darker the miso, the stronger the flavor)
2 tsps fresh lemon juice
Toasted baguette slices or crackers, for serving

Directions

1. Preheat oven to 375°F. Line a baking tray with parchment. Toss the mushrooms, shallots, garlic, tamari, olive oil, nutritional yeast, and rosemary together in a bowl. Transfer to baking tray and place in the oven to roast for about 25 to 30 minutes, or until vegetables are browned and most of the moisture released during roasting has evaporated. Remove tray from oven and let cool to room temperature.

2. Place the roasted vegetables in a food processor with ½ cup walnuts, miso, and lemon juice. Blend, scraping down the sides as necessary, until smooth. Serve in a small bowl or ramekin, garnished with the chopped walnuts, and alongside an array of toasted baguette slices or your favorite crackers.

Buffalo Cauliflower Bites

SERVES 6 TO 8

Chef Linda: Social gatherings include the unspoken promise that we will nibble before we dine. An appetizer should pique our interest and take the edge off of our hunger. These buffalo cauliflower bites are a compassionate riff on a Super Bowl staple. We developed the recipe for these spicy nibbles at cocktail parties and staff lunches, and it has what it takes to become an MVP. Tender, battered cauliflower is the perfect vehicle for a lip-smacking hot sauce and an outrageous dip.

Allergens: Contains gluten and soy
Make Ahead: The quick and creamy dip can be made 1 or 2 days in advance
Tip: Mirin, a type of rice wine, lends a sweetness and richness that for sauce indescribably delicious. Use extra cauliflower and dip for your next salad, sandwich, or pizza.

Ingredients

Batter
½ cup all-purpose flour
¼ cup cornstarch
2 Tbsps onion powder
1 Tbsp nutritional yeast
½ tsp salt
1 cup unsweetened nondairy milk
1 head of cauliflower, cut into bite-sized florets, about 5–6 heaping cups

Buffalo Sauce
4 Tbsps vegan butter
½ cup hot wing/buffalo sauce
2 Tbsps maple syrup
1 Tbsp tamari or soy sauce

Quick and Creamy Dip
½ cup vegan mayonnaise
2 Tbsps yellow miso
2 Tbsps nutritional yeast
2 Tbsps fresh lemon juice
2 Tbsps mirin
1 Tbsp tahini
¼ cup crumbled firm tofu

To Serve
Carrot and celery sticks
1 scallion, trimmed and sliced very thin diagonally

Directions

1. Preheat oven to 400°F. Line a baking tray with parchment.
2. To make the batter, mix together flour, cornstarch, onion powder, nutritional yeast, and salt in a medium bowl. Stir in milk until a smooth batter is formed. Dip each cauliflower into the batter, coating only the top, and place on the lined baking tray. Roast for about 20 minutes, until the batter is light brown and dry and the cauliflower stem is easily pierced with a knife.
3. To make the buffalo sauce, place all the ingredients in a small pot. Heat gently over low heat until the butter is melted.
4. Remove the cauliflower from the oven and brush each piece with buffalo sauce. Return tray to oven and roast for another 10 minutes until the sauce has darkened slightly and is bubbling.
5. To make the quick and creamy dip, mix the mayonnaise, miso, nutritional yeast, lemon juice, mirin, and tahini until smooth. Stir in crumbled tofu. The dip should be thick.
6. To serve, arrange cauliflower on a platter with carrot and celery sticks. Garnish with scallions, and serve the dip on the side.

Butternut-Sage Crostini

MAKES 16 TO 20 CROSTINI

Chef Sara: When it comes to classic pairings, butternut squash and sage are one of our favorites. This elegant fall appetizer, created for a Thanksgiving cooking class at the Sanctuary, has several steps, but most can be made well in advance to save time. Fried sage leaves are a simple and delicious garnish. This is a wonderful appetizer with drinks, but be warned: they disappear quickly!

Allergens: Contains gluten, nuts, and soy

Special Equipment: Food processor

Make Ahead: The tofu-cashew ricotta and squash can be made several days in advance. If making in advance, allow the squash to come to room temperature or warm it before assembling crostini.

Tip: Reserve the leftover sage-infused olive oil to use in other recipes where a subtle sage flavor is welcome. To simplify this dish further without sacrificing flavor, substitute an artisanal spreadable vegan cheese for the homemade tofu-cashew ricotta.

Ingredients

Tofu-Cashew Ricotta

1 cup raw cashews, soaked for 4–8 hours, drained

¼ cup fresh lemon juice, from about 2 lemons

2 Tbsps mellow white miso

2–4 Tbsps nondairy milk

½ pound extra-firm tofu

½ tsp dried Italian seasoning

½ tsp salt, plus more to taste

Ground black pepper, to taste

Squash

1 small butternut squash, about 1½ pounds, peeled, seeded, and cut into ½-inch pieces, about 3 cups

2 Tbsps olive oil

1 Tbsp maple syrup

Salt and pepper, to taste

Fried Sage Leaves

1 bunch fresh sage

¼ cup olive oil

Coarse salt, for sprinkling

To Assemble

1 baguette, sliced into ½-inch-thick slices, toasted

Directions

1. To make the tofu-cashew ricotta, combine the cashews, lemon juice, and miso in the bowl of a food processor. Process until mostly smooth, adding in nondairy milk as needed to keep the mixture moving. Add the tofu, Italian seasoning, salt, and pepper, and pulse a few times, until mostly blended but not completely smooth—a bit of texture is desirable. Taste, adjust seasoning if desired, and set aside until needed, or refrigerate.

2. To make the squash, preheat the oven to 425°F and line a baking tray with parchment. Pile the butternut squash on the baking tray and drizzle with olive oil and maple syrup. Toss together to coat and arrange in one layer on the baking sheet. Sprinkle generously with salt and pepper, transfer to the oven, and bake for 25 to 30 minutes, until the squash is tender and starting to caramelize. Allow to cool at room temperature or refrigerate.

3. To make the fried sage leaves, pinch the sage leaves from the thick stems, discarding the stems.

(continued on next page)

Line a large plate with paper towels. Heat the oil in a small pan over medium-high heat. Working in small batches of 6 to 8 leaves at a time, fry the leaves in the hot oil for 5 to 10 seconds on each side, flipping with a fork. The leaves should still be green, with no hint of browning. Lift the leaves out to drain on the paper towel-lined plate. Repeat with the remaining leaves. Sprinkle them with salt and allow to cool completely. They will crisp up as they cool. Fried sage leaves may be used immediately, or stored in an airtight container at room temperature for two to three days.

4. To assemble the crostini, spread a generous 1 tablespoon of cashew-tofu ricotta on a baguette slice, top with a few cubes of butternut squash, and place a sage leaf on top. Serve immediately. Store any remaining ricotta in the refrigerator for up to five days.

Roasted Grape Crostini with Cashew Ricotta

MAKES 16 TO 20 CROSTINI

Chef Linda: Crostini is a blank slate, ready to be adorned with whatever is seasonal, beautiful, and delicious. In this recipe, we roast fresh grapes with a drizzle of olive oil and salt to tame their boisterous, juicy sweetness, making them behave with a bit more sophistication. With just a few ordinary ingredients, we transform cashews into a luscious, savory vegan ricotta spread that serves as an excellent bridge between the crispy bread and tender grapes. These appetizers are lovely for company, but fuss-free enough to indulge in at any time.

Allergens: Contains gluten and nuts
Special Equipment: Food processor
Make Ahead: The cashew ricotta can be made several days in advance.
Tip: Substitute a spreadable vegan cheese for the homemade cashew ricotta.

Ingredients

2 cups seedless red grapes
1 Tbsp olive oil
¼ tsp coarse salt

Cashew Ricotta

1½ cups raw cashews, soaked in water for 15–30 minutes, drained
2 large cloves garlic, peeled
3 Tbsps fresh lemon juice
2 Tbsps nutritional yeast
1 tsp onion powder
½ tsp salt
⅓ cup water

To Serve

1 large baguette, about 14–16 inches long
2 Tbsps fresh thyme leaves

Directions

1. Preheat oven to 400°F and line a baking tray with parchment. Cut grapes in half lengthwise and place on the tray in a pile. Drizzle with the olive oil and sprinkle with the salt. Toss together and arrange cut-side down in a single layer. Roast for 10 to 12 minutes. Grapes should get a just little wrinkly and slightly browned along the edges. Remove from oven and let cool. Transfer to a bowl or plate and set aside the baking tray and parchment.

2. To make the cashew ricotta, drain and rinse the cashews. Place them in a food processor with garlic, lemon juice, nutritional yeast, onion powder, salt, and water. Blend, for several minutes until completely smooth, stopping to scrape down sides, and adding a little more water, as necessary. Taste and adjust seasonings, if desired.

3. Cut baguette into ¼-inch-wide diagonal slices. Lay slices on the same baking tray lined with parchment and broil in the oven for 1 to 2 minutes, watching carefully, until bread is lightly toasted. Flip slices over and put under broiler again for another minute or so. Remove from the oven and cool slightly.

4. To assemble, smear a generous tablespoon of cashew ricotta on each slice of bread. Top with several grapes and repeat. Arrange on plate and garnish with thyme leaves. Serve immediately. Store extra ricotta in the refrigerator for up to five days.

Greek Spanakopita Bites

MAKES 18 TO 20 PIECES

Chef Linda: Spanakopita, or spinach pie, is a traditional Greek dish made with phyllo dough, spinach-cheese filling, butter, and eggs. Consider this recipe an act of love . . . or showmanship. Working with phyllo may seem intimidating, but only until you've done it once. Look for vegan phyllo in the freezer case of well-stocked grocery stores; many brands are also "accidentally" vegan because they don't use eggs. Impossibly crispy and flaky on the outside, and tender and salty on the inside, this recipe demonstrates the possibilities that abound when you cook with compassion.

Allergens: Contains gluten and soy
Make Ahead: The tofu feta can be made several days in advance.
Tip: Substitute vegan cream cheese for tofu feta, though the result will be denser and moister. Extras freeze well or heat up quickly in a toaster oven for light dinner.

Ingredients

Tofu Feta
1 (14- to 16-ounce) package of firm tofu
3 Tbsps mellow white miso
3 Tbsps nutritional yeast
3 Tbsps fresh lemon juice
2 Tbsps olive oil
1 Tbsp apple cider vinegar
1 tsp garlic powder
1 tsp onion powder
1 tsp salt

Spanakopita
2 Tbsps olive oil, plus extra for brushing
½ medium onion, finely chopped, about ½ cup
½ tsp salt, plus extra for sprinkling
2 scallions, trimmed and finely chopped, about ¼ cup
10 ounces frozen, chopped spinach, thawed and squeezed to remove excess water
¼ cup nutritional yeast
¼ tsp ground nutmeg
1½ cups tofu feta (from recipe above)
1 pound package vegan phyllo dough, thawed in the refrigerator overnight

Directions

1. Drain, rinse, and press tofu (pg. 6).
2. To make the tofu feta, whisk together the miso, nutritional yeast, lemon juice, olive oil, vinegar, garlic powder, onion powder, and salt in a large bowl. The mixture will be thick. Cut tofu into ¼-inch cubes and add to the bowl with marinade. Stir gently to coat tofu. The tofu feta will be more flavorful if it's left to marinate for several hours or overnight, but proceed to baking if time does not allow.
3. Preheat oven to 350°F. Line a baking tray with parchment. Arrange tofu in a single layer and bake for about 25 minutes, or until cubes start to turn golden brown. Remove from oven and set aside to cool.
4. To make the spanakopita, increase oven temperature to 375°F. Line two baking trays with parchment. To make the filling, heat olive oil in a large pan over medium heat. Add onions and salt. Cook for 8 to 10 minutes or until they are soft and translucent. Add scallions and stir. Add spinach, nutritional yeast, and nutmeg. When spinach is hot and everything is fully combined, crumble tofu feta into the pan and gently mix, leaving chunks of cheese. Remove from heat and set aside to cool.

5. On a clean countertop, carefully unroll the phyllo dough, laying it out with the longest side horizontal to the edge of the counter. Take one sheet and lay it flat, then brush with a little olive oil (or use your hands to spread the oil). Place another sheet on top, brush again. Then place a third sheet on top and do not oil. Using a sharp knife, cut the stacked sheets horizontally into strips about 3½ inches wide. Place 1 tablespoon of filling in the bottom corner of one strip, closest to you. Fold the end corner over till it meets the opposite edge. Press gently to even out the filling inside. Take the triangle and fold it up and away from you, then continue to fold back and forth, making a triangle pocket. Place it on the prepared baking tray.

6. Repeat the process until all the filling is gone. Brush each triangle with a little olive oil and sprinkle with a bit of salt. Bake for about 20 minutes (with both trays in the oven) or until the phyllo turns golden brown. Remove from the oven and serve immediately.

Southern-Style Cheese Ball

MAKES 1 (4- TO 5-INCH) BALL OR SEVERAL SMALLER ONES, DEPENDING ON SIZE

Chef Sara: This smoky, pecan-crusted cheese ball—a veganized version of the cheese ball my grandmother, Lucy, used to serve friends and family—has achieved legendary status among its fans. Soaked cashews and coconut oil stand in for the traditional cream cheese, and a mix of bold, savory seasonings lend a rich, familiar flavor. Serve with crackers and crisp vegetables for a surefire hit at your next get-together.

Allergens: Contains nuts, soy, and ingredients that may contain gluten
Special Equipment: Food processor
Variation: Cranberry-Walnut Cheese Balls: begin the recipe as written, omitting the smoked paprika. After scraping the mixture into a bowl, fold in ½ cup chopped dried cranberries and 1 teaspoon finely chopped fresh thyme. Roll the chilled cheese ball in ½ cup chopped, toasted walnuts instead of pecans.

Ingredients

1½ cups raw cashews, soaked for 4–8 hours, and drained
¼ cup nutritional yeast
1 Tbsp mellow white miso
1 Tbsp apple cider vinegar
¾ tsp salt
½ tsp garlic powder
½ tsp onion powder
½ tsp smoked paprika
¼ cup water
¼ cup refined coconut oil, melted
½ cup chopped pecans, for coating

Directions

1. Drain and rinse the cashews. Place the cashews, nutritional yeast, miso, vinegar, salt, garlic powder, onion powder, smoked paprika, and water in the bowl of a food processor. Process on high speed for several minutes, scraping down the bowl as necessary, until mostly smooth. With the machine running, stream in the melted coconut oil, and process again until very smooth and creamy. This may take a few minutes. Use a spatula to scrape the mixture into a bowl. Cover and refrigerate for at least 4 hours, until firm enough to shape into a ball.

2. Place the chopped pecans on a plate. Scoop the cheese ball mixture out of its bowl, form into one large ball or several smaller ones (a flattened disc shape also works well), and roll in the chopped nuts, pressing the nuts gently into the surface of the cheese ball to help them stick. Refrigerate until ready to eat.

Baked Nut-Cheese Wheel

MAKES 1 (6-INCH) WHEEL

Chef Linda: Cheese seems to be the last holdout for many people who want to go vegan. Luckily, recipes like this will satisfy the craving for that creamy, salty, and rich flavor. We created this recipe for our popular Compassionate Cuisine cooking class "Life after Cheese" to demonstrate how versatile nuts can be in creating plant-based cheese. By baking, we get a dense, firm, sliceable result with a gorgeous toasted crust on the outside. The short list of ingredients and simple technique make it the perfect appetizer to serve at parties, crumble on salads, or keep in the fridge for your own secret pleasure. Add fresh, chopped herbs, like oregano or rosemary if you like. Do yourself a favor and make a double batch.

Allergens: Contains nuts
Special Equipment: Food processor or blender

Ingredients

1½ cups raw cashews (not soaked)
¼ cup nutritional yeast
3 Tbsps lemon juice
½ cup water
3 Tbsps olive oil
2 cloves garlic, roughly chopped
¾ tsp salt

Directions

1. Preheat oven to 350°F. Place all ingredients in a blender or food processor and blend until very smooth.

2. Oil a 6-inch oven-safe ceramic or glass bowl and pour the nut mixture into the bowl. Bake for about 25 minutes. It's ready when the top, puffs up, feels dry, and turns a light golden-brown. Remove from the oven and let stand for about 15 minutes. Slide a sharp knife around the perimeter of the bowl, then turn it upside down on a cutting board or plate. Serve immediately, or store sealed in the refrigerator for up to a week. This can also be frozen for up to three months.

Kale and Walnut Stuffed Mushrooms

MAKES 20 TO 25 APPETIZER-SIZED MUSHROOMS

Chef Linda: Stuffed mushrooms always cause a murmur in the room. Guests swoon at this perfect morsel, which is sure to appease their appetite. So often, recipes for the perfect stuffed mushroom obsess over cheesiness or meatiness while missing out on ingredients that complement the mushroom, choosing those that suffocate it instead. Our simple, inexpensive, and compassionate approach relies on walnuts and kale for the filling. While this recipe is easy enough to make on the day you need them, it can also be made in advance and baked just before your guests arrive, filling the house with the welcoming scent of herbs, garlic, and all that is right in the world.

Allergens: Contains nuts

Make Ahead: Follow the recipe without baking the stuffed mushrooms. Instead, cover and refrigerate for up to 2 days, then bake at 375°F for about 15 minutes before serving. The filling can also be made 1 or 2 days in advance.

Tip: To create a hearty main dish, stuff portobello mushrooms instead of button mushrooms.

Ingredients

20–24 ounces large button mushrooms

3 Tbsps olive oil, divided

1 tsp salt, divided

3 large cloves garlic, minced, about 1 Tbsp

1 cup finely chopped kale

¾ cup walnuts, finely chopped (or raw pumpkin or sunflower seeds)

½ cup breadcrumbs, regular or gluten-free

1 Tbsp nutritional yeast (optional)

1 tsp dried oregano

1 tsp dried thyme

Directions

1. Preheat oven to 375°F. Wipe dirt from mushrooms, remove stems, finely chop, and set aside. Place mushroom caps in a large bowl. Drizzle with 2 tablespoons of oil and sprinkle with ½ teaspoon of salt. Toss to coat and arrange stem-side down in a casserole dish. Bake for 10 to 12 minutes until mushrooms have released their moisture and turned dark brown.

2. While the mushrooms are baking, heat the remaining 1 tablespoon of oil in a large pan. Add the chopped mushroom stems, garlic, and remaining ½ teaspoon of salt. Cook, stirring occasionally, for 5 to 8 minutes, or until the stems have browned and released their liquid. Add kale, walnuts, breadcrumbs, nutritional yeast, oregano, and thyme. Stir and cook for 2 to 3 minutes more, or until the kale is bright green and herbs are fragrant.

3. Spoon walnut-kale mixture into the mushroom caps, packing it tightly. Return mushrooms to casserole dish, stuffed-side up, and bake for 12 to 15 minutes, until tops are lightly browned and crispy. Serve at room temperature.

Sanctuary Story
CHARLIE'S QUESTIONS

I am walking past the pond on my way to visit Leo, our special needs baby goat, when I bump into a "Family Tour" standing between two pastures: one where four horses live, the other occupied by four cows, including my "son" Tucker, a massive steer who's lived with us since a mother and daughter saved his life ten years ago when he was a young calf on his way to slaughter.

I stop, and tour guide Em invites me to say hello. There are few things in life I enjoy more than connecting kids with animals, so I happily oblige.

The group is comprised of one family of five, three additional families of two or three, and two adults who've joined this "G-rated" tour. We don't discuss agribusiness on this tour. We don't talk about the impact of our diet on the planet or the other species who inhabit it. We don't talk about how meat and dairy consumption wreak havoc on human health. Nope. Rather, the Family Tour is designed to foster meaningful connection. It's designed to show our guests, particularly the pint-sized ones, that cows, chickens, and pigs are as loving, affectionate, and uniquely wonderful as dogs and cats. We sit on the ground with the chickens. If they want to be held, we hold turkeys Michael and Imogen. We kiss the pigs. Well, *some* of us do. In other words, the Family Tour is a lovefest. We're planting seeds.

"Kids!" I say, facing the group. "Do you want to meet the cows?"

A chorus of voices responds, "YES!"

I introduce myself and ask the kids' names: Roxie, Henry, Lucy, Charlie, and Gina. All but Gina are names of current or past residents, which I explain by saying, "Lucy, we have a pig named after you," and so forth. Two other children, both infants, are both sacked out in Dads' backpacks. I forego the name game with them.

"I'm so glad you want to meet the cows, because I haven't seen them in about ten days, and I miss them!" I explain.

"Why do you miss them?" asks four-year-old Charlie. Charlie has deep brown eyes, fair skin, a smattering of freckles . . . and a twinkle in his eye. "Because they are my friends," I explain.

"Are the horses your friends?" Charlie asks.

"They sure are!"

"Are the chickens your friends?"

Mom shoots me a "You'd better nip this in the bud" glance, so I kneel down right in front of Freckle Face and say, "If we're gonna go out with the cows, we've got to practice something important." And then, gauging his size, I ask his age: Charlie is four.

"And do you ever get a little *silly* . . . a little *goofy?*"

"A lot!" Charlie offers.

"Well, there's a cow out in the field named Benjamin, and he's four years old, too. Boy, can he get goofy, just like you. He's a very, *very* sweet cow, but if he gets a little excited, we don't want him to hurt us by accident." This is the kid-friendly version of, "Parents, keep your eyes on this fella."

I demonstrate a quick, determined jump in place as I throw my hands skyward and shout a sharp, loud, "HAH!" We learned years ago that when a seven-hundred-pound young steer who has no idea of his own strength is barreling toward you, this is the best way to ensure that he stops *before* you're potentially in a heap of trouble. (Mind you, Benjamin has never acted like this with a tour. The activity is merely a precaution.)

Together, we practice. The grown ups shout "HAH!" and the kids shout "HAH!," though little Henry will only perform when hiding behind his mom. Good enough.

"Let's go," I instruct, reaching for a couple of small hands. Charlie offers his.

It's been an unusually wet late summer, so we have to pick our way through the pasture, avoiding small pools of water. "Also," I add, because kids find hyperbole about poop hilarious, "watch out for poop piles. Cows poop about nine million times a day."

"That's disgusting," Henry says.

"I have a feeling, Henry, that you would *not* want to live on a sanctuary," I say to the little man.

"No way," says Henry, who's clutching Monster, a pink unicorn with a neon green mane, in his hand while explaining that he wants to live in a castle.

Charlie has asked at least a dozen more questions on our walk out to Tucker and friends, and he doesn't stop when he lays eyes on the 2,500-pound-plus beast lying thirty feet in front of us. He wants to know if Tucker is "the mama horse."

I explain first that Tucker is a cow, and, second, that he is the stepdad in this family of four—stepparents Tucker and Sadie, and stepkids Benjamin and Blossom—who love each other very much. Big-hearted, gentle Tucker especially loves people and enjoys having visitors, so I sit directly in front of his massive head, legs crossed, and begin massaging his ears, his cheeks, his wide forehead. His eyes droop as he relaxes into my hands. As I tell his story and share cow facts that might be interesting to children, I tap my thigh.

"Come on guys, who wants to give Tucker a kiss?" I ask, and then by way of example plant a kiss above Tucker's right eye, another one on his cheek, another on his wet nose. Tucker responds with a scratchy kiss delivered to my cheek.

"I do!" shouts Charlie. "I want to kiss him!"

"That's disgusting," Henry says.

A single toss of Tucker's head would send Charlie sailing, but the tiny child walks confidently to me, settles into my lap, and sits a few inches in front of a cow head the size of his entire body. He plants a kiss on the bridge of Tucker's nose, and a wide smile spreads across his face.

We spend a couple moments, and then Lucy tiptoes over, working through her fear, and places her small hand on Tucker's neck. Even Henry, encouraged by his dad, comes eventually. He perches on the edge of my knee and tentatively strokes Tucker's face once before catapulting back towards Dad's reassuring embrace.

A few minutes later, these tiny hearts and I climb the fence and enter a pasture where horses Barclay, Arabelle, Destiny, and Julius live. We talk about

horse teeth and, again, about poop ("That's disgusting," Henry announces). We also talk about how soft the horses are and about their "hair." Henry, guardian of Monster the plastic pink unicorn with the flowing neon mane, is fascinated by the horses' manes and tails. Parents ask questions about the individual horses, and I offer abbreviated versions of their rescue stories because this group is worrisomely oblivious to the instructions about keeping their kids safe, and my focus has become more about watching the children.

One by one, I lift them to the horse's faces so they can, if they choose, safely plant more kisses.

We reassemble in front of one of five pig pastures next, and I ask, "Who wants to kiss pigs?!"

Henry says emphatically, "I definitely do not want to kiss pigs." Nor does his sister. Nor does Roxie, and the littlest children are still fast asleep. Charlie is the only taker.

"You're not going to believe how great this is," I say to him as we march out into the field. "I'm so excited I can hardly stand it! Are you excited, Charlie?"

"Yeah! I think my face is going to come off!"

I call to Moses, our sweet, spotted boy, who turns and ambles toward us. Charlie is all breath and rapt attention, sitting in my lap as we wait for the big moment. I wrap my arms around his chest; his tiny heart races.

But when the six-hundred-pound pig is before us, there's only time for a brief intro, because Moses has already spotted the rest of the group at the fence line. They're offering willow branches, a favorite treat for most of our species. No matter: Moses utters a friendly "hello" as Charlie places his hand flatly on the pig's cool, moist snout. For a few seconds, pig eyes meet human eyes, and I know this is a moment Charlie won't soon forget.

Cajoled by their parents, Henry and Lucy have entered the field not for pig kisses, but for pig butt scratches. I demonstrate how to scratch forcefully to penetrate Moses' thick skin, and though he uses "disgusting" a dozen times, Henry starts to giggle as Moses responds to the treatment by wiggling from side to side.

"Mmmph," says Moses.

"He's saying thanks," I tell Henry.

A smile, the first one I've seen, spreads across Henry's face.

An hour after I usurped Em's tour, I kneel down to be at eye-level with the children as we say goodbye. As Charlie's dad whispers to me, "Charlie wants to give you a hug," the freckle-faced imp comes over and envelopes me in his four-year-old arms. We stay that way for a long, long time. And then, to my astonishment, Henry comes toward me, arms outstretched. I can't see it, but I think I feel another smile.

Some days, a warm bowl of soup can feel like just the hug we need. Made with love and compassion, it can tease out even the most reluctant smile. Days like these were made for peanut-y sweet potato stew (pg. 62), Smoky Three-Bean Chili (pg. 74), and humble lentil stew (pg. 65). Got a little spring in your step? We've got a soup for that, too.

Soups and Stews

We believe in soup. Whether carefully constructed or made with lazy abandon, we think most days should have some soup in them. To cure or soothe, to nourish or indulge, soups and stews are a way to summon and invite a list of ingredients to work magic together. We could go on for pages, listing our favorites and making up new ones, but accept these selected recipes as an offering to whet your appetite, then go ahead and create your own.

African Sweet Potato Peanut Stew

SERVES 4 TO 6

Chef Linda: This inviting stew is a study in taste, ease, and satisfaction. Simple ingredients dispel the myth that vegan cooking is expensive and uses hard-to-find ingredients. The power in creating plant-based food comes not only from what we leave out, but also what we include. Fresh ginger and warming spices transform everyday sweet potatoes and ordinary peanut butter into a meal you'll hunger for again, before you even set your spoon down. Compassionate. Magical. Healthy. It's one of our favorites.

Allergens: Contains peanuts
Make Ahead: Use leftover rice or your favorite grain for an extra-hearty meal.

Ingredients

2 tsps coconut oil
1 medium onion, finely chopped, about 1 cup
1 tsp salt
3 large cloves garlic, minced, about 1 Tbsp
2-inch piece fresh ginger, peeled and grated, about 1 Tbsp
1 tsp ground cumin
½ tsp ground cinnamon
½ tsp ground turmeric
3 cups vegetable broth
⅓ cup unsalted, smooth peanut butter
¼ cup tomato paste
1–2 Tbsps sriracha or hot sauce
2 medium sweet potatoes, peeled and cut into ¼-inch cubes, about 2½ cups
1 (15.5-ounce) can chickpeas, drained and rinsed (or 1½ cups cooked)
¼ cup peanuts, salted or unsalted, roughly chopped
2 scallions, thinly sliced, about ¼ cup
Chopped cilantro, for garnish

For Serving

2–3 cups cooked rice or your favorite cooked grain, heated

Directions

1. Heat oil in a large pot over medium heat. Add onion and salt. Cook, stirring occasionally, for 8 to 10 minutes, or until onion is soft and translucent. Stir in garlic, ginger, cumin, cinnamon, and turmeric. Cook for another 2 to 3 minutes, until garlic is fragrant.

2. Add vegetable broth, peanut butter, tomato paste, and sriracha. Stir until combined. Add sweet potatoes and chickpeas. Bring to a gentle boil, reduce to a simmer, and cook covered for about 20 minutes, or until the sweet potatoes are fork-tender. To serve, scoop rice or grain into a large bowl, ladle stew over top. Top with chopped peanuts, scallions, and cilantro.

Dal Makhani (Indian Bean Stew)

SERVES 6 TO 8

Chef Linda: This is not your ordinary bean stew. At once, it is both exotic yet humble, boasting an intoxicating array of spices even as it uses economical, simple legumes. Dal is a broad term that refers to legumes (lentils, peas, and beans) that are cooked and spiced to perfection in Indian cuisine. The legumes used here can generally be found in the ethnic aisle of well-stocked grocery stores. Dal Makhani is traditionally made with clarified butter (ghee) and heavy cream, but we employ coconut cream as a healthy and compassionate replacement. The result is a luscious, decadent dish without the cruelty or the calories. Don't be put off by the list of ingredients. This recipe requires very little prep time and the ingredients are mainly spices that can be used again and again to lend excitement to soups, stews, and vegetable dishes. Using a slow cooker makes this a fuss-free dish, but cook it on the stovetop if you prefer.

> **Special Equipment:** Slow cooker, optional
> **Tip:** This blend of spices is superb, but substitute a curry spice blend like garam masala for the spices here if you have to.

Ingredients

1 cup urad/dry whole black lentils, soaked overnight in water, drained (or unsoaked green or French lentils)
½ cup rajma/dry kidney beans, soaked overnight in water, drained
1 medium onion, finely chopped, about 1 cup
1½ cups diced tomatoes (fresh or canned)
1–2 green chili peppers, depending on spice level, minced
2-inch piece fresh ginger, peeled and grated, about 1 Tbsp
3 large garlic cloves, minced, about 1 Tbsp
1 Tbsp ground coriander
2 tsps ground fenugreek
2 tsps chili powder
1½ tsps salt
1 tsp ground cardamom
½ tsp ground cinnamon
½ tsp ground turmeric
¼ tsp ground cloves
¼ tsp ground black pepper
4 cups water or vegetable broth
⅓ cup coconut cream
Chopped cilantro, chopped for garnish

Directions

1. Add all the ingredients except the coconut cream and cilantro to the slow cooker. Stir well. Cook on high for 8 hours. Add a little water to thin if necessary. If cooking on the stovetop, add all the ingredients except the coconut cream and cilantro into a large pot and simmer for about 50 to 60 minutes. If the beans are still firm, continue to simmer for another 10 to 15 minutes.

2. When done cooking, gently mash the beans against the side of the slow cooker or pot with the back of a wooden spoon. Stir in coconut cream and serve garnished with cilantro.

Chipotle Sweet Potato Lentil Stew

SERVES 4 TO 6

Chef Linda: There are days when almost nothing will warm or fill you up. This is a stew for those days. It's rustic, satisfying, full of wholesome ingredients, and has just enough heat to thaw you from the inside out. Sometimes the humblest ingredients take on new personalities when paired and spiced differently. Succulent sweet potatoes marry beautifully with tender and toothsome lentils. A couple of chipotle peppers, some chili powder, and cumin bring this dish to life. For a splendid topping that brings the flavors together, make Cashew Herb Cream (pg. 189). It's hardly optional, in fact, we urge you to make a double batch and use it on everything, from rice and beans to our Smoky Three-Bean Chili (pg. 74).

Allergens: Contains nuts
Special Equipment: Blender

Ingredients

2 Tbsps olive oil
2 medium carrots, peeled, sliced lengthwise, and chopped into ¼-inch pieces, about 1 cup
2 stalks celery, trimmed and chopped into ¼-inch pieces, about 1 cup
1 medium onion, finely chopped, about 1 cup
3 large cloves garlic, minced, about 1 Tbsp
1 tsp salt, divided
4 cups vegetable broth
2 medium sweet potatoes, about ¾ pound, peeled and cubed into 1-inch pieces, about 3 cups
1½ cups canned diced tomatoes with juice
¾ cup dried green or brown lentils
2 chilis in adobo sauce, chopped (or ½–1 tsp chipotle powder, depending on spice level)
1 Tbsp chili powder
1 tsp cumin
1 batch Cashew Herb Cream (pg. 189)
Chopped parsley or cilantro, for garnish

Directions

1. Heat oil in a large pot over medium-high heat. Add carrots, celery, onions, garlic, and salt. Cook, stirring occasionally, for about 10 minutes, or until vegetables have softened. Add vegetable broth, sweet potatoes, tomatoes, lentils, chilis, chili powder, and cumin. Cover, reduce heat to medium, and simmer for 20 to 25 minutes, until the lentils are cooked and the sweet potatoes are soft. Stir in cashews, remove from heat, and cover

2. To serve, spoon the stew into in bowls, top with a dollop of Cashew Herb Cream, and garnish with chopped parsley or cilantro.

Rustic Summer Gazpacho

SERVES 6 TO 8

Chef Linda: Warm weather and end-of-summer tomatoes are made for gazpacho. It's a simple, casual recipe that celebrates the flavors and colors of nature's bounty. The texture of this soup is completely up to you—some love it puréed; others like it chunky. (We like it on the chunky side with flecks of color.) Together, the tomatoes and vinegar create a bright, zesty flavor. If you've missed the peak of tomato season and still crave the tangy goodness of gazpacho, canned tomatoes are a perfectly acceptable substitution. We know from experience!

Allergens: Contains soy and ingredients that may contain gluten
Special Equipment: Blender
Tip: Serve this with a thick, crusty piece of bread slathered with good hummus

Ingredients

3 pounds fresh tomatoes, cored and cut into large chunks, about 3–4 cups
2 red bell peppers (or 1 red and 1 green), seeded and roughly chopped, about 2 cups
1 large cucumber, peeled, seeded, and cut into large chunks, about 2 cups
1 cup canned tomatoes with juice
2 scallions, trimmed, roughly chopped, about ¼ cup (or red onion)
3 large garlic cloves, peeled
1 jalapeño pepper, seeded and roughly chopped (or ¼ tsp crushed red pepper flakes)
¼ cup red wine or apple cider vinegar
¼ cup fresh lemon juice
¼ cup extra-virgin olive oil
2 Tbsps tamari or soy sauce
¼ cup tomato paste
1 tsp salt
½ tsp crushed red pepper flakes
½ tsp ground cumin
Ground black pepper, to taste

To Garnish

1 avocado, pitted and cut into ¼-inch cubes
Croutons

Directions

1. Place all the ingredients except the avocado and croutons in the blender. Blend until chunky-smooth, leaving small bits of ingredients unblended.
2. Chill for 1 hour. Serve in wine or margarita glasses or bowls. Garnish with avocado and/or croutons.

New Orleans Pecan Gumbo

SERVES 4 TO 6

Chef Linda: Gumbo originated from the Louisiana Creole people during the eighteenth century. Hearty, rich, and strongly seasoned, the dish combines the ingredients and culinary practices of several cultures and traditionally includes sausage, chicken, or shellfish. Remaking gumbo without animal products proved to be full of opportunities for creativity. This version relies on pecan halves for its meatiness. If you're transitioning to a plant-based diet and looking for something hearty and flavorful, give this gumbo a try.

Allergens: Contains nuts
Tip: Use sautéed vegan sausage for a nut-free version

Ingredients

Cajun Seasoning

1½ tsps smoked paprika
1½ tsps garlic powder
½ tsp ground black pepper
1 tsp dried oregano
1 tsp onion powder
1 tsp dried thyme
½ tsp salt
¼ tsp cayenne pepper

Gumbo

5 Tbsps olive oil, divided
2 heaping cups quartered button mushrooms
1 tsp salt
3 Tbsps all-purpose or gluten-free flour
½ medium onion, finely chopped, about ½ cup
2 celery stalks, finely chopped, about 1 cup
1 green bell pepper, chopped in ¼-inch pieces, about 1 cup
1 red bell pepper, chopped in ¼-inch pieces, about 1 cup
3 large cloves garlic, minced, about 1 Tbsp
3 Tbsps Cajun Seasoning (from recipe above)
3 cups vegetable broth
2 large zucchinis, trimmed and cut into ½-inch pieces, about 4 cups
1 cup raw pecan halves
1 Tbsp fresh lemon juice

To Serve

3–4 cups cooked white rice
2 scallions, thinly sliced, about ¼ cup

Directions

1. To make the Cajun seasoning, mix all the ingredients together in a jar or zip-top plastic bag.
2. To make the gumbo, heat 2 tablespoons of oil in a large, heavy-bottomed pot over medium heat. Add mushrooms and salt. Cook, stirring occasionally, for 8 to 10 minutes, or until mushrooms have browned and released their liquid. Transfer mushrooms to a bowl and set aside.
3. Heat remaining 3 tablespoons of oil in the same pot over low heat. Whisk in flour. Cook, stirring continually for about 5 minutes. It's important to stir continually and not allow the mixture to stick to the bottom and burn.
4. When the flour has turn a golden-dark brown, add onion, celery, bell peppers, and garlic. Cook for about 10 minutes, or until vegetables have softened. Add the Cajun seasoning, vegetable broth, zucchini, pecans, and cooked mushrooms.
5. Let the stew come to a simmer, stirring occasionally, until zucchini is tender, about 15 minutes. Stir in lemon juice. Taste and adjust seasonings if desired. To serve, spoon rice into the bottom of deep bowls and ladle the gumbo on top. Garnish with scallions.

Roasted Cauliflower Garlic Soup

SERVES 4 TO 6

Chef Linda: How we treat a vegetable like cauliflower depends on the season. In spring, when we crave lightness, we steam. Summer weather invites us outdoors where a grill makes quick and tasty work of our food. Colder weather beckons us to turn on the oven and roast. Roasting concentrates flavors and satisfies cold weather cravings. This soup was originally developed for a Thanksgiving cooking class to demonstrate that humble, versatile, and economical ingredients are often at the core of vegan cooking, and the soup's thick texture reminds us that we do not have to rely on dairy to add creaminess. This earthy soup is rich, flavorful, restorative, and shamefully simple to make. Just a few good reasons to make a double batch!

Special Equipment: Blender or immersion blender

Ingredients

1 large head cauliflower (about 2–2½ pounds) cut into florets

10–15 large cloves garlic, peeled

1 medium onion, peeled and thinly sliced, about 1 cup

1 Tbsp fresh thyme or 2 tsps dried

3 Tbsps olive oil

1 tsp salt

6 cups vegetable broth

1 Tbsp fresh lemon juice

Fresh thyme sprigs, for garnish

Directions

1. Preheat oven to 400°F. Line a baking tray with parchment. Place cauliflower, garlic, onions, and thyme on the baking tray and drizzle with the olive oil. Gently toss together and sprinkle with salt. Roast for about 30 to 35 minutes or until all the vegetables are soft and medium brown.

2. Heat the broth while the vegetables are roasting. When the vegetables are done, pick out a few small florets of browned cauliflower for garnish and set aside. Transfer remaining vegetables to a blender. Add the warm vegetable broth and lemon juice and carefully blend. Caution, it's hot, so remove the plastic handle in the lid and use a towel to gently cover the top of the hole in the blender lid to let steam escape during the blending process. Blend until chunky-smooth, leaving tiny bits and pieces of browned vegetables for visual appeal. Do not overblend into a purée. Alternatively, use an immersion/hand blender. To serve, ladle soup into bowls and place one or two small florets on top and a small sprig of thyme.

Moqueca (Brazilian Stew)

SERVES 6 TO 8

Chef Linda: Thick and luscious, and almost too good to share, this vegan Moqueca recipe was inspired by a Brazilian seafood stew. Our compassionate version uses fried plantains, tofu, hearts of palm, and diced potatoes to create a gorgeous and uniquely flavorful dish. Since this was originally a seafood stew, we used wakame, a sea vegetable, to create a mild broth that lends a subtle taste of the sea. Although the ingredient list may look lengthy and a little unfamiliar, this silky, tangy stew comes together fairly easily, and the result is more than worth the effort. We created this recipe for a multicultural wedding hosted at the Sanctuary. Guests came together from different countries, speaking different languages, to celebrate a joyous event. Like that wedding, our Moqueca is proof that the language of love is universal.

Allergens: Contains gluten and soy

Make Ahead: This stew can be served over rice that's been made in advance.

Tip: Farofa, the crunchy topping, is an essential condiment to many Brazilian dishes. It's made from manioc meal, the ground root of cassava, and can be found online or in ethnic markets. Panko breadcrumbs are a perfect substitute.

Ingredients

3 cups vegetable broth

½ cup dried wakame or other sea vegetable (like kombu, hijiki, or arame)

5 Tbsps coconut oil, divided

1 large ripe plantain, peeled and sliced into ¼-inch slices

3 Tbsps all-purpose flour (or cornstarch for gluten-free version)

½ medium onion, finely chopped, about ½ cup

1 red bell pepper, seeded and chopped into ¼-inch pieces, about 1 cup

2 large garlic cloves, minced, about 2 tsps

1 tsp ground paprika

1 tsps salt

½ tsp ground coriander

½ tsp crushed red pepper flakes

2 large tomatoes, seeded and chopped into ¼-inch pieces, about 2 cups

1 cup thickly sliced hearts of palm

4 ounces firm tofu, cut into ½-inch cubes

1 large potato, peeled, and cut into ½-inch cubes

1 (14.5-ounce) can coconut milk

2 Tbsps fresh lime juice

Chopped cilantro or parsley, for garnish

4–6 cups cooked rice for serving, optional

Topping (Farofa)

2 Tbsps coconut oil

1 large garlic clove, minced, about 1 tsp

½ cup manioc meal or breadcrumbs (regular or gluten-free)

¼ tsp salt

Directions

1. In a small pot, simmer vegetable broth with wakame for about 10 minutes. Pour the broth into a bowl through a mesh strainer to remove the sea vegetables, if desired, or leave some in for extra taste, texture, and nutrition.

2. Heat 2 tablespoons of coconut oil in a pan over medium-high heat. When the oil is hot, lay plantain slices in a single layer in the pan and cook

(continued on next page)

for 2 to 3 minutes per side, until nicely browned. Plantains should be fork-tender when done. Transfer to a paper towel-lined plate to drain. Set aside the pan.

3. Heat the remaining 3 tablespoons of coconut oil in a large pot over medium heat. Add flour and cook for about 2 minutes, while stirring, until it darkens slightly. Add onions, peppers, garlic, paprika, salt, coriander, and crushed red pepper flakes. Cover and cook until onions and peppers have softened slightly, about 8 minutes. Add tomatoes, hearts of palm, tofu, potatoes, vegetable broth, and coconut milk. Simmer for 25 to 30 minutes, until all the vegetables have softened and potatoes can be pierced with a fork. Stir in lime juice and plantains.

4. To make the farofa, use the pan from the plantains. Heat oil over medium heat. Add garlic, manioc meal or breadcrumbs, and salt. Cook, while stirring, for about 5 minutes until light golden brown and fragrant. Be careful not to burn as it goes from golden to dark brown quickly. Empty into a small bowl and serve with the moqueca, as a garnish.

5. Serve in bowls garnished with farofa and cilantro.

Slow-Simmered Cannellini Beans and Collard Greens

MAKES 8 SERVINGS

Chef Sara: Some of our Compassionate Cuisine cooking classes are designed to focus on certain techniques, ingredients, or nutritional concerns. This flavorful stew was created for a class on plant-based iron and calcium sources. Aside from being incredibly delicious and quick to assemble, it is a nutritional powerhouse. Iron-rich cannellini beans mingle with calcium-rich collard greens, while the addition of tomatoes and red bell peppers contribute the vitamin C necessary for aiding in the absorption of plant-based iron. Served over quinoa, another great source of iron, this is a nourishing dinner you'll turn to again and again.

Ingredients

2 Tbsps olive oil

2 medium red onions, chopped, about 2 cups

2 medium red bell peppers, chopped, about 2 cups

1-inch piece of fresh ginger, peeled and minced, about 1 tsp

4 large cloves garlic, minced, about 1⅓ Tbsps

1 tsp chili powder

½ tsp smoked paprika

¼–½ tsp cayenne pepper, to taste

3 cups vegetable stock or water

1 (15.5-ounce) can diced tomatoes

1 large bunch collard greens, chopped into bite-size pieces, 6–7 cups

1 tsp salt, plus more to taste

Ground black pepper, to taste

2 (15.5-ounce) cans cannellini beans, drained and rinsed (or 3 cups cooked)

Directions

1. Heat the olive oil in large pot oven over medium-high heat. Add the onions and a pinch of salt, and cook until softened and translucent, 8 to 10 minutes. Add the bell peppers, ginger, and garlic, and cook a few minutes more, until the peppers are just beginning to soften. Stir in the spices, stock, tomatoes, collard greens, and salt and pepper to taste, and mix well. Bring to a boil, cover, reduce the heat to low, and simmer for 20 minutes.

2. Add the cannellini beans and simmer, covered, for an additional 10 minutes to allow the flavors to blend. Taste, adjust salt and pepper as needed, and serve.

Smoky Three-Bean Chili

MAKES 6 TO 8 SERVINGS

Chef Sara: If you're like us and always have sweet potatoes, frozen corn, canned beans, and tomato purée on hand, this recipe practically makes itself! The result is a mildly to moderately spicy chili. Feel free to substitute whatever beans you have for the three we've chosen, but you'll need a total of 4½ cups cooked beans. For a real treat, make our Cashew Sour Cream (pg. 188) and serve with a generous dollop on top.

Tip: Poblano chiles can be tricky to find; if so, substitute green or red bell peppers for a slightly different, though no less delicious, flavor.

Ingredients

Spice Blend

1 Tbsp chili powder
2 tsps ground cumin
1½ tsps ground coriander
1 tsp ground chipotle powder
½ tsp dried oregano

Chili

1 Tbsp olive oil
1 medium yellow onion, chopped, about 1 cup
2 poblano or bell peppers, seeded and chopped in ½-inch pieces, about 1 cup
1 jalapeño pepper, seeds and veins removed, minced
4 cloves garlic, minced, about 1⅓ Tbsps
1 large or 2 small sweet potatoes, peeled and cut into ½-inch pieces, about 1½ cups
1 cup frozen corn, thawed
1 (15.5-ounce) can black beans, drained and rinsed (or 1½ cups cooked)
1 (15.5-ounce) can kidney beans, drained and rinsed (or 1½ cups cooked)
1 (15.5-ounce) can chickpeas, drained and rinsed (or 1½ cups cooked)
1 (28-ounce) can tomato purée
1½ cups vegetable broth or water
1 tsp salt, plus more to taste
1 Tbsp fresh lime juice
Chopped cilantro, for garnish
1 lime, cut into wedges for serving

Directions

1. To make the spice bend, mix together the chili powder, cumin, coriander, chipotle powder, and oregano in a small bowl. Set aside until needed.

2. To make the chili, heat the olive oil a large pot over medium-high heat. Add the onion and a pinch of salt, and cook until it begins to soften, 4 to 5 minutes. Add the poblano and jalapeno peppers, and cook for an additional 3 to 4 minutes. Stir in the garlic and spice blend. Cook for an addition minute or two, until fragrant.

3. Stir in the sweet potato, corn, beans, tomatoes, broth, and salt. Bring to a boil. Reduce heat to low and cover. Simmer for 25 to 30 minutes, until the sweet potatoes are fork-tender. Add the lime juice, taste and adjust seasonings as desired. To serve, garnish with cilantro and serve with lime wedges. The chili will keep in the refrigerator for five days. Cooled portions freeze beautifully and are best enjoyed within three months.

Shiitake Hot and Sour Soup

SERVES 4 TO 6

Chef Linda: In our popular global cuisine cooking class, we tackled a vegan version of a Chinese takeout favorite: hot and sour soup. Traditionally made with pork, eggs, and beef broth, our recipe eliminated those ingredients while still coming alive with flavor, texture, and zing. To achieve the true essence of the soup, you must find harmony between the hot and the sour; an imbalance will be most disagreeable. White pepper is essential, and you'll know when it's just right. The first bite may singe your sensibilities, but by the second, that fire will feel more like embers warming you from the inside out. And when the third bite follows, you'll wonder whether you have enough ingredients to make another batch.

Allergens: Contains soy and ingredients that may contain gluten

Ingredients

6 cups vegetable broth

1 cup thinly sliced shiitake mushrooms

½ pound firm tofu, drained and rinsed

½ cup bamboo shoots, cut into thin strips

½ cup tamari or soy sauce, plus more to taste

5 Tbsps distilled white vinegar (or rice vinegar)

½ tsp granulated sugar

4-inch piece fresh ginger, peeled and grated, about 2 Tbsps

1 tsp salt

¼ tsp garlic powder

1 tsp ground cayenne pepper

1 tsp ground white pepper

2 Tbsps cornstarch

½ cup water

2 Tbsps scallions, finely chopped, about ¼ cup

1 tsp toasted sesame oil

Directions.

1. Bring the broth to a boil in a large pot. Add the mushrooms, tofu, bamboo shoots, ½ cup tamari, vinegar, sugar, ginger, salt, garlic powder, cayenne pepper, and white pepper. Simmer for 15 to 20 minutes. Taste and add more tamari if desired.

2. Make a slurry with the cornstarch by mixing it in a small bowl with the water. Add the slurry to the pot slowly, stirring constantly. Cook for another 2 to 3 minutes so the cornstarch can thicken the soup. Ladle the soup into bowls, and serve garnished with scallions and a drizzle of toasted sesame oil.

Stovetop White Bean Cassoulet

MAKES 6 TO 8 SERVINGS

Chef Sara: Traditional cassoulet is a slow-cooked French specialty typically containing several types of meat and white beans. In our vegan version, the beans take center stage, and the cooking happens on the stovetop instead of the oven. The finished stew is rich with fresh herbs, chunks of vegetables, and tender beans. Toasted breadcrumbs add crunch to each piping hot bowl of stew.

Allergens: Contains gluten
Special Equipment: Food processor
Tip: For additional texture and flavor, you can stir in sliced vegan sausages during the last 5 minutes of cooking.

Ingredients

Toasted Breadcrumbs
2 thick slices stale bread, cut into cubes, about 1½ cups cubes (or 1 cup vegan breadcrumbs)
1 Tbsp olive oil

Cassoulet
2 Tbsps olive oil
4 medium shallots, chopped, about 1 cup (or 1 medium yellow onion)
3 medium carrots, sliced, about 1½ cups
3 stalks celery, diced, about 1½ cups
6 cloves garlic, minced, about 2 Tbsps
1 pound brown button mushrooms, halved and thickly sliced, about 4 cups
3 medium red potatoes, cut into ½-inch pieces, about 1¼ cups
2 (13.5- 15.5 ounce) cans cannellini beans, drained and rinsed (or 3 cups cooked)
1 (14.5-ounce) can diced tomatoes
3 cups vegetable broth
1 Tbsp chopped fresh thyme (or 1½ tsps dried)
2 tsp chopped fresh rosemary (or 1 tsp dried)
1 tsp dried Herbes de Provence
½ tsp salt, plus more to taste
Ground black pepper, to taste
½ cup fresh parsley, leaves only, chopped

Directions

1. To make the toasted breadcrumbs, place the bread cubes in a food processor and pulse until finely chopped. Transfer to a medium pan, drizzle with olive oil, and cook over medium heat, stirring frequently, until the breadcrumbs are lightly browned. Place the finished breadcrumbs in a bowl and set aside until needed.

2. To make the cassoulet, heat the oil in a medium pan over medium-high heat. Add the shallots, carrots, celery, and a pinch of salt, and cook until the vegetables are beginning to soften, about 5 minutes. Add the garlic and mushrooms, and cook for an additional 5 minutes, until the garlic is fragrant and the mushrooms have released their liquid.

3. Add the potatoes, beans, canned tomatoes, broth, herbs, salt, and a few grinds of black pepper. Bring to a boil, then lower to heat to a simmer, cover the pot, and allow to cook gently for 30 to 40 minutes, until the potatoes are tender. Taste and adjust seasonings as desired. Just before serving, stir in the fresh parsley.

4. The cassoulet will keep in the refrigerator for up to five days. Cooled portions can be frozen for up to three months.

Sanctuary Story
BREAKING THE RULES

In 2018, we discovered that our supporters actually love to squish around in the mud with pigs, tiptoe through the coolness of the main barn in order not to wake Hannah, our elderly blind sheep, and step into the turkey barn to feel what we mean when we say, "You're about to have an experience you'll remember for the rest of your lives." I lead these aptly named "Break All the Rules" tours, and it's a toss-up as to who enjoys them more: the guests, the animals, or me.

The weather, which of the animals are most accessible, the composition of the group, and the personality and energy level of its members: these things and more make each "Break All the Rules Tour" entirely unique. Group dynamics help inform whether we climb fences or open gates, sit in a

semi-circle surrounding giant Tucker or stand a respectful distance, have a full-out love-fest with the pigs versus me being the only one doing all the pig kissing.

In general, though, these unconventional tours lean heavily toward love-fests. We focus on the animals who crave affection and who give back as much or more love than is offered them. Tucker's head droops and his eyes blink slowly as he accepts gentle scratches on his cheeks, forehead, neck, and shoulders. Jasmine the pig stares without guile into the souls of those who sit in front of her. Turkeys Michael and Imogen nestle fully into the laps of unsuspecting guests, who typically sit silently, tears rolling down their cheeks, often uttering a sentence that begins with "I had no idea . . ."

"Yes," I say. "Turkeys are love on two legs."

Catskill Animal Sanctuary tours change lives. We speak the truth, always with love, about the urgency of veganism, not only for the animals, not only for our precious planet, but also for our very survival.

But it's *the animals*—these precious animals with their glorious individuality, their capacity to forgive, their breathtaking full-heartedness—who speak with a clarity that simply cannot be misunderstood. Ninety-three percent of our non-vegan guests say they intend to reduce or eliminate animal products from their diet as a result of visiting Catskill Animal Sanctuary. We have Tucker, Jasmine, Michael, and so many more to thank for that.

And just like our tours changes lives, so do our recipes. Whether you're feeling famished or peckish, our sides and salads will satisfy all kinds of appetites and all kinds of eaters. From Chickpea Waldorf Salad (pg. 86) to Stovetop Mac and Cheese (p. 105), these dishes can play a supporting or starring role—you decide.

Sides and Salads

Call it a side dish or a salad. Make it your main meal of the day or a midday lunch. These dishes are made to either stand obediently at the sidelines or to march right in to take center stage—it's up to you.

COLD

Eggless Egg Salad   82

Asian-Style Quinoa and Chickpea Salad   83

Caribbean Sweet Potato Black Bean Salad   85

Chickpea Waldorf Salad   86

Curried Cashew Tofu Salad   87

Mediterranean Orzo   88

Black Bean Mango Salad   89

Greek Watermelon Salad   91

Kale Caesar Salad with Polenta Croutons   93

Lemon Hearts of Palm Salad   95

South of the Border Quinoa Salad   96

Simple Sweet and Tangy Coleslaw   97

Forbidden Rice and Edamame Salad   99

HOT

Cashew Fried Rice   101

Blistered Green Beans with Leeks and Shiitake Crisps   103

Stovetop Mac and Cheese   105

Spiced Cabbage and Cauliflower   106

Confetti Cauliflower "Rice" and Beans   107

Farro and Wild Mushroom Pilaf   109

Eggless Egg Salad

SERVES 4

Chef Linda: Whatever the reason, whether it be taste, comfort, or ease, it seems eggs and dairy are the most challenging foods to eliminate from our diets. Thankfully, it's easier than ever to live happily without them. When we make this eggless egg salad for visitors and summer campers at Catskill Animal Sanctuary, we prove it with every bite. Tofu takes on the familiar flavor of this family favorite, while turmeric gives it a sunny, yellow hue. Sulphur-scented black salt adds the authentic taste and smell of eggs. Enjoy this creamy, comforting salad on top of fresh greens, stuffed in a pita, rolled up in a wrap, or on your favorite crackers.

Allergens: Contains soy

Tip: Buy a pouch of black salt online or in a well-stocked healthy grocery store and use it for this recipe as well as in our Ultimate Tofu Scramble (p. 34) and Deviled Potatoes (pg. 41).

Ingredients

1 (14- to 16-ounce) package firm tofu

½ cup vegan mayonnaise

2 Tbsps nutritional yeast

1 Tbsp yellow mustard

1 tsp ground turmeric

½–1 tsp black salt or regular salt

Ground black pepper, to taste

2 stalks celery, chopped into ¼-inch pieces, about 1 cup

½ small red onion, finely chopped, about ¼ cup

2 Tbsps chopped fresh parsley

Optional Add-Ins

Chopped dill pickles

Chopped fresh dill or tarragon

Cayenne pepper

To Serve

Sliced bread or pita bread

Fresh salad greens

Crackers

Directions

1. Drain, rinse, and press the tofu (see pg. 6).
2. In a medium bowl, whisk together mayonnaise, nutritional yeast, mustard, turmeric, black salt, and pepper. Using your hands, crumble tofu in small pieces into the bowl with the dressing and mix.
3. Stir in celery, onion, and parsley. Mix in other optional add-ins and serve immediately or chill until ready to serve.

Asian-Style Quinoa and Chickpea Salad

MAKES 6 TO 8 SERVINGS

Chef Sara: Quinoa and chickpeas are a powerhouse duo, providing protein plus tons of fiber, as well as great taste. When combined with a flavorful Asian-style dressing, colorful vegetables, and crunchy sunflower seeds, they are sure to delight your taste buds. Make a batch of this simple salad to serve as a cool lunch on a hot day. If you're up for experimenting, use this recipe as a springboard for your own creative grain and bean salad ideas, combining whatever grains, beans, veggies, nuts, seeds, and dressings you like best. How wonderful it is to have so many delicious options!

> **Allergens:** Contains soy
> **Make Ahead:** Quinoa can be made several days in advance.

Ingredients

Quinoa

1 cup quinoa, rinsed
½ tsp salt

Dressing

2 Tbsps extra-virgin olive oil
1 Tbsp toasted sesame oil
2 Tbsps tamari or soy sauce
2 Tbsps rice wine vinegar
1 clove garlic, minced, about 1 tsp
1-inch piece fresh ginger, peeled and minced,
    about 1 tsp
½ tsp salt
Ground black pepper, to taste

Salad

1 (14-ounce) can chickpeas, drained and rinsed (or
    1½ cups cooked)
4 scallions, thinly sliced, about ½ cup
4 celery stalks, chopped, about 2 cups
4 medium carrots, grated, about 2 cups
1 medium red bell pepper, chopped in ¼-inch pieces,
    about 1 cup
½ cup raw unsalted sunflower seeds
½ cup chopped fresh parsley
Salt, to taste
Ground black pepper, to taste

Directions

1. To cook the quinoa, bring 1½ cups water to a boil in a small pot. Add the quinoa and salt. Return to a gentle boil, then reduce heat, cover, and cook for 15 to 20 minutes. Remove from the heat, let sit for 5 minutes, then fluff with a fork and allow to cool.

2. To make the dressing, whisk together all the ingredients. Set aside.

3. To make the salad, in a large bowl, mix the cooked quinoa, chickpeas, scallions, celery, carrots, bell pepper, sunflower seeds, and parsley. Pour in the dressing and mix well. Add salt and pepper to taste. Serve immediately or chill. Stored in the refrigerator, the salad will keep for up to five days.

Caribbean Sweet Potato Black Bean Salad

SERVES 6 TO 8

Chef Linda: Like a tropical breeze that beckons you to linger in your lounge chair, this festive warm-weather dish invites you to slow down and dine on island time. In one mouthful, you'll taste the caramel soulfulness of the roasted sweet potatoes; in another, the spiciness of the cayenne and garlic; and then the crunch of the salty peanuts. Wait, what's that? Oh yes! The sweet, fresh, creamy burst of corn. Perfection!

Allergens: Contains peanuts

Ingredients

Sweet Potatoes
2 large sweet potatoes, peeled and cut into ½ inch cubes, about 4 cups
3 Tbsps extra virgin olive oil
1 tsp ground cumin
1 tsp ground cinnamon
¼ tsp ground cayenne pepper
1 tsp salt

Dressing
¼ cup fresh lime juice
3 Tbsps extra-virgin olive oil
2 Tbsps fresh lemon juice
2 Tbsps maple syrup
2 large cloves garlic, minced, about 2 tsps
1 tsp yellow mustard
1 tsp salt

Salad
1 (15.5-ounce) can black beans, rinsed and drained, about 1½ cups
1 cup fresh (cooked or uncooked) or frozen and thawed corn kernels
2 scallions, sliced thinly on the diagonal, about ¼ cup
1 cup roasted, salted peanuts, roughly chopped

Garnish
Chopped cilantro or parsley, for garnish

Directions

1. Preheat oven to 425°F. Line a baking tray with parchment. Place sweet potatoes on the baking tray in a pile. Drizzle with the olive oil and sprinkle with cumin, cinnamon, cayenne, and salt. Toss together with your hands then arrange in a single layer on the tray. Roast for about 20 minutes, until fork-tender.

2. To make the dressing, in a large bowl, whisk together the lime juice, oil, lemon juice, syrup, garlic, mustard, and salt. When potatoes are done, set aside to cool for about 10 minutes then place them in the bowl with the dressing.

3. To make the salad, add black beans, corn, scallions, and peanuts. Toss to combine. Garnish with fresh cilantro or parsley. Serve immediately or chill before serving.

Chickpea Waldorf Salad

SERVES 6 TO 8

Chef Linda: When Oscar Tschirky, the maître d'hôtel of the Waldorf-Astoria hotel, developed his acclaimed salad recipe in 1896 for a charity ball, dairy-free yogurt and egg-free mayonnaise probably didn't exist. If they had, his recipe surely would have been vegan. Created as a fruit and nut salad, ours takes it a step further with the addition of chickpeas. Crunchy and tender, sweet and salty—all at the same time—this salad begs you to slow down and savor each bite. Serve on a bed of crisp salad greens or tuck it into a pita pocket with peppery sprouts. We originally created this sweet, playful salad for children attending our summer camp, but quickly noticed that the adults liked it just as much by the way they gobbled it up at our food demonstrations.

Allergens: Contains nuts and ingredients that may contain soy

Ingredients

⅓ cup unsweetened, plain nondairy yogurt

⅓ cup vegan mayonnaise

2 Tbsps fresh lemon juice

½ tsp salt

3 cups cooked chickpeas or 2 (15.5-ounce) cans, drained and rinsed

1 medium apple, chopped in ½-inch pieces, about 1 cup

2 stalks celery chopped into ½-inch pieces, about 1 cup

2 cups seedless green grapes, halved lengthwise (red grapes discolor the chickpeas after several hours)

1 cup dried cranberries

1 cup walnuts, roughly chopped

To Serve

Salad greens

Pita bread

Sprouts

Directions

1. Whisk yogurt, mayonnaise, lemon juice, and salt in a large bowl. Add chickpeas, apple, celery, grapes, cranberries, and walnuts to the bowl and toss to combine. Serve immediately. Salad is best eaten within two days when stored in the refrigerator.

Curried Cashew Tofu Salad

SERVES 3 TO 4

Chef Linda: Lunchtime is often a guilty, stolen moment crammed between meetings, errands, or other demands. But it doesn't have to be that way. Even in the midst of a hectic day, we all need to nourish and renew our bodies and spirits. Steal a moment and enjoy this luscious dish. Treated right, tofu is a willing partner and chameleon, changing its nature and demeanor depending on who it's keeping company with. Smoky curry infuses this creamy dressing with warmth, while sweet cashews and shredded carrot provide a welcome crunch amidst the velvety-soft tofu. A sublime pleasure.

Allergens: Contains nuts and soy

Ingredients

1 (14- to 16-ounce) package organic extra-firm tofu

3 Tbsps vegan mayonnaise

2 Tbsps tahini

3 Tbsps fresh lemon juice

2 tsps mild or hot curry powder

2 tsps toasted sesame oil

1 tsp maple syrup

1 tsp salt

⅛ tsp cayenne, plus more to taste

Ground black pepper, to taste

2 medium carrots, peeled and grated, about 1 cup

2 scallions, finely chopped, about ¼ cup

½ large cucumber, peeled, seeded, sliced lengthwise and cut into ¼-inch pieces

½ cup raw or roasted and salted cashews

¼ cup raisins or dried apricot (optional)

Chopped cilantro or parsley, for garnish

For Serving

Pita bread, tortillas, crackers

Lettuce cups

Directions

1. Drain, rinse, and press the tofu (see pg. 6).
2. In a medium bowl, stir together mayonnaise, tahini, lemon juice, curry powder, toasted sesame oil, syrup, salt, cayenne, and black pepper. Using your hands, crumble tofu into the bowl with the dressing. Add carrot, scallions, cucumber, cashews, and dried fruit. Mix and garnish with fresh herbs. Serve immediately or chill in refrigerator.

Mediterranean Orzo

SERVES 8 TO 10

Chef Linda: We created this tasty orzo salad to showcase the flavors of Mediterranean food and introduce guests to feta cheese made with tofu. Briny and lemony, colorful and vibrant, this combination of common ingredients creates a distinctive salad that's perfect for a weeknight dinner but festive enough for entertaining. The tofu is marinated in a salty, pungent paste and baked to intensify the flavors. You can make this dish without the tofu feta, but then you'd miss out on the creamy, salty chunks! The directions call for making the dressing in a food processor or, but you can chop ingredients with a knife for a chunkier effect.

Allergens: Contains soy
Special Equipment: Food processor or blender
Make Ahead: Make tofu feta 1 or 2 days in advance.

Ingredients

Tofu Feta

1 (14- to 16-ounce) package of firm or extra-firm tofu
3 Tbsps mellow white miso
3 Tbsps nutritional yeast
3 Tbsps fresh lemon juice
2 Tbsps extra-virgin olive oil
1 Tbsp apple cider vinegar
1 tsp garlic powder
1 tsp onion powder
1 tsp salt

Salad

12–16 ounces orzo pasta
1 (15-ounce can) chickpeas, rinsed and drained (or
    1½ cups cooked)
1 cup cherry tomatoes, halved
1 (12-ounce) jar kalamata olives, pitted and chopped
1 (12-ounce) jar marinated artichoke hearts, drained
    and chopped
1 cup packed fresh basil, chopped

Dressing

½ cup extra virgin olive oil
½ cup fresh lemon juice
1 cup capers, drained
⅓ cup sun-dried tomatoes, dry- or oil-packed, chopped
2 large cloves garlic, peeled
2 medium shallots, peeled

Freshly ground black pepper
½ tsp salt

Directions

1. Drain, raise, and press the tofu (see pg. 6).
2. To make the tofu feta, stir together the ingredients except the tofu in a large bowl. Cut tofu into 1-inch cubes. Add to the bowl and stir to coat. The tofu will be more flavorful if left to marinade for several hours or overnight, but proceed if time does not allow.
3. Preheat oven to 350°F. Arrange tofu in a single layer on a baking tray lined with parchment. Bake for 20 to 25 minutes, or until cubes turn light brown. Set aside to cool.
4. To make the salad, cook orzo according to package directions. Rinse with cold water, drain, and empty into a large bowl. Stir in chickpeas, tomatoes, olives, artichoke hearts, and basil.
5. To make the dressing, place all of the ingredients, except for the salt, in a food processor and pulse into a chunky blend; do not purée. Taste and add more salt and lemon juice if desired. Dressing should have a strong flavor so that it stands up to the orzo. Pour dressing over orzo and toss to combine. Add tofu feta and toss again. Serve immediately or chill in the refrigerator and serve cold.

Black Bean Mango Salad

SERVES 4 TO 6

Chef Linda: If you could eat with your eyes, you'd be full before taking even one bite of this vibrantly colored salad. Deep purple black beans, sunny-yellow mangos, verdant green scallions, and bright red peppers create a glorious medley of hues. Then there's the taste—sweet, salty, tangy, and tart. With only a few simple ingredients and a bit of prep work, this salad makes for a satisfying warm-weather weeknight dinner or festive addition to any potluck.

> **Tip:** Select mangos that give slightly when squeezed, indicating they are ripe. Frozen mango is not a good substitute.

Ingredients

3 ripe mangos
2 Tbsps olive oil
2 Tbsps apple cider vinegar
3 Tbsps fresh lime juice
1 tsp toasted sesame oil
½ tsp salt
Pinch of crushed red pepper flakes
2 (15.5 ounce) cans black beans, drained and rinsed
   (or 3 cups cooked)
1 red bell pepper, chopped into ¼-inch pieces, about
   1 cup
2 scallions, thinly sliced on the diagonal, about ¼ cup
Salad greens (optional)

Directions

1. To dice the mango into ½-inch cubes, slice it in half by cutting on each side, lengthwise, just outside the hard pit in the center. Using a paring knife, cut a grid pattern creating ½-inch cubes on each mango half, being careful not to cut through the skin. Turn the skin inside out so the cubes pop. Use a spoon or paring knife to scoop the flesh into a bowl.

2. In a medium bowl, whisk together olive oil, apple cider vinegar, lime juice, toasted sesame oil, salt, and crushed red pepper flakes. Add mangos, beans, bell pepper, and scallions. Toss gently. Serve in bowls or over fresh salad greens.

Greek Watermelon Salad

SERVES 6 TO 8

Chef Linda: This cool and refreshing salad swells with summer goodness. Sweet, juicy watermelon and cherry tomatoes are a tasty contrast to the salty olives and tofu feta, and a modest but lovely dressing coaxes out the season's best flavors. This recipe was developed to showcase tofu feta in our popular Compassionate Cuisine vegan cheese class. It may seem like an unusual combination of flavors, but we've never had leftovers!

Allergens: Contains soy and ingredients that may contain gluten
Make Ahead: Make tofu feta 1 or 2 days in advance for easy assembly.

Ingredients

Tofu Feta
1 (14- to 16-ounce) package of firm tofu
3 Tbsps mellow white miso
3 Tbsps nutritional yeast
3 Tbsps fresh lemon juice
2 Tbsps extra-virgin olive oil
1 Tbsp apple cider vinegar
1 tsp garlic powder
1 tsp onion powder
1 tsp salt

Salad
3 heaping cups of cubed 1-inch-piece watermelon
2 cups cherry tomatoes, halved
1 medium cucumber, peeled, seeded, halved
    lengthwise and sliced
1 small red onion, thinly sliced, about ½ cup
⅓ cup pitted kalamata olives, roughly chopped
1½ cups tofu feta
½ cup fresh parsley, mint, or basil, roughly chopped
3 Tbsps extra-virgin olive
3 Tbsps fresh lemon juice
Coarse salt, to taste
Ground black pepper, to taste

Directions

1. Drain, rinse, and press tofu (see pg. 6).
2. To make the tofu feta, prepare marinade paste by stirring together remaining ingredients in a large bowl. Cut tofu into 1-inch cubes and add to the bowl. Stir to gently to coat tofu. Result will be more flavorful if it's left to marinade for several hours or overnight, but proceed to baking if time does not allow.
3. Preheat oven to 350°F. Arrange tofu in a single layer on a baking tray lined with parchment. Bake for about 25 minutes, or until cubes start to turn light brown. Remove from oven and let cool completely or refrigerate.
4. To assemble the salad, gently toss together in a large bowl the watermelon, tomatoes, cucumber, onion, olives, tofu feta, and fresh herbs. Drizzle with the olive oil and add lemon juice. Sprinkle with pinch of salt and pepper. Toss again and serve chilled. Salad is best eaten the same day it's made.

Kale Caesar Salad with Polenta Croutons

SERVES 8 TO 10

Chef Linda: Italian immigrant and restaurateur, Caesar Cardini, is said to have invented a tasty salad made with the remaining ingredients left in his kitchen after a Fourth of July rush depleted his supplies. Originally, Caesar salad included anchovies, coddled eggs, and parmesan. Apologies, Mr. Cardini, you won't find those ingredients in our kitchen. In our version, adored by staff and guests at the Sanctuary, kale takes center stage because of its nutritional content, color, and curly leaves that cradle the luscious dressing. Capers, miso, and kelp granules provide the briny-salty punch in place of the anchovies. We used polenta to make the croutons to put a tasty spin on something familiar (and to make it gluten-free), but use cubed bread if you prefer.

Allergens: Contains nuts, soy, and ingredients that may contain gluten
Special Equipment: Food processor or blender
Make Ahead: Nut parmesan and dressing can be made 2 to 3 days in advance
Tip: Find kelp granules in the ethnic aisle of well-stocked grocery stores. You can also substitute with dulse flakes or ½ sheet of nori paper, crumbled into tiny pieces.

Ingredients

Polenta Croutons

1 (18-ounce) tube of pre-made polenta, cut into ½-inch cubes
2 Tbsps olive oil
½ cup nutritional yeast
1 Tbsp onion powder
1 Tbsp garlic powder
½ tsp salt

Nut Parmesan

1 cup unsalted nuts (walnuts, almonds, or Brazil nuts)
⅓ cup nutritional yeast
2 medium cloves garlic, peeled, plus more to taste
¼ tsp salt, plus more to taste

Dressing

1 cup raw cashews, soaked in water for 30 minutes, drained
4 large cloves garlic, peeled
4 Tbsps extra virgin olive oil
3 Tbsps fresh lemon juice
2 Tbsps white or yellow miso
2 Tbsps Dijon mustard
2 Tbsps kelp granules

2 Tbsps capers, drained
½ cup water

Salad

1 bunch kale, stems removed and torn or cut into small, small bite-sized pieces, about 5–6 cups
1 head of romaine lettuce, chopped into small bite-sized pieces, about 4 cups

Directions

1. To make polenta croutons, preheat oven to 425°F. Line a baking tray with parchment. Place cubed polenta in a large bowl and toss with the olive oil. Add nutritional yeast, onion powder, garlic powder, and salt. Toss to coat. Arrange polenta in a single layer on the baking tray and roast for 15 to 20 minutes stirring midway through baking. The croutons are done when the sides are golden brown.

2. To make the nut parmesan, place all the ingredients in a food processor and pulse until mixture resembles coarse sand. Taste and adjust seasonings, adding more salt or garlic, if you choose.

(continued on next page)

3. To make the dressing, place all the ingredients in a blender and blend until smooth. Add more water to thin, if necessary, 1 tablespoon at a time. Dressing should taste very strong. It will mellow when the salad is assembled.

4. To assemble the salad, place kale and romaine in a large bowl. Add the desired amount of dressing and toss to combine. Store leftover dressing in a covered container for up to one week. Top salad with polenta croutons and sprinkle with nut parmesan. Store leftover parmesan in the refrigerator for several weeks or freeze.

Lemon Hearts of Palm Salad

SERVES 3 TO 4

Chef Linda: Here's a light and lovely lunch you'll look forward to eating that is full of beautiful colors, bright flavors, and interesting textures. Hearts of palm, which are the tender, inner trunks of young palm tree trunks planted and replanted to harvest as food, can be found in most grocery stores. This salad is a delightful combination of both crunchy and soft textures with a light and lemony dressing. Serve it on toasted English muffins, stuffed in a pita, over fresh salad greens . . . or right out of the mixing bowl.

Allergens: Contains ingredients that may contain soy

Ingredients

2 Tbsps vegan mayonnaise

1 Tbsp whole grain or yellow mustard

2–3 Tbsps fresh lemon juice (start with 2 and add more if desired)

⅛ tsp cayenne pepper

1 (14- to 16-ounce) jar or can of hearts of palm, drained, rinsed, and roughly chopped

1 red bell pepper, chopped into ¼-inch pieces, about 1 cup

1 avocado, pitted and diced into ¼-inch pieces, about 1 cup

2 scallions, finely chopped, about ¼ cup

2 stalks celery, chopped into ¼-inch pieces, about 1 cup

¼ cup chopped fresh parsley

2 Tbsps capers, drained and chopped

½ tsp salt

Ground black pepper, to taste

To Serve

Toasted English muffins

Pita bread

Crackers

Fresh salad greens

Directions

1. In a medium bowl, whisk together the mayonnaise, mustard, lemon juice, and cayenne. Add hearts of palm, bell pepper, avocado, scallions, celery, parsley, capers, salt, and black pepper. Gently toss to combine.
2. Serve immediately with English muffins, pita bread, crackers, or fresh salad greens—or chill in refrigerator.

South of the Border Quinoa Salad

SERVES 6 TO 8

Chef Linda: Nutty-tasting quinoa, a seed related to spinach (yes, really!), has become the ubiquitous staple for vegans. Quinoa is not only versatile and quick-cooking, but it also makes an excellent and compassionate protein choice. Perfect for potlucks or lunch boxes, this recipe is fuss-free, flavorful, and fun to eat. Zesty with lime and crushed red pepper flakes, you can adjust the flavors by adding them a little at time until it tastes just right. Roasted and salted pumpkin (or sunflower) seeds add a burst of saltiness and crunch, but use raw if you prefer. This salad is forgiving and flexible.

> **Make Ahead:** Quinoa can be made 2 to 3 days in advance for easy assembly.
>
> **Tip:** For simplicity, we recommend frozen corn, but use fresh when it's in season. Cut the kernels from the cob and add them raw or use leftover from corn on the cob.

Ingredients

1 cup quinoa, rinsed

1¾ cups water

1½ tsps salt, divided

⅓ cup extra-virgin olive oil

⅓ cup fresh lime juice, from 3–4 limes

1 Tbsp maple syrup

½–1 tsp crushed red pepper flakes, depending on spice level

½ tsp ground cumin

1 (15.5-ounce) can black beans, drained and rinsed (or 1½ cups cooked)

1 (15.5-ounce) can red or white kidney beans, drained and rinsed (or 1½ cups cooked)

1 cup frozen corn kernels, thawed (or fresh corn kernels, raw or cooked)

¼ cup chopped cilantro leaves

2 scallions, thinly sliced, about ¼ cup

¼ cup roasted pepitas/pumpkin seeds or sunflower seeds

Directions

1. Bring quinoa, water, and 1 teaspoon of salt to a boil in a medium pot. Reduce heat to low, cover, and simmer until quinoa is tender, but still has a little bite to it and the liquid has been absorbed, about 15 minutes.

2. In a large bowl, whisk together oil, lime juice, syrup, crushed red pepper flakes, cumin, and remaining ½ teaspoon of salt. Add beans, corn, cilantro, and scallions. Empty quinoa into the bowl with the beans and dressing. Toss to combine. Garnish with pepitas or sunflower seeds. Serve immediately or chill in the refrigerator.

Simple Sweet and Tangy Coleslaw

SERVES 4 TO 6

Chef Linda: Like a simple black dress, everyone should have a go-to coleslaw recipe. When you do, you'll find yourself using it with burgers, BBQ, and just about anything that welcomes its bright, tangy flavor and crisp texture. This version works well in a team because it doesn't go overboard with its own flavors, but rather plays a supporting role to more dominant flavors. Make it once or twice, and you'll have it memorized for life.

> **Tip:** Cabbage has lots of water and can dilute the taste of the best dressings. Put the cabbage in a bowl and sprinkle with a little salt about 1 hour before making the coleslaw. Toss and keep it in the refrigerator. Drain excess water before using.

Ingredients

1½ tsps salt

¼ cup apple cider vinegar

¼ cup maple syrup

¼ cup olive oil

1 Tbsp yellow mustard

1 tsp celery seed

Ground black pepper, to taste

1 (10- to 16- ounce) package shredded cabbage, or 1 small head of red or green cabbage, thinly shredded

Directions

1. In a small bowl, mix together all ingredients except the cabbage. Pour the dressing over the cabbage and toss to coat evenly. Taste and adjust seasonings. Chill for 30 minutes, then toss again and serve.

Forbidden Rice and Edamame Salad

SERVES 6 TO 8

Chef Linda: We eat with our eyes first, which is why food should beckon and tempt—and this salad does all of that and more. Legend tells us that black rice was referred to as "forbidden" because it was once eaten exclusively by the emperors of China to enrich health and ensure longevity. Thankfully, we can all enjoy the taste, beauty, and health benefits of black rice today. This heirloom rice is treasured for its delicious roasted, nutty taste and beautiful deep-purple color. The addition of vibrant-green edamame beans and toasted pistachios add to the visual appeal and complement the nutritional value of the rice. Enjoy this salad as a side dish or a complete meal—good for a weeknight dinner but also impressive enough for entertaining.

Allergens: Contains nuts, soy, and ingredients that may contain gluten
Make Ahead: Shiitake crisps can be made 1 day in advance and stored in a sealed container in the refrigerator.

Ingredients

¾ cup black rice
½ tsp salt
½ cup white or multi-colored quinoa, rinsed
2 cups frozen shelled edamame, thawed

Shiitake Crisps

½ pound shiitake mushrooms, stemmed, caps very
    thinly sliced
3 Tbsps olive oil
½ tsp salt
½ tsp smoked paprika (optional)

Vinaigrette

¼ cup fresh lime juice, plus more to taste
3 Tbsps mild vinegar (like rice or apple cider)
3 Tbsps tamari or soy sauce
2 Tbsps extra-virgin olive oil
2 Tbsps toasted sesame oil
1 Tbsp maple syrup
2-inch piece of ginger, peeled and grated, about 1
    Tbsp
Salt, to taste

To Assemble

½ cup shelled, salted pistachios
2 scallions, thinly sliced, about ¼ cup

Directions

1. Bring 3½ cups water to a boil. Add rice and salt. Reduce heat, cover, and simmer for about 15 minutes. Add quinoa. Stir and cover again. Cook for another 10 to 15 minutes, or until the rice and quinoa are tender. Drain excess water and empty into a very large bowl or onto a baking tray to cool.

2. While the rice and quinoa are cooking, cook edamame according to package instructions. Drain and rinse in cold water. Avoid overcooking edamame or it will result in a dull green color instead of bright green.

3. To make the shiitake crisps, preheat oven to 375°F. Line a baking tray with parchment. Place sliced mushrooms in a mound on the baking tray. Drizzle with the oil. Toss to coat and arrange in a single layer. Sprinkle with salt and paprika. Roast for about 25 minutes, stopping to stir about halfway through cooking time. Mushrooms are done when they are dark brown, almost burnt. Transfer to a paper towel–lined plate to cool.

(continued on next page)

4. While rice, quinoa, and mushrooms are cooking, make the vinaigrette by whisking lime juice, vinegar, tamari, olive oil, toasted sesame oil, syrup, and ginger together in a large bowl. Taste and adjust with salt or more lime juice.
5. Add the cooled rice and quinoa, edamame, pistachios, and scallions to the bowl with the dressing. Toss to combine. Serve immediately, topped with shiitake crisps, or chill before serving.

Cashew Fried Rice

SERVES 4 TO 6 AS A MAIN DISH, 6 TO 8 AS A SIDE DISH

Chef Linda: Fried rice, a vibrant medley of flavors, colors, and textures, is a satisfying and compassionate dish when you leave out eggs and animal protein. This vegan version, developed for our Compassionate Cuisine Asian cooking class "Better Than Takeout," is the perfect dish for when you have leftover rice. Seasoned scrambled tofu replaces the eggs and contributes plant-based protein and calcium. Meaty cashews add texture and heartiness to this dish. We used our favorite ingredients here, and you can use your own to create endless variations of one of the most popular Chinese takeout dishes.

> **Allergens:** Contains nuts and soy, and ingredients that may contain gluten
> **Make Ahead:** Cook the rice 1 or 2 days in advance.

Ingredients

1 Tbsp oil
½ medium onion, finely chopped, about ½ cup
1 red bell pepper, chopped in ¼-inch pieces, about 1 cup
2 medium carrots, peeled and finely chopped or shredded, about 1 cup
1 cup frozen peas, thawed
3 large cloves garlic, minced, about 1 Tbsp
2-inch piece of fresh ginger, peeled and grated or minced, about 1 Tbsp
1 (14- to 16-ounce) package firm tofu, drained and rinsed
¼ cup nutritional yeast
2 tsps onion powder
1 tsp ground turmeric
½ tsp salt, plus more to taste
3 cups cooked rice
1 cup raw or roasted and salted cashews
¼ cup water
3 Tbsps tamari or soy sauce
1 Tbsp toasted sesame oil
2 scallions, thinly sliced, about ¼ cup
Chopped cilantro, for garnish

Directions

1. Heat the oil in a large pan or wok over medium heat. Add onion, bell pepper, and carrots and cook, stirring occasionally, until softened, about 10 minutes. Add peas, garlic, and ginger and cook about for about 3 minutes more. Transfer vegetables to a bowl.

2. Crumble tofu into the pan and add nutritional yeast, onion powder, turmeric, and salt. Cook, stirring frequently, for about 5 minutes, until tofu and spices are incorporated and tofu is yellow.

3. Add rice, cooked vegetables, cashews, water, and tamari. Continue to cook for about 5 minutes until everything is heated through. Taste and add more salt if desired. Turn off heat. Stir in toasted sesame oil, sprinkle with scallions, and garnish with cilantro. Serve immediately.

Blistered Green Beans with Leeks and Shiitake Crisps

SERVES 4 TO 6

Chef Linda: Blistered and adorned with buttery leeks and roasted shiitake, these aren't your average green beans. Bringing out the best in each other, the ingredients harmonize to create a flavorful, textured savory dish. The green beans are cooked quickly on high heat—the charred taste adds a smokiness that marries beautifully with a mess of sautéed leeks and garlic. A hearty splash of balsamic and maple syrup add lively notes. These green beans are simple enough for weeknights and sublime for special occasions.

Make Ahead: Shiitake crisps can be made up to 1 day ahead and stored in a sealed container in the refrigerator.

Ingredients

Shiitake Crisps

½ pound shiitake mushrooms, stems removed and very thinly sliced

3 Tbsps olive oil

½ tsp salt

¼ tsp smoked paprika, optional

Green Beans

2 Tbsps high-heat oil (like refined coconut, grape seed, avocado, or sunflower)

1½ pounds green beans or haricot verts (a long, thin variety), hard stems trimmed, if necessary

2 leeks, cut in half lengthwise and very thinly sliced, white and light green parts only, about 1½ cups

3 large cloves garlic, thinly sliced or minced, about 1 Tbsp

½ tsp salt

2 Tbsps balsamic vinegar

1 Tbsp maple syrup

Ground black pepper, to taste

Directions

1. To make the shiitake crisps, preheat oven to 375°F. Line a baking tray with parchment. Place sliced mushrooms in a mound on the baking tray. Drizzle with the oil. Toss to coat and arrange in a single layer. Sprinkle with salt and paprika. Roast for about 25 minutes, stopping to stir about halfway through cooking time. Mushrooms are done when they are dark brown, almost burnt. Transfer to a paper towel–lined plate to cool.

2. To make the green beans, heat oil over medium-high in a large (12-inch) frying pan; cast iron works very well. Let the oil get hot enough so that a green bean sizzles when added. Working in batches, add enough green beans to cover the bottom of the pan. Let them cook for a several minutes without stirring so that they blacken and blister a little. Cook, stirring occasionally, for about 8 minutes, until green beans are partly charred and mostly crisp, but a little tender to the bite. Transfer green beans to a plate and repeat until all the green beans are cooked.

3. Add the leeks, garlic, and salt to the pan. Cook, stirring occasionally, until the leeks are softened and translucent, another 5 minutes. Return all the green beans to the pan and stir in balsamic, syrup, and black pepper. Serve immediately with shiitake crisps on top.

Stovetop Mac and Cheese

SERVES 6 TO 8

Chef Linda: For many people considering a plant-based diet, it's not the meat but the cheese they can't imagine living without. Well, we'll let you in on a little secret . . . you don't have to live without it! Take this mac and cheese recipe—it's simple and economical, and it uses everyday ingredients, so you can dig into this creamy family-favorite anytime you want. Our approach is deceptively delicious: carrots, potatoes, and chickpeas are blended to silky-smooth perfection, and, together with few additional ingredients, they create a sauce that is undeniably cheesy. This dish is so good you may want to make it when the kids are *not* around. We encourage you to make extra sauce and eat it with broccoli, or baked potatoes, or your fingers . . .

Allergens: Contains ingredients that may contain gluten and soy. Nut parmesan contains nuts.
Special Equipment: Blender and food processor
Make Ahead: Nut parmesan can be made several days in advance.

Ingredients

Cheese Sauce

4 medium carrots, peeled and roughly chopped, about 2 heaping cups

2 medium waxy potatoes, peeled and cubed, about 2 heaping cups

½ medium onion, roughly chopped, about ½ cup

3 large cloves garlic, peeled

2 Tbsps vegan butter

2 cups unsweetened nondairy milk

1 (15.5-ounce) can chickpeas, drained and rinsed (or 1½ cups cooked)

¼ cup nutritional yeast

2 Tbsps fresh lemon juice, plus more to taste

2 tsps yellow mustard

¾ tsp ground turmeric

1 tsp salt, plus more to taste

Macaroni

1 pound elbow or shell macaroni, regular or gluten-free
Salt

Nut Parmesan

1 cup raw almonds, walnuts, or Brazil nuts

⅓ cup nutritional yeast

2 medium cloves garlic, peeled

¼ tsp salt

Directions

1. To make the cheese sauce, place carrots, potatoes, onion, garlic, and butter in a small pot and cover with milk. Simmer until the vegetables are soft, about 10 minutes. Remove from heat and carefully pour into the blender. Add the chickpeas, nutritional yeast, lemon juice, mustard, turmeric, and salt. Do not blend right away. Let the mixture cool while you start the macaroni.

2. Boil the macaroni in salted water, according to package directions.

3. Blend the cheese sauce for about 1½ minutes, until smooth and glossy. Taste and add more salt or lemon juice if you like.

4. To make the nut parmesan, put all of the ingredients in a food processor and pulse until finely ground.

5. When the pasta is done, drain and return it to the pot. Add most of the cheese sauce and stir to combine. It will seem very saucy, but the pasta will absorb the sauce as it sits. Serve immediately, drizzled with additional sauce and garnished with nut parmesan. Store the remaining nut parmesan in a sealed container in the refrigerator for up to one month. Extra sauce can be stored in the refrigerator for up to five days or frozen for up to six months.

Spiced Cabbage and Cauliflower

SERVES 4 TO 6

Chef Linda: In this Indian-inspired recipe, we use two vegetables that belong together, especially when combined with rich, warming spices—cabbage and cauliflower. Together, they create a lovely blank canvas to absorb rich flavors, while standing up in their own right. Garam masala, a common Indian blend of spices, boasts a warm, sweet flavor that transforms these ordinary vegetables into a magical experience. *Garam* refers to the intensity and heat of the spices, though it doesn't necessarily mean spicy, and *masala* is a term used for a mixture of spices. Served over rice or your favorite cooked whole grain, this humble dish is surprisingly addictive. In our Compassionate Cuisine Indian food class, we add a generous dollop of Cashew Sour Cream (pg. 188) to add a creamy, satisfying finish.

Ingredients

1 Tbsp coconut oil

1 tsp cumin seed

1 tsp mustard seeds

2 tsps garam masala

¼ tsp crushed red pepper flakes

2-inch piece of fresh ginger, grated, about 1 Tbsp

3 large cloves garlic, minced, about 1 Tbsp

1 head cauliflower, about 1½ pounds, cut into florets, about 6 cups

1 red bell pepper, seeded and sliced into thin strips, about 1 cup

1 medium head of cabbage, about 1½ pounds, very thinly sliced, about 6 cups

2 Tbsps fresh lemon juice

1½ tsps salt

Chopped cilantro, for garnish

Directions

1. Heat the oil in a large, deep pan or pot over medium heat. Add the cumin and mustard seeds, garam masala, crushed red pepper flakes, ginger, and garlic. Cook while stirring, for a minute or two, until fragrant. Add cauliflower as the bottom layer, then pepper strips, then cabbage, sprinkling a little salt on each layer as you go. Cover tightly and cook for about 25 minutes. Tightly covering the pot creates steam which helps to cooks the vegetables through.

2. When done, the cabbage and cauliflower should be tender, but not mushy. Check the texture about midway through cooking. Add lemon juice then toss gently in the pan and taste. Adjust seasonings if necessary, adding more heat or salt. Transfer to a serving platter and sprinkle with chopped cilantro.

Confetti Cauliflower "Rice" and Beans

SERVES 6 TO 8

Chef Linda: Is there anything that cauliflower can't do? This healthy cruciferous vegetable has worked its way onto the main stage and can be enjoyed as a plant-based alternative to steak, puréed to make cream sauces, or roasted with hot sauce to make vegan Buffalo Cauliflower Bites (pg. 45). Cauliflower can also serve as a lower-carb substitute for rice. All you need is a food grater or food processor to turn a head of cauliflower into a heaping bowl of "rice." In this recipe, you'll get the comforting texture and "south of the border" flavors without overdoing the carbs on your plate.

Special Equipment: Food processor or box grater

Ingredients

1 large head cauliflower cut into florets, or 2 (12 ounce) bags pre-cut, about 6 cups

2 Tbsps olive oil

1 red bell pepper, chopped into ¼-inch pieces, about 1 cup

1 medium zucchini, chopped into ¼-inch pieces, about 1½ cups

½ medium onion, chopped, about ½ cup

3 large garlic cloves, minced, about 1 Tbsp

2 tsps dried oregano

1 tsp chili powder

1 tsp ground cumin

¼ tsp crushed red pepper flakes

1½ tsps salt

1 cup frozen corn, thawed

1 (15.5 ounce) can black beans, rinsed and drained (or 1½ cups cooked)

2 Tbsps fresh lime juice, plus 1–2 extra limes, quartered, for garnish

Chopped cilantro, for garnish

Directions

1. Working in batches, place cauliflower chunks into food processor bowl, filling it only about halfway. Pulse until finely chopped.

2. Heat oil in large pan over medium heat. Add pepper, zucchini, and onion. Cook, stirring occasionally, until vegetables begin to soften, 8 to 10 minutes. Add cauliflower, garlic, oregano, chili powder, cumin, red pepper flakes, and salt. Cook for about 5 minutes, until cauliflower is just tender. Stir in corn, black beans, and lime juice. Cook several minutes more until heated through. Serve garnished with cilantro and extra limes.

Farro and Wild Mushroom Pilaf

MAKES 6 TO 8 SIDE-DISH SERVINGS

Chef Sara: Farro is an ancient form of wheat that has a nutty flavor and a texture similar to barley. When cooked, it retains a pleasant, slightly chewy texture that holds up beautifully in soups, salads, and side dishes. In this recipe, we've paired farro with flavorful mushrooms, pecans, dried cranberries, and fresh herbs to make a delicious and elegant pilaf, perfect for the holiday season.

Allergens: Contains gluten and nuts
Make Ahead: Farro can be cooked 1 or 2 days in advance.
Tip: Oyster mushrooms are our favorite here, but feel free to substitute cremini, portobello, or even white button mushrooms.

Ingredients

1½ cups farro, rinsed and drained
4¼ cups water
1 Tbsp olive oil
1 medium yellow onion, chopped, about 1 cup
8 ounces oyster, brown button or portobello
    mushrooms, trimmed and chopped, about 2 cups
3 cloves garlic, minced, about 1 Tbsp
¼ cup white wine (or ¼ cup apple juice and 1 tsp
    mild vinegar)
1½ tsps salt, plus more to taste
½ cup dried cranberries
½ cup chopped pecans
1 Tbsp chopped fresh sage (or 1 tsp rubbed sage)
1 Tbsp chopped fresh thyme (or 1 tsp dried thyme)
3 Tbsps chopped fresh parsley
Ground black pepper, to taste

Directions

1. Combine the farro and water in a large pot. Bring to a boil over medium-high heat. Reduce the heat to low, cover, and allow to simmer for 30 to 40 minutes, until the farro is tender but not mushy. Drain excess water and set the farro aside.

2. Heat the oil in a large pan over medium-high heat. Add the onion and cook until softened and translucent, about 10 minutes. Add the mushrooms and garlic, and cook for an additional 3 to 5 minutes, until the mushrooms have released their liquid and the garlic is fragrant. Pour in the wine and allow it to bubble and reduce for another minute or so, scraping up any flavorful bits from the bottom of the pan. Add the salt, cooked farro, cranberries, pecans, fresh herbs, and a few grinds of black pepper, and mix well. Taste, adjust seasonings as desired, and serve. The pilaf will keep in the refrigerator for up to five days.

Sanctuary Story
ON LOVE, LOSS, AND HOT DOGS

When a local fundraiser Go Dog Go was held to support dog rescue efforts, I was invited to be one of three judges of their "show." I jumped at the opportunity—there was fun to be had.

I was in the company of Bruce Littlefield, best-selling author and "arbiter of fun," and Pia Salk, a psychologist, animal lover, and live wire. Judging spackle would have been fun with these two, but when you add the fact that the divisions of this "dog show" were "Bad Hair Day," "Most Mysterious Heritage," "I Look Like My Mama," and so on, and that dog kisses were available on demand, *well*

. . . the day was custom made for me. In fact, Go Dog Go is the only kind of dog show I could ever support.

While Go Dog Go would have been my idea of a good time anytime, on this day, it was especially meaningful after a tough week of saying good-bye to my beloved Babe, a seventeen-year-old steer who touched thousands of lives at Catskill Animal Sanctuary and whom I loved every bit as much as I love The Great Dog Chumbley, who sleeps at the foot of my bed every night. If ever there was a big, hairy ball of lovableness, it was Babe.

Babe, all 1,800-ish pounds of him, arrived at Catskill Animal Sanctuary in 2003. We were a fledgling organization . . . and we looked it. We had just purchased our property, a forlorn, forgotten farm that needed rescuing every bit as much as the animals who would soon arrive, when big Babe barreled down the drive.

Babe's human friend had rescued him at an auction, wanting to save one life. She'd bottle-fed him, kept him in her backyard until he simply grew too big, then boarded him, rather ironically, at a beef farm. When she divorced, she could no longer afford his board, and the farmer gave her a month to find him a home. Fortunately for Babe, and fortunately for us, his human found Catskill Animal Sanctuary.

I am flooded with memories of the placid being with the soft eyes and the tongue that reached out expertly to grab one carrot, then another, and then another until a five-pound bag was gobbled up.

Among my favorite memories:

BABE THE HOMEBODY

I'm not sure why—maybe our fencing didn't stand a chance against our new "moose"—but for a short while, Babe was a free-ranger. Only he never went *anywhere*. Free to roam the entire farm, Babe instead stood in the middle of the barn aisle, motionless as Peepers the duck patrolled the barn by waddling frantically back and forth under Babe's belly. "Quack-*QUACK!!*" Peepers said, rushing under the black giant, who stood unfazed as he eyed the feed room. Surrounded by free-ranging ducks, chickens, goats, sheep, and a growing human fan club, Babe seemed supremely at peace.

BABE THE BRUTE

Once, a bunch of us were cleaning the cow field. I stood atop the tractor bucket to bellow instructions to volunteers who were spread throughout the large pasture. Babe wandered up to say hello, but got so close that when he turned his head to flick a fly away, he sent me sailing through the air. I landed with a thud, gathered my breath, then laughed hysterically. Babe startled, but then walked over and licked my head.

BABE THE RINGLEADER

6:30 a.m. Two police cars pulled down our driveway. "Are you missing somebody?" a young cop asked. I remember the wry smile on his face; somehow I knew that this was code for "Your cows are in town." And in the town they were, all right—Babe had led his herd through the woods, down our local rural lane, and onto the *very busy* Rt. 9W . . . and then he'd just stood there. The escapade, and our return walk home (I put a bright green draft horse halter on Babe and led him down the road while the others followed) was on the evening news.

BABE THE WISEMAN

Several summers ago, the renowned Omega Institute invited us to bring animals for their animal communication workshop. We don't typically oblige such requests, and have turned down dozens more to provide animals for school fairs, Nativity scenes, and even a movie shoot in Central Park. But this felt different. We'd be outside, by the pond, where the animals could relax, graze, and essentially be loved for a weekend. So we took our best ambassadors, and our most social friends—the ones we felt would truly enjoy the experience. Whether or not we learned how to "communicate" with them (I believe all of us are communicating all the time but am ambivalent about how "animal communication" is often taught), I wanted our animal friends to open the hearts of those whose previous experiences had only included dogs and cats.

I didn't expect that Babe would want to join us. Like many of us, cows are frightened of unfamiliar situations. Yet when I opened the trailer door, *he evidently did* because he stepped right in and cozied up next to Chester the horse. That he had absolute trust was remarkable enough. And while maybe it's a stretch to say that on some level he knew we needed him, that's surely what it felt like.

Throughout the weekend, the communicator guided us through various relaxation techniques, after which we would open ourselves to the messages our friends wished to share. I was blown away by our animals' comfort level and their obvious connection to their Catskill people (six staff members had been given the chance to attend the workshop)—how much we learned from them!

The instructor decided that Babe would be the final animal with whom we'd practice. This is exactly what happened: we had just finished "speaking with" our old, hilarious Appaloosa named Chester, who put his head down to graze in the meadow where we'd gathered. "Let's turn our attention now to this big guy," the teacher said, gesturing toward Babe, and as she suggested that we form a circle around him, Babe walked right into the middle. Then, as she'd done with each of the animals, she invited us to close our eyes. As she spoke softly and we breathed slowly and deeply, my eyes stayed open, and I watched a huge black head droop. "Relax," she whispered, and he did. Babe's giant head dropped lower, and lower still, until right before his knees were about to buckle, he folded his legs and lay down.

And that's when I received a clear and plaintive and powerful message. "We don't want to be hamburger," is one part I remember, along with: "I hope I'm doing a good job. Thank you for choosing me."

To this day, I'm not sure what to make of that moment.

I don't recall what anyone said about what Babe "communicated" to them. But I do recall many of them weeping, one woman sitting in front of him and cradling his massive head as he licked her face, and another woman draping her body over Babe's back (after she saw me do it). And I remember the thought that struck me like a lightning bolt: "These people will never eat meat again."

Back to my story: I suppose the organizers of Go Dog Go thought it would be clever to sell "hot dogs" (and nothing more) at a "dog show." But the "hot dogs" were not "hot" (as in cooked) "dogs" (as in the animal) at all. They were cooked cows. I'm fairly certain that our Babe, and every other cow or pig who's ever lived, if given the "Bad Hair Day" or "Become a Hot Dog" choice, would have chosen the former.

I stood in line behind half a dozen animal lovers, all of whom ordered cooked cows.

"I'll have the veggie burrito," I said to the vendor, who in the eleventh hour had put them on her menu at my request.

"I have a pet pig," she said as we chatted briefly about my special request. "He's really something."

"They're remarkable animals," I responded. "Are you vegan?"

"Me?" she laughed. "Never. I love my meat."

Eating vegan does not mean forsaking hearty, meaty foods. Consider a Cuban Jackfruit Sandwich, crispy and oozing with cheese (pg. 117), a Shepherd's Pie piled high with mashed potatoes (pg. 161), or a thick slice of Meatless Meatloaf doused in gravy (pg. 145). We, too, love our meat—ours just happens to be made from plants.

Main Meals

Without the hope of something delicious or familiar to hitch our hunger to, eating vegan might seem elusive. We'll wish for a burger piled high with toppings to sink our teeth into. We'll pine for meatballs smothered in sauce. And the day will come when nothing short of creamy fettuccine will tame our passions. Luckily, eating vegan doesn't mean foregoing any of these. These main meals have been created to soothe and gratify, to delight and surprise, and to reassure us that choosing compassion eliminates only the suffering, not the satisfaction.

BURGERS AND SANDWICHES

HEARTY FARE

Sensational Sloppy Joes

SERVES 4 TO 6

Chef Linda: For some, the Sloppy Joe is a bad memory—an oily, mysterious, loose meat sandwich served in school cafeterias. Thanks to the humble lentil, this version gets a scrumptious, meat-free makeover. Cooked right, lentils are tender with a just a little bite. But texture is only half of the equation. Sloppy Joes have a distinct flavor: sweet, sour, and tangy—a playful cross between tomato sauce and BBQ sauce. To achieve it, we use vinegar, mustard, syrup, and, yes, molasses! Add your favorite hot sauce for a spicy kick. Your Sloppy Joe won't be truly complete unless it's served on a lightly toasted bun with a "schmear" of vegan butter and a side of potato chips to scoop up what will inevitably fall out.

Allergens: Contains ingredients that may contain gluten
Make Ahead: Lentils can be cooked several days in advance.
Tip: Worcestershire sauce traditionally includes anchovies to give it a salty punch, so look for a vegan version in the aisle with BBQ sauce. Use it to add a tangy zing to dressings and sauces.

Ingredients

1 cup lentils
2 tsps salt, divided
2 Tbsps olive oil
1 medium onion, finely chopped, about 1 cup
1 large red bell pepper, chopped in ¼-inch pieces, about 1 cup
3 cloves garlic, minced, about 1 Tbsp
1 cup water
2 Tbsps tomato paste
2 Tbsps ketchup
2 Tbsps maple syrup or brown sugar
2 Tbsps apple cider vinegar
1 Tbsp vegan Worcestershire sauce
1 Tbsp yellow mustard
1 Tbsp molasses
1½ tsps smoked paprika
1 tsp chili powder

To Serve

Soft buns or rolls
Vegan butter
Potato chips
Dill pickles

Directions

1. Pick over the lentils, discarding any withered ones or stones. Place in a medium saucepan, cover generously with water, add 1 teaspoon of salt and bring to a boil. Lower the heat and simmer for about 20 minutes, until tender. Avoid overcooking. Drain and set aside.

2. Heat oil in a medium pot over medium-high heat. Add the onion, bell pepper, garlic, and the remaining 1 teaspoon of salt. Cook, stirring occasionally, until vegetables begin to soften, 8 to 10 minutes. Add the water, tomato paste, ketchup, syrup, vinegar, Worcestershire sauce, mustard, molasses, smoked paprika, and chili powder. Lower heat to medium and simmer for about 10 minutes more, until sauce has thickened.

3. Remove pan from heat. Lightly toast buns and spread with vegan butter. Place buns on plates and spoon lentil mixture on top. Serve with potato chips and pickles.

Cuban Jackfruit Sandwiches

MAKES 4 SANDWICHES

Chef Linda: A variation of a ham and cheese sandwich that includes roast pork, the Cuban sandwich was a common lunch for workers in the cigar factories and sugar mills in Cuba. It's made with crispy bread, pressed on a grill top, and held fast with oozing cheese and tangy pickles. We just had to remake this classic with compassion, and jackfruit fit the bill to take the place of the pork. A zesty marinade perks up this versatile, canned fruit. We like roasting the jackfruit—we think it deepens the flavors—but fry it in a pan if you prefer. Vegan sliced cheese is essential to the gooey, scrumptious texture of this sandwich—thank goodness there are so many brands to choose from! Complete this compassionate remake with a good "schmear" of spicy mustard and a crisp dill pickle.

Allergens: Contains gluten and ingredients that may contain soy
Special Equipment: Food processor recommended

Ingredients

¼ cup orange juice
¼ cup lime juice
¼ cup vegan mayonnaise
3 Tbsps maple syrup
2 Tbsps tamari or soy sauce
3 large cloves garlic, minced, about 1 Tbsp
1 Tbsp chopped cilantro, optional
2 tsps onion powder
1 tsp ground cumin
1 tsp salt
Ground black pepper, to taste
2 (20-ounce) cans jackfruit in brine, drained and rinsed

To Assemble

4 Cuban rolls (or a large baguette or crusty sandwich rolls)
Yellow mustard
8 slices of your favorite vegan sliced cheese
8 slices of vegan ham (optional)
Dill pickles slices
2 Tbsps vegan butter

Directions

1. Preheat oven to 375°F. Line a baking tray with parchment.
2. To make the marinade, in a large bowl, whisk together orange juice, lime juice, mayonnaise, syrup, tamari, garlic, cilantro, onion powder, cumin, salt, and pepper. Use a food processor to chop the jackfruit. Alternatively, chop the jackfruit with a sharp knife. You may have to cut out hard centers of the jackfruit pieces and discard before chopping. Add chopped jackfruit to the bowl with the marinade. Mix well. Spread the jackfruit on the lined baking tray and bake for about 30 minutes until edges start to brown slightly.
3. To assemble the sandwiches, split the bread and spread mustard liberally on both sides. Place one slice of cheese on the top of the roll and one on the bottom, then layer the sandwich with ham, pickles, and jackfruit in between. To cook, melt butter in a large pan (cast iron works well) over medium heat. Depending on the size of your pan, place one or two sandwiches in the pan and top with another heavy pan or pot, then put something heavy in the top pan or pot to help press the sandwiches down as they cook; canned beans or tomatoes work well. Sandwiches should be pressed to about half their original thickness. Cook for about 5 minutes per side, pressing down occasionally, until the sandwiches have flattened, the bread is toasted, and the cheese has melted. Alternatively, use an electric panini grill. Cut in half and serve immediately.

Sweet Potato Black Bean Burritos with Cashew Herb Cream

MAKES 6 TO 8 BURRITOS

Chef Linda: Sassy and sweet, this dish was a hands-down favorite in our Compassionate Cuisine "Budget-Friendly Vegan Meals" class. Shattering the myth that eating vegan is costly and difficult, this is just one of many recipes made from easy-to-find, economical ingredients. And unlike many burritos, they boast healthy ingredients. Plus, they taste great! Maybe it's the combination of gently spiced roasted sweet potatoes and earthy salsa black beans. Or it could be the luscious cashew herb cream on top. We can't decide, because we think that this whole is definitely greater than the sum of its parts!

Allergens: Contains gluten and nuts
Special equipment: Blender

Ingredients

Sweet Potatoes

2 medium sweet potatoes, peeled and cut into
½ -inch cubes, about 3 cups
1 red bell pepper, chopped into ¼-inch pieces, about
1 cup
½ medium onion, finely chopped, about ½ cup
2 Tbsps oil
1 Tbsp chili powder
½ tsp ground cumin
½ tsp ground cinnamon
½ tsp salt
¼ tsp ground cayenne pepper

Black Beans

2 (15.5-ounce) cans black beans, drained and rinsed
¾ cup jarred salsa, divided
½ tsp salt

To Assemble

6–8 large (10-inch) tortillas
2 ripe avocados, pitted and sliced
1 batch Cashew Herb Cream (pg. 189)
Chopped cilantro or parsley, for garnish

Directions

1. Preheat oven to 400°F. Line a baking tray with parchment. Lightly oil a 9-inch square baking dish and set aside.

2. To make the sweet potatoes, place them along with the bell pepper and onion on the baking tray in a pile. Drizzle with the oil. Sprinkle with chili powder, cumin, cinnamon, salt, and cayenne. Use your hands to toss together, coating everything with spices and oil. Arrange in a single layer. Place the tray in oven and roast for about 20 minutes, or until sweet potatoes are fork-tender, but not mushy, and the bell peppers and onions are tender. When done, remove from oven and reduce temperature to 375°F.

3. To make the black beans, place them in a bowl with ½ cup of salsa and salt. Use a wooden spoon or fork to mash the beans and the salsa together so that you end up with a spreadable filling.

4. To assemble, lay a tortilla flat on a cutting board. Spread about ¼ cup of black bean–salsa mixture on the tortilla, leaving a ¼-inch border. Arrange ⅓ to ½ cup of sweet potato mixture evenly over the black beans about a third of the way up from the bottom edge closest to you. Lay 2 to 3 slices of avocado across the sweet potatoes. Using a

firm hand, begin rolling away from you, while folding and tucking the ends in. Place burritos seam side down in the prepared baking dish and repeat until ingredients have been used.

5. Spoon about half of the cashew-herb cream over burritos. Place the baking dish in the oven and bake for about 15 minutes, to heat through. Serve immediately, garnished with the remaining half of the cashew cream and remaining ¼ cup tomato salsa. Garnish with cilantro. Alternatively, you can serve without baking.

White Bean, Artichoke, Arugula Wraps

MAKES 4 LARGE WRAPS

Chef Linda: Do you remember eagerly awaiting lunchtime in grade school? Discovering and devouring neatly packed sandwiches and treats in our paper bags or lunch boxes was a welcome break in the day. Bring back the excitement that made you watch the clock so closely by making yourself one of these wraps! Wholesome white beans and tangy artichoke hearts join forces with peppery arugula and radishes, cooling cucumber, and creamy avocado. This wrap will give you a hearty dose of protein, a serving of your daily greens, and the delight in knowing that you are the envy of the lunch room.

Allergens: Contains gluten
Special Equipment: Food processor
Make Ahead: Shiitake crisps can be made 1 day in advance and stored in a covered container in the refrigerator.

Ingredients

Shiitake Crisps

4 ounces shiitake mushrooms, stemmed and very
 thinly sliced
3 Tbsps olive oil
½ tsp salt
¼ tsp smoked paprika (optional)

Filling

2 (15.5-ounce) cans white beans, drained and rinsed
 (or 3 cups cooked)
2 cups marinated artichoke hearts, drained
¼ cup sun-dried tomatoes (dry- or oil-packed),
 chopped
2 Tbsps fresh lemon juice
½ tsp salt

To Assemble

4 cups arugula, lightly chopped
2 small radishes, very thinly sliced
2 Tbsps fresh lemon juice
1 Tbsp olive oil
½ large cucumber, peeled, seeded, and cut lengthwise
 into thin spears
1 avocado, pitted and cut into thick slices
4 (10-inch) tortillas

Directions

1. To make the shiitake crisps, preheat oven to 375°F. Line a baking tray with parchment. Place sliced mushrooms on the baking tray in a pile. Drizzle with olive oil and mix together with your hands. Arrange in a single layer and sprinkle with salt and paprika. Roast for about 25 minutes. Mushrooms are done when they are dark brown, almost burnt. Transfer to a paper towel–lined plate to cool.

2. To make the filling, place white beans, artichoke, sun-dried tomatoes, lemon juice, and salt in the food processor. Pulse several times to combine into a thick, chunky mixture.

3. To assemble, place the arugula and radishes in a medium bowl. Drizzle with the lemon juice and oil and toss. Lay tortillas, one at a time, on a cutting board. Spread about ¾ cup of the white bean mixture on the tortilla, leaving a ½-inch border. Place arugula over the bean mixture. Lay 2 cucumber spears and a couple of avocado slices on the bottom third of each tortilla. Sprinkle shiitake crisps on top. Roll, while tucking in the ends, into a burrito shape. Cut each wrap in half, on the diagonal, to serve.

Tempeh Reuben Sandwich

MAKES 4 SANDWICHES

Chef Linda: The Reuben Sandwich is traditionally made with corned beef, Swiss cheese, and Russian dressing, and it delivers 40 grams of fat, 1,600 milligrams of sodium, and 770 calories. Ouch! A more compassionate approach, for you and the animals, is our Tempeh Reuben Sandwich. Always a favorite at our special events, it's made with heart-healthy tempeh, avocado, and sauerkraut, and dressed up with a quick and tasty dressing. Tempeh is often maligned because of its texture and bitter tones, but if simmered in a little water and soy sauce or tamari, it becomes recipe-ready! Add a side of fries or a bowl of soup, and this tangy, succulent sandwich will work its way onto your shortlist of easy favorites.

Allergens: Contains gluten and soy

Ingredients

Tempeh

1 (8-ounce) package of tempeh
1¼ cup water
3 tsps tamari or soy sauce

Marinade

2 Tbsps olive oil
2 Tbsps tamari or soy sauce
2 Tbsps apple cider vinegar
1 Tbsp maple syrup
1 Tbsp yellow mustard
1 tsp liquid smoke (optional)

Dressing

⅓ cup vegan mayonnaise
2 Tbsps capers, rinsed and chopped (or relish)
2 Tbsps ketchup
1 Tbsp fresh lemon juice
1 tsp hot sauce or sriracha

To Assemble

8 slices rye bread
1 ripe avocado, pitted and thinly sliced
1 cup sauerkraut, room temperature or hot

Directions

1. Preheat oven to 375°F. Lay tempeh on cutting board horizontally. Place your palm on the top of the tempeh and hold while cutting horizontally, creating two, long, thin cutlets. Keep the two pieces together and cut it width-wise, in half, then cut each half in half again. You should end up with 8 cutlets. Place tempeh, water, and tamari in a small pot over medium heat. Simmer for about 10 minutes. Using a slotted spoon, gently remove the tempeh cutlets from the pot and place them on a plate lined with a clean paper towel to dry.

2. To make the marinade, whisk together the oil, tamari, vinegar, syrup, mustard, and liquid smoke in a baking dish. Arrange tempeh in a single layer in the baking dish and spoon marinade over slices to ensure even coating. Bake for 25 to 30 minutes, or until tempeh is medium to dark brown. Remove from oven.

3. To make the dressing, stir together the mayonnaise, capers, ketchup, lemon juice, and hot sauce.

4. To assemble the sandwiches, slather 4 pieces of bread with dressing. Place two tempeh slices each on of the four slices. Top each with a few slices of avocado and 1 or 2 tablespoons of sauerkraut. Top each slice of bread with another slice. Cut in half and serve.

BBQ Jackfruit Sandwiches

MAKES 4 TO 6 SANDWICHES

Chef Linda: When brainstorming for Father's Day recipes, BBQ—and its layers of rich, hearty, and familiar flavors—was top of mind. Our challenge was to deliver on those worthy expectations while keeping the meal kind. Luckily, we have jackfruit, the perfect vehicle for all the flavors in a BBQ sandwich. Cooked first in a delicious marinade, then finished off with traditional BBQ sauce (store-bought or homemade, see our recipe on pg. 186), the smoky, spicy scent will surely make your mouth water and reassure you that compassion is always the best ingredient. For a different spin on nachos, use this recipe on tortilla chips with your favorite vegan toppings.

Allergens: Contains ingredients that may contain gluten
Special Equipment: Food processor

Ingredients

2 (20-ounce) cans green jackfruit, in water or brine (not syrup)
3 large cloves garlic, minced, about 1 Tbsp
2 Tbsps maple syrup
2 Tbsps yellow mustard
2 tsps smoked paprika
2 tsps chili powder
1 tsp ground cumin
1 tsp salt
1 tsp liquid smoke (optional)
¼–½ tsp cayenne pepper
2 Tbsps olive oil
1 cup store-bought BBQ sauce, plus extra for topping (or use our BBQ sauce recipe on pg. 186)

To Serve

Soft buns
Simple, Sweet and Tangy Coleslaw (pg. 97)
Dill pickles

Directions

1. Empty jackfruit into a strainer and rinse. Place jackfruit in a food processor and pulse to chop. You can also chop the jackfruit by hand, but remove tough center cores first.
2. In a medium bowl, mix together garlic, syrup, mustard, paprika, chili powder, cumin, salt, liquid smoke, and cayenne pepper. Add the jackfruit into the bowl and toss together.
3. Heat oil in a medium pan over medium heat. Add jackfruit and cook for about 15 minutes, stirring occasionally. When the jackfruit is darkened and somewhat dried out, add the BBQ sauce and stir. Cook for another 8 to 10 minutes to ensure flavor is distributed throughout. Serve on buns topped with another dollop of BBQ sauce.

Compassionate "Crab" Cakes with Remoulade Sauce

SERVES 4 TO 6 AS A MAIN COURSE

Chef Linda: If your heart swoons for crab cakes in the summer, but you want a more compassionate solution to your craving, this recipe is a must. There are two options to replace the crab—hearts of palm, an ingredient found jarred or in cans in most grocery stores; or jackfruit, a tropical fruit most often purchased in cans. Both have their merits, and both are delicious. We use kelp flakes to add a bit of briny, seaside taste. Light, crispy, and so flavorful, these compassionate "crab" cakes are always the hit of the party when we serve them at the Sanctuary. Lovely as an appetizer or main course served with fries or salad greens.

Allergens: Contains ingredients that may contain soy
Special Equipment: Food processor recommended if using jackfruit
Make Ahead: Mixture can be made 1 day in advance.
Tip: Depending on which brand of canned jackfruit you use, you may have to cut out the tough core at the center of each piece before chopping by hand.

Ingredients

"Crab" Cakes

1½ cups breadcrumbs, regular or gluten-free, divided
¼ cup vegan mayonnaise, plus 1 heaping Tbsp if using jackfruit
2 Tbsps capers, rinsed and chopped
2 Tbsps fresh lemon juice
2 tsps kelp flakes
1 Tbsp yellow mustard
1 tsp Old Bay Seasoning
½ tsp salt
Ground black pepper, to taste
Dash of cayenne pepper
1 (14- to 16-ounce) jar of hearts of palm, drained, rinsed, and roughly chopped, or 1 (20-ounce) can of jackfruit in brine, drained and pulsed 2–3 times in a food processor or finely chopped
½ red bell pepper, finely chopped, about ½ cup
2 large celery stalks, finely chopped, about 1 cup
¼ cup minced fresh parsley
1 large shallot, minced, about 3 Tbsps

Assembly

2–3 Tbsps olive oil
1 batch Remoulade Sauce (pg. 186)

Directions

1. To make the "crab" cakes, measure out ¾ cup of the breadcrumbs into a shallow dish and set aside. In a medium bowl, stir together the mayonnaise, capers, lemon juice, kelp flakes, mustard, Old Bay Seasoning, salt, ground pepper, and cayenne. Add hearts of palm or jackfruit, bell pepper, celery, parsley, shallots, the remaining ¾ cup of breadcrumbs, and stir to combine. If using jackfruit, add an extra 1 heaping tablespoons of vegan mayonnaise. Let stand for about 10 minutes to allow the breadcrumbs to bind everything together.

2. Gently shape "crab" cake mixture into patties, about 3 inches wide and ½ inch thick. Dredge the patties in breadcrumbs. Heat oil in a large skillet over medium heat. Fry cakes until golden brown and crisp, about 3 to 4 minutes per side. Alternatively, to bake the cakes, preheat oven to 375°F. Line a baking tray with parchment. Brush parchment with oil and arrange cakes on it several inches apart. Bake for 20 to 25 minutes, carefully flipping midway through.

3. Serve immediately with a dollop of remoulade sauce on top.

Scarlet Black Bean Burgers

MAKES 8 TO 10 BURGERS

Chef Linda: Veggie burgers are a healthy, compassionate way to include variety in your plant-based diet. Flexibility and creativity are hallmarks of homemade burgers—use what you have on hand, make substitutions, and let the spices and flavors work for you. The delightfully chunky texture in this recipe comes from humble whole foods like mushrooms, oats, walnuts, and black beans. Beets provide earthy flavor and color, and even the most committed beet-haters won't be able to discern their flavor while enjoying their wholesome nutrients. Baked in the oven, these burgers are ample, satisfying, and hold together on a bun or on a bed of salad greens. Serve with Avocado-Scallion Sauce (pg. 185), and thank us later.

Allergens: Contains nuts and ingredients that may contain gluten and soy
Special Equipment: Food processor

Ingredients

2 Tbsps oil
1 medium beet, peeled and cut into chunks, about 1 cup
2 medium carrots, peeled and cut into large pieces, about 1 cup
½ medium onion, peeled, cut into chunks, about ½ cup
5 ounces button mushrooms, with stems
3 large cloves garlic, peeled
1 cup old-fashioned oats
½ cup walnuts
2 tsps chili powder
2 tsps smoked paprika
1 tsp ground cumin
1 tsp salt
1 (15.5-ounce) can black beans, drained and rinsed (or 1½ cups cooked)
½ cup vegan mayonnaise

For Serving

Buns, lettuce, tomato, avocado
1 batch Avocado-Scallion Sauce (pg. 185)

Directions

1. Preheat oven to 375°F. Line a baking tray with parchment. Brush oil on the parchment.
2. Place beets, carrots, onion, mushrooms, and garlic in the bowl of a food processor. Pulse until finely chopped. Empty into a large bowl. Next, place oats, walnuts, chili powder, paprika, cumin, and salt into the processor and pulse several times, leaving some texture to the nuts and oats. Empty into bowl with beet mixture. Finally, place beans and mayonnaise in the processor and pulse to combine, leaving some texture to the beans. Empty into the bowl with the other ingredients and mix everything together.
3. Use a medium portion scoop or ⅓ measuring cup to form each patty. Use an offset spatula or knife to flatten and create uniform burgers that are 1½ inches thick and about 3 inches wide. Place burgers on tray in oven and bake for about 30 minutes. Remove tray from oven and let burgers sit for about 5 minutes to set.
4. Serve alone or on buns with all of the fixings—lettuce, tomato, avocado, and avocado-scallion sauce. Refrigerate extra cooked burgers for up to five days, or freeze between layers of parchment paper in a covered container.

Seaside Summer Rolls

SERVES 4 TO 6

Chef Linda: Summer tickles us with the notion that the beach is the place to be. Sandy feet, briny breezes, and easy living. If you could wrap up that feeling and eat it, you'd have these Seaside Summer Rolls. Perfect for the beach-blanket lunches or lazy picnics in your backyard, two winning texture combinations (tender, chunky hearts of palm and chewy mushrooms) make this sandwich reminiscent of a lobster roll, but without the cruelty. Filling and satisfying, but playfully light, you might serve these rolls with some chips and and ice-cold lemonade on the side.

Allergens: Contains ingredients that may contain gluten and soy
Tip: If King Oyster mushrooms are hard to come by, substitute shiitake mushroom caps cut into thick strips.

Ingredients

½ pound King Oyster or trumpet mushrooms
2 Tbsps oil
2 Tbsps vegan mayonnaise
2 Tbsps fresh lemon juice
1½ tsps Old Bay Seasoning
Ground black pepper, to taste
Salt, to taste (optional)
1 (14.5-ounce) jar or can of hearts of palm, drained, rinsed, and very roughly chopped
2 large stalks celery, finely chopped, about 1 cup
1 Tbsp fresh herbs, finely chopped, like dill, chives, or parsley
4–6 split-top vegan hot dog buns
2 Tbsps vegan butter or oil
1 lemon, sliced, for serving

Directions

1. Chop mushroom caps and stems into large pieces. Heat oil in a large pan over medium-high heat. Add mushrooms to the pan and cook, stirring occasionally, for several minutes until lightly golden brown all over. Sprinkle with a little salt, then cover tightly and continue to cook for about 5 minutes longer. Remove from heat and set aside.

2. In a medium bowl, stir together mayonnaise, lemon juice, Old Bay Seasoning, and black pepper. Taste and add salt, if desired. Add hearts of palm, celery, and herbs to the bowl with the dressing. Add cooked mushrooms to the bowl with the hearts of palm and dressing. Gently toss to combine.

3. To toast the rolls, heat vegan butter in the mushroom pan on medium-high heat. Open the rolls and place face down on the hot pan to toast for several minutes. Remove from heat. To serve, spoon filling into toasted buns. Serve with lemon wedges.

BBQ Tempeh Sandwiches

MAKES ABOUT 4 SANDWICHES

Chef Linda: Nothing says summer like the flavors of BBQ. Smoky, tangy, sweet, or hot, there's good reason to love anything slathered in BBQ sauce, especially when it's healthy and compassionate. Why settle for a store-bought bottle of sauce when you can make your own? Made mostly with pantry ingredients, this BBQ sauce has a distinct, clean flavor, made with less sugar than most store-bought versions and no preservatives. You'll also enjoy the freedom to adjust the flavors to suit your taste. Tempeh is a wonderful canvas for this sassy sauce and stands up mightily to your favorite buns and vegan coleslaw—but cauliflower, tofu, or portobello work just as well.

Allergens: Contains soy and ingredients that may contain gluten
Make Ahead: BBQ sauce can be made in advance and stored for up to 3 months.
Tip: Worcestershire sauce typically contains anchovies, so look for a vegan version in the aisle where you would find BBQ sauce.

Ingredients

1 (8-ounce) package tempeh
1¼ cup water
3 Tbsps tamari or soy sauce
1 batch The Only BBQ Sauce You'll Ever Need (pg. 186)

To Serve

Buns
Simple, Sweet and Tangy Coleslaw (pg. 97)

Directions

1. Place tempeh on a cutting board, horizontally. Slice tempeh across into ¼-inch-wide strips. Place water, tamari, and tempeh in a small pot. Simmer for about 10 minutes. Transfer tempeh to a plate lined with a paper towel to dry.

2. Preheat oven to 375°F. Line a casserole dish or baking pan with parchment for easy cleanup. Pour enough BBQ sauce to just cover the bottom of the casserole dish. Arrange tempeh slices in a single layer and spoon on a few more tablespoons of BBQ sauce. Spread to cover each slice.

3. Place dish in the oven and bake for about 20 to 25 minutes. Tempeh is done when sauce begins to turn dark brown on top and around the edges of the pan. Alternatively, line a grill with heavy-duty foil. Coat tempeh with BBQ sauce and arrange in a single layer over medium heat, turning once during cooking. Grill for several minutes on each side. Serve on rolls with coleslaw. Store extra BBQ sauce in a covered container in the refrigerator for several weeks.

Nutty Protein Burgers with Avocado-Scallion Sauce

MAKES 6 (3-INCH) BURGERS

Chef Linda: This recipe comes from the Compassionate Cuisine cooking class "Where Will I Get My Protein?" Tasty recipes made from everyday sources of plant-based protein allow us to easily get all the healthy proteins we need without harming any animals. Loaded with 15 grams of protein per serving, these hearty and satisfying burgers also boast generous amounts of calcium, healthy fat, iron, and fiber. They're even great on the grill because they hold together so well. Go bun-less for a lighter meal and serve the burgers on a bed of crisp salad greens dressed with lemon juice. Our Avocado-Scallion Sauce (p. 185) adds a boost of nutrition and a vibrant color and bright flavor.

Allergens: Contains nuts, soy, and ingredients that may contain gluten
Special Equipment: Food processor
Tip: Keep the ratios about the same and you can use your favorite nuts and seeds. For variety, add different spices or herbs and experiment with your favorite dressings.

Ingredients

Burger
2 large cloves garlic, peeled
1 cup raw walnuts or almonds
1 cup ground flaxseed
½ cup hulled hemp seeds
½ cup raw pumpkin seeds
¼ cup balsamic vinegar
3 Tbsps extra-virgin olive oil
2 Tbsps tamari or soy sauce
1 Tbsp nutritional yeast (optional)

To Serve
Fresh salad greens, dressed in oil and lemon juice
Buns, with sliced tomato and avocado
1 batch Avocado-Scallion Sauce (pg. 185)

Directions

1. Preheat oven to 375°F. Line a baking tray with parchment. To make burgers, pulse garlic in the food processor until finely chopped. Add walnuts, flaxseed, hemp seeds, and pumpkin seeds. Pulse again until finely chopped. Add vinegar, oil, tamari, and nutritional yeast, and pulse again until blended. The mixture should be moist and hold together when pinched between two fingers. Using a portion scoop or spoon, form the mixture into 3-inch-wide patties that are about ¾-inch thick. Bake for about 15 minutes, or until lightly browned on the bottom, flipping burgers midway through cook time. These burgers also work well on a grill set at medium heat.

2. Serve burgers on greens dressed in oil and lemon juice or on buns with tomato and avocado with a generous dollop of avocado-scallion sauce.

Artichoke-Cannellini Fettuccine Alfredo with Pan-Fried Tomatoes and Shiitake Crisps

SERVES 4 TO 6

Chef Linda: This recipe was developed for an Italian cooking class at the Sanctuary and uses artichoke hearts, cannellini beans, and cashews to create a thick, creamy, and compassionate alternative to traditional alfredo sauce. It comes together easily in a blender and would be just fine tossed with your favorite pasta, but we encourage you to make the tomatoes and shiitake crisps to get the full effect of the complementary flavors, colors, and textures. The tangy pan-roasted tomatoes burst in your mouth, while shiitake crisps deliver a salty, smoky, crunchy finish. We'll warn you: you'll want to use this sauce everywhere . . . on pasta, with vegetables, or even as a dip for a crusty loaf of warm bread.

Allergens: Contains nuts
Special Equipment: Blender

Ingredients

Shiitake Crisps
4 ounces shiitake mushrooms, stems removed and thinly sliced
3 Tbsps olive oil
½ tsp salt
¼ tsp smoked paprika

Pasta
1 pound regular or gluten-free dried fettuccine or pasta
Salt, for the water

Sauce
1 (15.5-ounce) can cannellini beans, drained and rinsed
1 cup marinated artichoke hearts, drained
½ cup raw cashews, soaked in water for 30 minutes, drained
⅓ cup nutritional yeast
2 large cloves garlic, peeled
2 Tbsps extra-virgin olive oil
2 Tbsps fresh lemon juice
¾ tsp salt
Ground black pepper, to taste

Pan-Roasted Tomatoes
1 Tbsp olive oil
2 cups cherry tomatoes, halved
¼ tsp coarse salt
3 large cloves garlic, thinly sliced or minced, about 1 Tbsp

Garnish
Chopped parsley

Directions

1. To make shiitake crisps, preheat oven to 375°F. Line a baking tray with parchment paper. Place shiitake slices in a mound on the baking tray and drizzle with oil. Toss to coat with oil. Arrange in a single layer and sprinkle with salt and paprika. Roast for about 25 minutes, or until mushrooms are very dark, almost burnt. Remove tray from oven and let cool. Mushrooms will crisp up as they cool.

2. Start the pasta by bringing a large pot of salted water to a boil.

(continued on next page)

3. Meanwhile, make the sauce. Place beans, artichoke hearts, drained cashews, nutritional yeast, garlic, olive oil, lemon juice, salt, and pepper in a blender and purée until velvety and smooth.
4. While the pasta is cooking, make the pan-roasted tomatoes. Heat oil in a pan over medium-high heat. Add tomatoes and salt. Cook, stirring occasionally, for about 5 minutes, or until tomatoes become just soft. Add garlic and cook for another 2 to 3 minutes.
5. When pasta is done, drain, reserving about ½ cup of cooking water, and return to the pot. With the pot over medium heat, add sauce and toss to combine, adding reserved water to thin to your desired consistency. Serve pasta in individual bowls or in a large serving bowl. Top with tomatoes, shiitake crisps, and garnish with parsley.

Coconut Maple Squash Bowls

SERVES 4 TO 6

Chef Linda: Harmony is the combination of musical notes that produce a pleasing effect. The same can be said for food. When just the right colors, tastes, and textures are combined, there is harmony in our mouths and bellies. In this recipe, the vibrant-green kale, bright-orange butternut squash, and pearly white coconut rice are a feast for the eyes. After one bite, you'll see that these uncomplicated ingredients hit all the right notes together—salty, sweet, crunchy, and soft. Ahh, music to your mouth. And don't be surprised if you break into song when you taste the candied pumpkin seeds.

> **Tip:** When winter squash is unavailable, substitute with sweet potatoes. If you can't find the raw, green pumpkin seeds (also called pepitas), use sliced raw sliced almonds or sunflower seeds.

Ingredients

Squash

3 Tbsps maple syrup

2 Tbsps olive oil

1 tsp ground cinnamon

1 tsp salt

1 medium (about 2½–3 pounds) butternut squash, peeled, seeded, and cut into 1-inch cubes, about 4 cups

1 cup raw pumpkin seeds

Rice

1 cup water

1 (13.5-ounce) can coconut milk

1½ cups long grain white rice

½ cup shredded, unsweetened coconut

½ tsp salt

Greens

1 Tbsp olive oil

1 bunch hearty greens (like kale or chard), about 1 pound, stems removed, chopped or torn into bite-sized pieces, about 5–6 cups

3 large cloves garlic, minced or thinly sliced, about 1 Tbsp

¼ tsp salt

Garnish

Toasted coconut chips (optional)

Directions

1. Preheat oven to 400°F. Line a baking tray with parchment. In a large bowl, mix together syrup, oil, cinnamon, and salt. Add squash and pepitas. Toss to coat. Empty contents of bowl onto prepared baking tray. Place tray in oven and roast for 25 to 30 minutes, or until the squash is fork-tender, but not mushy. Stir and flip squash midway through cooking.

2. While squash is roasting, make the rice. Put water and coconut milk into a medium pot. Add rice, coconut, and salt. Cover and simmer on medium-low heat for about 15 to 20 minutes, or until rice is tender. Remove from heat when done, fluff with a fork, and keep covered.

3. To make the greens, heat oil in a medium pan over medium-high heat. Add the chopped greens, garlic, and salt. Cook for about 5 to 7 minutes, while stirring occasionally. Remove from heat when kale is bright green and wilted.

4. To serve, scoop rice into a large bowl, top with greens and squash. Garnish with toasted coconut chips.

Breaded Eggplant Cutlet Lasagna

SERVES 4 TO 6

Chef Linda: Noodles are nice, but eggplant is better! If you love lasagna but want a new twist on this beloved comfort dish, use breaded eggplant slices instead of lasagna noodles. We developed this recipe for a Compassionate Cuisine Italian cooking class to demonstrate that there are plant-based solutions even to techniques like breading food, which usually involves milk and eggs. The eggplant is baked to crispy perfection and layered with a tofu ricotta that serves as a compassionate and healthy alternative to dairy-based ricotta cheese. Delightfully rich, luscious, and creamy, you'll lose nothing in terms of taste. This dish is perfect for family dinners or potlucks.

Allergens: Contains soy and ingredients that may contain soy
Make Ahead: Breaded eggplant and tofu ricotta can be made 1 or 2 days in advance for easy assembly. The entire recipe can be made 1 or 2 days in advance, then reheated in a 350°F oven for 20 to 25 minutes. Freeze baked lasagna for up to 3 months.
Tip: Enjoy extra cutlets on a roll with lettuce, tomato, and mayonnaise.

Ingredients

Breaded Eggplant

2 Tbsps olive oil
¼ cup all-purpose flour or gluten-free flour
½ cup unsweetened nondairy milk
1 cup regular or gluten-free breadcrumbs
1 Tbsp nutritional yeast
½ tsp garlic powder
½ tsp dried oregano
½ tsp dried basil
¼ tsp onion powder
¼ tsp salt
Ground black pepper, to taste
1 large eggplant, about 2 pounds, peeled and sliced into in ⅛-inch-thick round slices (about 12 slices in total)

Tofu Ricotta

1 (14- to 16-ounce) package of firm tofu, drained, rinsed, and pressed (pg. 6)
¼ cup nutritional yeast
2 Tbsps fresh lemon juice
2 tsps olive oil
2 tsp onion powder

1 tsp garlic powder
½ tsp salt

To Assemble

1 (24- to 32-ounce) jar marinara sauce, or about 3–4 cups homemade sauce
1½ cups shredded vegan mozzarella cheese, divided

Directions

1. Preheat oven to 400°F. Line a baking tray with parchment. Brush or spread oil on the parchment and set aside.

2. To make the breaded eggplant, place flour and milk in two separate bowls. In a third bowl, mix together the breadcrumbs, nutritional yeast, pepper, garlic powder, oregano, basil, onion powder, salt, and pepper. To bread the eggplant, dredge slices in flour, dip in the milk, then dredge in breadcrumbs. Place eggplant slices in a single layer on the baking sheet. Bake for 10 minutes then flip each slice and bake for another 10 minutes, until the eggplant is soft. (The key is cutting eggplant into thin slices.) Remove from the oven and reduce heat to 375°F.

3. While eggplant is baking, make the tofu ricotta. Finely crumble the tofu into a medium bowl. Add nutritional yeast, lemon juice, olive oil, onion powder, garlic powder, and salt. Mix until all ingredients are thoroughly combined.
4. To assemble, lightly oil a 9-inch square baking dish. Spread about ¾ cup of the marinara sauce on the bottom of the dish. Arrange slices of eggplant over the sauce in order to cover the bottom of the dish. Spread half the tofu ricotta mixture on top of the eggplant and sprinkle with ½ cup of mozzarella. Make a second layer by adding another ¾ cup sauce and arranging eggplant over the sauce. Spread the remaining half of the tofu ricotta over the eggplant and sprinkle ½ cup of mozzarella, and top with another ¾ cup of sauce. Finish with a final layer of eggplant, the remaining sauce, and remaining mozzarella.
5. Cover with foil and bake for 30 minutes, until bubbling around the sides. Let sit for about 5 minutes to set before cutting and serving.

Pecan-Crusted Tempeh Cutlets

MAKES 8 CUTLETS (4 SERVINGS)

Chef Sara: These festive tempeh cutlets, with their rich pecan coating, make a gorgeous main dish for your holiday table. We've updated the classic breading process by using flaxseed instead of eggs, and a gluten-free flour blend instead of traditional all-purpose flour (though you can certainly use all-purpose flour). Taking the extra steps to do a three-step breading—seasoned flour, a flax egg, then pecans—ensures that the pecans won't fall off the cutlets after they're baked. Serve with mashed potatoes, gravy, and cranberry sauce for a simple, delicious holiday feast—no turkey required. You can also try this recipe using our seitan cutlets (pg. 138).

Allergens: Contains, nuts, soy and ingredients that may contain gluten

Ingredients

2 Tbsps ground flaxseed
½ cup water
1 (8-ounce) package tempeh
1½ cups water, enough to cover the tempeh
3 Tbsps tamari or soy sauce
¼ cup all-purpose or gluten-free flour
1 Tbsp nutritional yeast
1 tsp salt
1 tsp dried thyme
½ tsp dried sage
½ tsp dried marjoram
Ground black pepper, to taste
2 cups whole pecans, finely chopped

Directions

1. In a wide, shallow bowl, whisk together the ground flaxseed and water, and set aside.
2. Preheat the oven to 375°F and line a baking tray with parchment.
3. Cut the block of tempeh in half horizontally, making two thin planks. Cut each plank into four triangles or rectangles to yield a total of 8 cutlets. Place the tempeh in small pot with water and tamari. Bring to a boil, cover, reduce the heat, and allow to simmer for about 10 minutes.
4. Meanwhile, prepare the three-part breading station. Arrange three wide, shallow bowls on your counter. In one bowl, stir together the flour, nutritional yeast, salt, thyme, sage, marjoram, and pepper. In the second bowl, you'll have the thickened flaxseed mixture. Finally, place the finely chopped pecans in the third bowl.
5. Transfer the tempeh from its simmering liquid to a plate and allow to cool briefly. Dip a cutlet into the flour mixture and shake off any excess. Next, dip it into the flaxseed mixture. Finally, dip it in the chopped pecans and place on the prepared baking sheet. Repeat with the remaining cutlets until everything is coated.
6. Place the tray in the oven and bake for 15 minutes. Flip the cutlets and bake for an additional 10 to 15 minutes, until golden brown. Remove from the oven and serve.

Tender Seitan Cutlets

MAKES 4 CUTLETS

Chef Sara: These savory cutlets, inspired by recipes by Isa Chandra Moskowitz and Miyoko Schinner, are great to keep on hand in the fridge or freezer. You can add them to a bowl, burrito, or salad by slicing a cutlet into strips and quickly sautéing them in a little oil. You'll find so many uses for these versatile, fun-to-make cutlets!

Allergens: Contains gluten and soy
Tip: Vital wheat gluten is the wheat protein found in wheat. This flour-like substance is found in well-stocked grocery stores or online.

Ingredients

1 (15.5-ounce) can chickpeas, drained and rinsed (or 1½ cups cooked)
1 cup vegetable broth
2 Tbsps olive oil
3 Tbsps tamari soy sauce
¼ cup nutritional yeast flakes
2 tsps onion powder
1½ tsps garlic powder
1 tsp poultry seasoning
Freshly ground black pepper, to taste
1½ cups vital wheat gluten

Directions

1. Place the chickpeas in a large bowl and mash with a fork or potato masher until the chickpeas are mostly broken down. Alternatively, use a food processor to pulse the chickpeas, leaving a finely ground texture. Add in the vegetable broth, olive oil, tamari, nutritional yeast, onion powder, garlic powder, poultry seasoning, and black pepper and mix thoroughly. Stir in the wheat gluten until the mixture begins to pull together, then use your hands to gently knead the dough right in the bowl.

2. Divide the dough into fourths and press each piece of dough into an oval patty roughly 4 to 5 inches wide. Place a patty on a square of aluminum foil and wrap snugly. Repeat with the remaining pieces of dough.

3. Transfer the foil-wrapped cutlets to a steamer basket set over boiling water. Cover the pot, reduce the heat to medium-low, and allow the cutlets to steam for 40 minutes. When finished, remove from the steamer, allow to cool briefly, then remove the foil. The cutlets can be used immediately or allowed to cool, wrapped in plastic wrap to store in the refrigerator or freezer. Extra cutlets will keep in the fridge for up to five days, and in the freezer for up to three months.

Italian-Style Lentil Meatballs

MAKES ABOUT 16 TO 18 (2-INCH) BALLS

Chef Linda: Some meals elicit feelings of comfort, familiarity, and home. Eating compassionately doesn't mean missing out on these important aspects of food. These savory, hearty lentil meatballs prove we can enjoy all of those feelings without causing harm to animals, our bodies, or the environment. These meatless meatballs are firm, plump, and flavorful. Made with humble ingredients, we've served them to kids, college students, and adults, and never had a meatball to spare. Try them on a roll smothered with tomato sauce or on top of a pile of spaghetti—but most important, share them with people you love.

Allergens: Contains ingredients that may contain gluten
Special Equipment: Food processor

Ingredients

Olive oil for the baking tray, plus 2 Tbsps for the pan
¾ cup dried green or brown lentils (or 2 cups cooked)
2 cups water, plus more if needed
1½ tsps salt, divided
½ pound of button mushrooms chopped, about 2 cups
½ medium onion, peeled and chopped into chunks, about ½ cup
3 large cloves garlic, peeled
1 cup old-fashioned oats or breadcrumbs
2 Tbsps finely chopped fresh parsley
2 tsps dried oregano
2 tsps dried basil
¼ tsp black pepper

To Serve

Cooked pasta, cooked spaghetti squash, or rolls
Prepared tomato sauce

Directions

1. Preheat oven to 375°F. Line a baking tray with parchment and brush lightly with oil.
2. Place lentils, water, and ½ teaspoon of the salt in a small pot on the stove. Bring to a boil then reduce heat and simmer, partially covered, for 20 to 25 minutes or until lentils are tender. Add water as needed to make sure lentils are just barely covered. Remove from heat and drain excess water, if necessary. Set aside.
3. In a food processor, pulse mushrooms, onion, and garlic until chopped. Heat 2 tablespoons of oil in a large pan over medium heat. Empty contents of food processor into the pan and add remaining 1 teaspoon of salt. Cook, while stirring occasionally, for about 10 minutes, or until the onions have softened, mushrooms have browned, and moisture has nearly evaporated.
4. While the mushroom mixture is cooking, place the cooked lentils, oats, parsley, oregano, basil, and pepper in the food processor. Pulse several times but don't overblend as some texture is desired. Add the cooked mushroom mixture to the food processor and pulse to combine. Taste and adjust seasonings. Let the meatball mixture sit for about 10 minutes, until it holds together when formed into a ball.
5. Use a tablespoon or portion scoop to measure out the desired sized balls, and roll. Arrange on the baking tray. Bake for 25 to 30 minutes, turning occasionally to ensure all sides are browned and the balls are firm on the outside. Alternatively, the lentil meatballs can be fried in a little oil on the stovetop. Serve over pasta, spaghetti squash, or on a roll. Make sure to add your favorite tomato sauce.

Japanese Curry with Winter Squash, Potatoes, and Roasted Tofu

MAKES 6 TO 8 SERVINGS

Chef Sara: Most people think of India when they hear the word *curry*, but curry is also extremely popular in Japan. In fact, Japan actually celebrates National Curry Day on June 2, and there are restaurants that serve nothing else! Our curry, developed for a Compassionate Cuisine cooking class, parts with tradition by including winter squash cubes, which break down during cooking to thicken the delicious gravy. Serve this comforting, mildly sweet curry over rice with a side of steamed broccoli for a cool-weather supper.

Allergens: Contains soy and ingredients that may contain gluten
Make Ahead: Tofu can be roasted 1 or 2 days in advance.

Ingredients

Roasted Tofu

1 (14- to 16-ounce) package extra-firm tofu
1 Tbsp tamari or soy sauce
2 tsps toasted sesame oil

Curry

2 Tbsps oil
2 medium onions, finely chopped, about 2 cups
2 cloves garlic, minced, about 2 tsps
1-inch piece of fresh ginger, peeled and minced, about 1 Tbsp
2 Tbsps mild curry powder
¼ cup gluten-free flour blend, or ⅓ cup unbleached all-purpose flour
4 cups vegetable stock, heated
4 Tbsps tamari or soy sauce
1 small apple, peeled and finely chopped, about 1 cup
1 small winter squash, like butternut, Kabocha, or buttercup, peeled, seeded, and cut into 1-inch chunks, about 3 cups
1 pound (about 3) Yukon Gold potatoes, cut into 1-inch chunks, about 3 cups
3 medium carrots, cut into 1-inch chunks, about 2 cups

Directions

1. Drain, rinse, and press tofu (see pg. 6).
2. To make the roasted tofu, preheat the oven to 425°F and line a baking tray with parchment. Cut the tofu lengthwise into three slabs, then cut each slab into 1-inch cubes. Toss gently with the tamari and sesame oil. Arrange in a single layer on the prepared baking tray, and transfer to the oven. Roast for 25 to 30 minutes, until the tofu is brown and the texture is firm.
3. To make the curry, heat the oil in a large pot over medium-high heat. Add the onions and a pinch of salt, and sauté until softened, translucent, and just beginning to brown, 7 to 10 minutes. Add the garlic and ginger and cook for 1 or 2 minutes. Add the curry powder and flour, cooking for an additional 2 to 3 minutes, until fragrant. Whisk in the hot vegetable stock and tamari, stirring well to help the sauce thicken evenly. Stir in the apple, squash, potatoes, and carrots, then bring to a boil. Cover, reduce to low-medium heat, and allow to cook for 25 to 30 minutes, until the vegetables are tender.
4. Stir in the roasted tofu, taste and adjust seasonings as necessary, and serve. Leftovers will keep in the refrigerator for three to five days.

Mushroom and Walnut Bolognese with Polenta and Greens

SERVES 6 TO 8

Chef Linda: Ragù alla bolognese, or bolognese sauce, is a slow-cooked Italian meat sauce with a creamy finish that originated in Bologna, Italy. On this side of the ocean, order pasta with bolognese sauce and you'll likely get tomato sauce with ground beef. In our version, ground mushrooms and walnuts replace the meat for a hearty and healthy base. In addition to the creamy finish, the absence of herbs like basil and oregano reiterate that bolognese sauce is *not* regular tomato sauce. Bolognese is often served on tagliatelle, a wide-noodle pasta, but here we've served it on creamy polenta, which makes this dish the ultimate comfort food (and gluten-free, too!). Make this for a special occasion, a special someone, or just because you long for something soul-satisfying.

Allergens: Contains nuts, soy, and ingredients that may contain gluten
Special Equipment: Food processor
Tip: A food processor or a good sharp knife is key to the final texture of this sauce. Ensuring that the ingredients are finely chopped is the difference between bolognese and a vegetable sauce.

Ingredients

Bolognese

10 ounces button mushrooms
1 cup walnuts
2 Tbsps olive oil
2 Tbsps tamari or soy sauce
1 medium yellow onion, finely chopped, about 1 cup
2 large carrots, finely chopped, about 1 cup
2 celery stalks, finely chopped, about 1 cup
3 large garlic cloves, minced, about 1 Tbsp
¾ tsp salt, plus more to taste
¼ tsp crushed red pepper flakes
Ground black pepper, to taste
1 (14- to 15-ounce) can plain tomato sauce
1 cup vegetable broth, plus more to thin
1 cup unsweetened nondairy milk
3 Tbsps tomato paste
1 Tbsp nutritional yeast
1 Tbsp fresh lemon juice

Polenta

6 cups water
2 Tbsps olive oil or vegan butter
2 Tbsps nutritional yeast
1 tsp salt
2 cups instant polenta

Greens

1 Tbsp olive oil
1 bunch hearty greens (like kale or chard), chopped into small pieces
3 cloves garlic, minced, about 1 Tbsp
¼ tsp salt
1 Tbsp fresh lemon juice

Directions

1. To make the bolognese, pulse the mushrooms and walnuts in a food processor until finely chopped. Heat the olive oil in a large pan over medium heat. Add the mushrooms and walnuts. Cook, stirring occasionally, until mushrooms start to give off moisture and darken, about 8 minutes. Add tamari and continue to cook until mushrooms are dark brown and moisture has evaporated.

(continued on next page)

2. Add the onions, carrots, celery, garlic, salt, crushed red pepper flakes, and black pepper. Cook, stirring occasionally until the vegetables are soft, about 10 minutes. Add tomato sauce, vegetable broth, milk, tomato paste, nutritional yeast, and lemon juice. Simmer, stirring occasionally, for about 15 minutes, until the sauce has thickened but is still loose enough to ladle onto the polenta. Add a little more broth by the tablespoon to thin, if necessary. Taste and add more salt and pepper, if necessary.

3. To make polenta, bring water to a boil in a large pot over medium heat. When water begins to boil, add olive oil, nutritional yeast, and salt. Reduce heat to low. Gradually pour in the polenta, whisking continuously until it has thickened and is soft and creamy, 1 or 2 minutes. Remove from heat and cover.

4. To make the greens, heat oil in a large pan over medium-high heat. Add greens, garlic, and salt. Cook for 3 to 5 minutes, until greens have wilted but are still bright green. Sprinkle lemon juice over greens and toss.

5. To serve, scoop polenta into a bowl, add a hearty spoonful of bolognese sauce, and top with greens. Extra sauce can be stored in the refrigerator for up to 1 week or frozen for up to six months. When reheating, thin the sauce with a little water or vegetable broth.

Marinated Portobello Strips with Rosemary Beans

SERVES 4

Chef Linda: The portly portobello mushroom is a hearty ingredient that can easily take center stage for a main course. Marinating and roasting bring out its best, creating a deep, rich flavor and meaty texture. And, as if made for each other, a bed of creamy, rosemary-infused white beans is the perfect canvas for these juicy slices of mushroom. Done drooling yet?

Allergens: Contains soy and ingredients that may contain gluten
Make Ahead Note: Marinate mushrooms for at least 30 minutes or overnight.
Tip: Serve with your favorite vegetable . For example, sauté kale or chard in a pan with oil, garlic, and salt.

Ingredients

Marinated Portobello

½ cup olive oil

3 Tbsps balsamic vinegar

2 Tbsps tamari or soy sauce

1 Tbsp vegan Worcestershire sauce

3 large garlic cloves, minced, about 1 Tbsp

6 large portobello mushroom caps, stems and gills removed, cut into ¼-inch thick strips

Rosemary Beans

2 Tbsps olive oil

½ medium onion, chopped, about ½ cup

3 large cloves garlic, minced, about 1 Tbsp

2 Tbsps minced fresh rosemary

1 tsp salt

2 (14-to 15.5-ounce) cans cannellini beans, drained and rinsed (or 3 cups cooked)

½ cup vegetable broth, plus more to thin if necessary

1 Tbsp fresh lemon juice

Ground black pepper, to taste

Chopped parsley, for garnish

Directions

1. To make the marinade for the portobello, put oil, vinegar, tamari, Worcestershire, and garlic in a zip-top plastic bag and add mushroom strips. Gently shake to combine. Place bag of mushrooms in the refrigerator to marinate for at least 30 minutes or overnight.

2. Preheat oven to 400°F. Line a large baking tray with parchment. Remove the mushrooms, reserving ¼ cup of the marinade. Arrange slices in a single layer on the tray and pour the reserved marinade over the mushrooms. Roast for about 25 minutes, or until mushrooms are smaller and very dark. They should be thick and juicy.

3. While mushrooms are roasting, make the rosemary beans. Heat olive oil in a large pan over medium heat. Add onion and cook, stirring occasionally, for 8 to 10 minutes or until onions are translucent and soft. Add garlic, rosemary, and salt and cook a few minutes more, until the rosemary and garlic are fragrant. Stir in beans, broth, and lemon juice, and cook for another 5 minutes. Use a fork to mash the beans in the pan into a thick, chunky mixture or purée them in a food processor. Add more broth if you prefer a thinner consistency. Season with ground black pepper.

4. Top beans with roasted mushroom slices and remaining juice from the baking tray. Garnish with chopped parsley. Serve immediately.

Meatless Meatloaf with Simple Golden Gravy

MAKES 2 SMALL LOAVES (5.75-BY-3.25 INCHES) OR 12 MUFFIN-SIZED PORTIONS

Chef Linda: For many, meatloaf is a comfort food that elicits nostalgic memories of family dinners. This meatless meatloaf recipe was developed for our "Vegan 101" cooking class to demonstrate that from the moment we choose to go meat-free, we can still enjoy our most beloved meals—and they'll taste every bit as delicious as we remember. This hearty vegan version uses protein-rich lentils, mushrooms, and nuts—along with the familiar flavors of celery, onions, carrots, and herbs that begs to be smothered in gravy.

Allergens: Contains nuts and ingredients that may contain gluten and soy
Special equipment: Food processor
Make Ahead: Lentils can be cooked several days in advance.

Ingredients

Lentil Meatloaf

¾ cup dried green or brown lentils (or 2 cups cooked)
2 tsps salt, divided
1 medium onion, peeled and cut into small chunks, about 1 cup
2 medium carrots, peeled and chopped, about 1 cup
2 large stalks celery, chopped, about 1 cup
3 large cloves garlic, peeled
2 Tbsps oil
2 tsps dried thyme
1 tsp dried sage
Ground black pepper, to taste
10 ounces button mushrooms, quartered
1 cup walnuts
2 Tbsps vegan Worcestershire sauce (or ketchup)
1 cup regular or gluten-free breadcrumbs
1 batch Simple Golden Gravy (pg. 189)

Directions

1. Lightly oil two 5¾-by-3¼-inch mini loaf pans. Alternatively, you can shape loaves with your hands and place on a parchment–lined baking tray or use a muffin pan so each person has an individual serving. Bake time will be slightly less when using a muffin pan.

2. Pick over the lentils, discarding any withered ones or stones. Place in a medium saucepan with 1 teaspoon of salt, cover generously with water, and bring to a boil. Lower the heat and simmer for 20 to 25 minutes, until tender. Drain the lentils.

3. Preheat oven to 375°F. Place chopped onion, carrots, celery, and garlic into the bowl of a food processor. Pulse until vegetables are finely chopped, leaving some texture. Heat the oil in a large pan over medium-high heat. Transfer vegetables to the pan. Add thyme, sage, remaining 1 teaspoon of salt, and ground black pepper. Cook until the vegetables have softened, about 10 minutes.

4. While the vegetables are cooking, place mushrooms, walnuts, cooked lentils, and Worcestershire sauce into the bowl of the food processor. Pulse until ingredients are just combined, retaining visible chunks and texture. Do not over-process or the result will be too mushy to hold together when sliced. Transfer mushrooms to the pan with chopped vegetables and cook for about 5 minutes more. Add breadcrumbs and stir to combine. Let

(continued on next page)

mixture sit in the pan for about 15 minutes, until the breadcrumbs have softened and can bind the loaves together.

5. Divide the mixture equally between the two prepared loaf pans and pack down very firmly using the back of a spoon. Cover with foil. Bake for 20 minutes then remove foil and bake for an additional 15 minutes, or until top and sides have browned and the lentil loaves have started to pull away from the sides of the loaf pans.

6. When loaves are done, they will be brown along the edges and firm to the touch. Remove from oven and let rest for 5 minutes; resting will help the loaf to keep its shape when slicing. Slide a knife along the edges and invert on a serving plate or cutting board. Flip back over so the tops are right side up. Cut into slices and serve immediately with simple golden gravy.

Moroccan Vegetable and Chickpea Tagine

MAKES 6 TO 8 SERVINGS

Chef Sara: Long before transitioning to a vegan lifestyle, I once made a chicken tagine with the most incredible blend of spices during a New York snowstorm that etched itself into my memory forever. Named after a Moroccan clay cooking vessel of the same name, this recipe, with its tasty combination of vegetables, briny olives, and bright, fresh lemon, makes a quick and easy stew that tastes far more complex than the sum of its parts. Follow the recipe to mix your own spices or purchase a Moroccan blend such as *ras el hanout*.

Ingredients

Spice Blend

1½ tsps ground cumin
1½ tsps ground coriander
1 tsp ground ginger
1 tsp ground turmeric
¼ tsp ground cinnamon
½ tsp hot paprika
½ tsp sweet paprika
Generous pinch of saffron threads

Tagine

1 Tbsp olive oil
1 medium red or yellow onion, chopped, about 1 cup
4 cloves garlic, minced, about 1½ Tbsps
2 Tbsps tomato paste
3 medium carrots, cut into ½-inch chunks, about 1½ cups
1 small head cauliflower, cut into bite-size florets, about 3 cups
1 small eggplant, un-peeled, cut into ½-inch chunks, about 3 cups
4 cups vegetable broth
1½ tsps salt, plus more to taste
1 (15.5-ounce) can chickpeas, drained and rinsed (or 1½ cups cooked)
½ cup sliced green olives
Zest and juice of 1 lemon

To Serve

¼ cup chopped mint

Directions

1. To make the spice mix, stir together all the spices in a small bowl and set aside until needed.

2. To make the tagine, heat the olive oil in a large pot over medium-high heat. Add the onion and a pinch of salt and cook until softened and just beginning to brown, 8 to 10 minutes. Add the garlic and cook for an additional minute or so, until fragrant. Stir in the spice mix and tomato paste. Add the carrots, cauliflower, and eggplant, and stir well. Pour in the vegetable broth and sprinkle in the salt. Bring to a boil, reduce the heat, and cover. Allow to simmer for 20 minutes, until the vegetables are nearly tender.

3. Stir in the chickpeas, olives, and lemon zest and juice, and allow to simmer for an additional 10 to 15 minutes, or until the vegetables are fork-tender. Taste and adjust seasonings as desired. Serve alone or over a grain, and garnish with fresh mint. The tagine will keep in the refrigerator for up to five days. Cooled portions freeze beautifully, and are best enjoyed within three months.

Butternut Harvest Roll

SERVES 6 TO 8 (TWO 2-INCH SLICES PER PERSON)

Chef Linda: This recipe was developed for a Thanksgiving feast at the Sanctuary when the bounty of the harvest season and affection for loved ones (human and nonhuman!) filled our hearts. Seasonal butternut squash makes a luscious filling, especially when combined with plump chickpeas, crunchy walnuts, and warming spices. Roll it all up in a flaky vegan puff pastry, and you've got a centerpiece festive enough for any special meal. We like to serve this with sautéed greens for the vibrant color contrast, as well as to balance the richness of the puff pastry. While savoring this festive dish, reflect on how humble ingredients that come from the ground can create harmony and beauty on our tables and in our hearts.

Allergens: Contains gluten, nuts, and ingredients that contain soy
Make Ahead: Filling can be made 1 or 2 days in advance.
Tip: Add crumbled vegan sausage to the filling for a heartier meal.

Ingredients

Roll

2 Tbsps olive oil
1 medium onion, chopped finely, about 1 cup
1 tsp salt, plus more to taste
1 medium butternut squash, about 2 pounds, peeled and cut into ½-inch pieces, about 4–5 cups
1 (15.5-ounce) can chickpeas, drained and rinsed
½ cup finely chopped walnuts
3 large cloves garlic, minced, about 1 Tbsp
1 Tbsp minced fresh sage (or 1 tsp rubbed sage)
1 Tbsp fresh thyme leaves (or 1 tsp dried thyme)
1 tsp cumin
½ tsp ground cinnamon
3 Tbsps water

To Assemble

1 sheet of vegan puff pastry dough, thawed for 2 hours or overnight in the refrigerator
Olive oil, for brushing
Pinch of coarse salt

To Serve

Sautéed or steamed greens
Peanut Butter Miso Sauce (optional) (pg. 185)

Directions

1. To make the filling, heat 2 tablespoons of oil in a large pan over low-medium heat. Add onion and salt. Cook, stirring occasionally, for about 8 minutes, or until onion has softened and turned translucent. Add the squash, chickpeas, walnuts, garlic, sage, thyme, cumin, cinnamon, and water. Cover pan and cook, stirring occasionally, for about 20 minutes, or until squash is fork-tender. When done, remove from heat, keep covered, and set aside.

2. To assemble the roll, preheat the oven to 400°F. Lay out a piece of parchment paper about the size of your baking tray. Unfold one sheet of puff pastry on the parchment. Roll the pastry sheet into a 16-by-12-inch rectangle. With the longest side horizontal to the counter, spoon the butternut filling onto the bottom half of the pastry sheet to within 1 inch of the edge. Starting at the side closest to you, roll the pastry sheet and filling up like a jelly roll. Tuck the ends under to seal. Lift the parchment paper up and onto the baking sheet. Brush with oil and sprinkle a little coarse salt on top. Cut 3 or 4 diagonal slits several inches apart in the pastry to allow steam to escape.

3. Bake for 25 minutes or until the pastry is golden brown all over. Remove the oven and let cool for about 5 minutes. Use a serrated knife to slice into desired-sized portions.

Mushroom Bourguignon (Mushroom Stew)

SERVES 4

Chef Linda: Julia Child is known for her dedication and thoroughness in developing exquisite recipes for the home cook. Her Boeuf Bourguignon recipe is the stuff of legends. Bourguignon refers to the Burgundy region of France, as well as the wine used in braising the stew. While noted for her impeccable taste in French cooking, her palate lacked sensitivity to animal suffering. By using meaty mushrooms instead of beef and bacon, our Mushroom Bourguignon is a compassionate makeover of the original French beef stew. We prepare pearl onions separately, according to tradition. Serve this over noodles, rice, or potatoes to soak up the sauce, or along a side dish of buttered (vegan, of course) spring peas or sautéed summer cherry tomatoes to add a bright note to a rich meal. Plan to make this when you've got time to enjoy the process, as well as the leftover wine; I have a feeling Julia did.

Make Ahead: Serve this dish with cooked pasta, rice, or mashed potatoes, all of which can all be made in advance and reheated.

Ingredients

4 Tbsps olive oil, divided
2 (10-ounce) packages of button mushrooms, quartered
1½ tsps salt, divided, plus more to taste
2 large carrots, peeled and sliced ¼-inch-thick, about 1 cup
1 medium onion, finely chopped, about 1 cup
2 Tbsps all-purpose, gluten-free flour, or cornstarch
1½ cups vegetable broth
½ cup red wine, Burgundy, Chianti, or other full-bodied wine (or 1 cup vegetable broth and 1 Tbsp apple cider vinegar)
1 Tbsp tomato paste
2 large cloves garlic, minced, about 2 tsps
2 tsps dried thyme
¼ tsp ground black pepper, plus more to taste
1 bay leaf

Braised Onions

1 Tbsp olive oil
1 cup frozen pearl onions, thawed
½ cup vegetable broth
1 tsp dried thyme
½ tsp salt
1 bay leaf

To Serve

Cooked mashed potatoes, rice, or noodles
Chopped parsley, to garnish

Directions

1. Heat 2 tablespoons of oil in a large pot over medium-high heat. Add mushrooms and ½ teaspoon of salt. Cook over medium-high heat, stirring occasionally, for about 15 minutes, until mushrooms have reduced in size and turned medium brown. The pan should be hot enough so that the mushrooms "squeak" when stirred. Transfer mushrooms to a bowl.

2. In the same pot, add remaining 2 tablespoons of oil. Add carrots and onions. Cook, stirring occasionally, until softened, about 10 minutes. Add the mushrooms back into the pot and sprinkle the flour over vegetables and stir again. Stir in broth, wine, tomato paste, garlic, thyme, remaining 1 teaspoon of salt, black pepper, and bay leaf. Cover, then simmer over low-medium heat for about 30 minutes. When done, sauce should be thick enough to coat the back of a spoon and carrots should be fork-tender. Taste and adjust salt and pepper, if desired.

3. To make the braised onions, heat oil over medium-high heat in a large pan. Add pearl onions and

cook, rolling them around to brown evenly, for about 5 minutes. Add broth, thyme, salt, and bay leaf. Cover and simmer over low heat for 20 to 25 minutes, or until onions are tender and most of the broth has evaporated. Onions and mushrooms should be done at about the same time.

4. While both the onions and the mushrooms are cooking, prepare potatoes, rice, or noodles. Remove bay leaf and thyme sprigs from mushrooms and onions. To serve, place potatoes, rice, or noodles in a bowl, ladle on mushrooms and sauce, and place several onions on top. Serve immediately, garnished with parsley.

Miso Mushroom Squash Bowl with Toasted Sesame Peanut Sauce

SERVES 4

Chef Linda: Some of the best dishes combine ordinary ingredients in a way that makes them seem exciting and new. That's how we feel about this dish. It confirms the truth that eliminating animals from our diets doesn't diminish our options—it expands them! You've probably had squash and mushrooms. But when you dress them together in rich miso, spicy garlic, and sweet syrup, then roast them to intensify the flavors, you create a complex and powerful combination of flavors that are enhanced with a simple but delectable sauce.

Allergens: Contains peanuts, soy, and ingredients that may contain gluten

Ingredients

Squash and Mushrooms
2 Tbsps yellow miso
2 Tbsps oil
3 large cloves garlic, minced, about 1 Tbsp
2 tsps maple syrup
2 tsps tamari or soy sauce
1 small (about 1½ pounds) butternut squash, peeled and cut into ½-inch pieces, about 3 cups
1 (10-ounce) package sliced button mushrooms

Rice and Kale
1½ cups white or brown rice (or your favorite whole grain)
3 cups water
¼ tsp salt
1 bunch kale, about 1 pound, stems removed and finely chopped

Sauce
4 Tbsps smooth, unsalted peanut butter
3 Tbsps tamari or soy sauce
1 Tbsp toasted sesame oil
2 tsps real maple syrup
1–2 tsps hot sauce (optional)
Up to ½ cup warm water

Garnish
2 scallions, trimmed and thinly sliced, about ¼ cup
½ cup salted peanuts, chopped

Directions

1. Preheat oven to 400°F. Line a baking tray with parchment.
2. To make the squash and mushrooms, stir together miso, oil, garlic, syrup, and tamari in a large bowl. Add squash and mushrooms to the bowl with the miso mixture and toss to coat evenly. The mixture will be thick, so use a big spoon or rubber spatula, but be gentle so as not to break the mushrooms. Empty onto the prepared baking tray and roast for about 25 minutes. Stir midway through the cooking time. Cook until the squash is fork-tender and lightly browned and the mushrooms are dark brown.
3. While the squash and mushrooms are roasting, make the rice and kale. Place rice, water, and salt in a large pot. Bring to a boil, then reduce heat, cover, and simmer for about 10 minutes. Place the chopped kale on top of rice to steam and continue cooking, covered, for about 8 minutes

more, or until the liquid has evaporated. Remove from heat and keep covered for 5 minutes. Fluff the rice and kale with a fork.

4. To make the sauce, whisk together peanut butter, tamari, toasted sesame oil, syrup, and hot sauce. Slowly add water, by the tablespoon, and whisk continuously until a thick, pourable consistency is reached.

5. To serve, scoop rice and kale into bowls, top with squash and mushrooms. Garnish with scallions and peanuts and drizzle sauce over everything. Serve immediately.

Tempeh, Shiitake, and Green Tea Noodle Bowls

MAKES 6 TO 8 SERVINGS

Chef Sara: Packed with immunity-boosting ingredients, this savory broth is nothing short of magical. Sip it straight up as a light and savory tea that's a great home remedy for a cold, or serve over rice noodles, fresh greens, and roasted tempeh for a full, yet light, meal.

Allergens: Contains soy and ingredients that may contain gluten
Make Ahead: Tempeh and broth can be made 1 or 2 days in advance, as can the broth: simply reheat when ready to serve.

Ingredients

Broth

8 cups water
1 ounce (approximately 1 cup) dried shiitake mushrooms
3-inch piece fresh ginger root, peeled and thinly sliced
10 cloves garlic, peeled and smashed
1 (4- to 5-inch) piece kombu seaweed
4 bags green tea
2 Tbsps tamari or soy sauce
½ cup mellow white miso

Roasted Tempeh

1 (8-ounce) package tempeh, cut into 1-inch cubes
2 tsps tamari or soy sauce
2 tsps toasted sesame oil

To Assemble

1 (8- to 12-ounce) package thin rice noodles, prepared according to package instructions and rinsed
4 cups very thinly sliced baby spinach or lacinato kale leaves
Toasted sesame oil, for drizzling
Sauerkraut or kimchi, for garnish
2–3 scallions, thinly sliced, for garnish
White and/or black sesame seeds, for garnish

Directions

1. To make the broth, in a large pot, combine the water, mushrooms, ginger, garlic, and kombu. Bring to a boil, cover, and simmer on low heat for about an hour.

2. While the broth is simmering, prepare the tempeh. Preheat the oven to 425°F and line a baking tray with parchment. Place the tempeh on the tray in a pile and drizzle with tamari and sesame oil. Toss to coat all the pieces. Bake for 15 to 20 minutes, flipping halfway through the cooking time until the tempeh is golden brown. Remove from the oven and allow to cool.

3. Remove the broth from the heat, add the green tea bags, and let sit for 5 minutes. Strain the broth, reserving the mushrooms. Thinly slice the mushrooms and add back to the broth. Stir in the tamari and miso. Reheat over medium to low heat until the broth is steaming but not boiling.

4. To assemble the noodle bowls, place a small handful of cooked noodles in wide soup bowl. Add a handful of spinach or kale and a small serving of roasted tempeh. Ladle the hot broth over the noodles, greens, and tempeh, and drizzle with toasted sesame oil. Garnish with the sauerkraut or kimchi, scallions, and sesame seeds, and serve immediately.

Sofrito Tofu-Bean Bowls

SERVES 6 TO 8

Chef Linda: Sofrito, used in so many dishes with Cuban, Puerto Rican, or Spanish influence, is that special something you can't quite put your finger on. It's a unique flavor that turns a boring dish of rice and beans into a lively affair. Flavorful and sometimes spicy, this sauce typically consists of onions, garlic, peppers, and tomatoes, depending on what part of the world your recipe originates. In this recipe, the sauce is used to braise spiced tofu and beans, creating a complex and delicious combination. A dollop of cool, creamy Cashew Sour Cream (p. 188) provides the perfect balance.

Allergens: Contains soy
Special Equipment: Food processor or blender
Tip: Make a double batch of sofrito and freeze it in ice cube trays. Pop a couple of cubes in your rice, beans, or soup when you want a little extra south-of-the-border zing.

Ingredients

Sofrito

2 red bell peppers, roughly chopped, about 2 cups
1 medium onion, roughly chopped, about 1 cup
¼ cup cilantro or parsley leaves, packed, plus more for garnish
4 cloves of garlic, peeled, about 1½ Tbsps
1 jalapeño pepper, roughly chopped
2 Tbsps olive oil
2 Tbsps fresh lime juice
¾ tsp salt

Rice

1½ cups uncooked white or brown rice
3 cups water
½ tsp salt
2 Tbsps fresh lime juice

Tofu

1 Tbsp olive oil
1 (14- to 16- ounce) package of extra-firm tofu, drained and rinsed
2 tsps ground cumin
2 tsps dried oregano
2 tsps chili powder
2 tsps maple syrup
1 tsp salt

¼ tsp ground cayenne
1 (15.5 ounce) can pinto beans, drained and rinsed (or 1½ cups cooked)
1 (15.5 ounce) can black beans, drained and rinsed (or 1½ cups cooked)
½ cup sliced black olives

To Serve

Diced avocado or prepared guacamole
Shredded lettuce
Shredded vegan cheddar cheese
Cashew Sour Cream (pg. 188), or your favorite brand
Cilantro, chopped for garnish

Directions

1. To make the sofrito, add the bell peppers, onion, cilantro, garlic, jalapeño, oil, lime juice, and salt to a food processor or blender. Pulse ingredients until finely chopped, but not completely blended.

2. To make the rice, place rice, water, and salt in a pot. Bring water to a boil, then cover and reduce to a simmer. Cook for about 18 minutes or until all the water is absorbed. Remove from heat and keep covered for 5 minutes. Remove cover, sprinkle rice with lime juice, and fluff with a fork. Cover to keep warm and set aside.

3. To make the tofu, heat oil in a large pan over medium heat. Crumble the tofu into the pan. Add cumin, oregano, chili powder, syrup, salt, and cayenne. Toss to coat the tofu with the spices, and cook, stirring occasionally, for about 5 minutes until spices are fragrant. Add beans, olives, and sofrito. Stir to combine and cook for about 20 minutes, until sofrito is cooked and flavors are combined.

4. To serve, build bowls with rice, tofu and bean sofrito, avocado, lettuce, and cheese. Finish with a dollop of sour cream and garnish with cilantro.

Spinach Pesto Pasta with Chili-Roasted Sweet Potatoes

SERVES 4 TO 6

Chef Linda: What strange bedfellows these chili-spiced sweet potatoes and pesto-dressed pasta make, but to dismiss this recipe on that account is to miss out on a tantalizing combination. When we develop recipes for Compassionate Cuisine classes, we often look for ways to boost the nutritional value without losing out on taste. This dish fits that bill with vitamin- and mineral-rich sweet potatoes and a punchy spinach pesto that would make Popeye proud. This sweet, salty, and spicy dish is easy enough for a weeknight dinner but also lovely enough to make for guests.

Allergens: Contains nuts
Special Equipment: Food processor
Tip: For a variation, use cubed butternut squash (if in season) in place of the sweet potatoes.

Ingredients

Sweet Potatoes

2 Tbsps olive oil
1 tsp chili powder
2 tsps onion powder
1 tsp maple syrup
1 tsp ground cumin
1 tsp garlic powder
1 tsp salt, plus more for cooking pasta
¼–½ tsp ground cayenne pepper
2 medium sweet potatoes, peeled and cut into ¼-inch cubes, about 3 cups
½ cup raw pumpkin seeds (or sunflower seeds or sliced almonds)
1 pound of your favorite regular or gluten-free pasta (choose a shape that will catch the pesto nicely)
1 batch Spinach Pesto (pg. 187)

Directions

1. Preheat oven to 375°F. Line a baking tray with parchment paper.
2. To make the sweet potatoes, stir together the oil, chili powder, onion powder, maple syrup, cumin, garlic powder, salt, and cayenne in a large bowl. Add cubed sweet potatoes and pumpkin seeds. Toss to coat. Arrange in a single layer on the baking tray. Roast for 20 to 25 minutes, until sweet potatoes have started to turn light brown and are fork-tender.
3. While the sweet potatoes are roasting, bring a large pot of salted water to a boil. Add pasta and cook according to package directions.
4. When pasta is done, drain and reserve about 1 cup of cooking water. Return pasta to the pot and add the spinach pesto. Gently toss to combine, using reserved cooking water to thin pesto, if necessary. To serve, transfer pesto-dressed pasta to a large serving platter or individual bowls and top with roasted sweet potatoes and pumpkin seeds.

Sausage and Spinach Stuffed Shells

MAKES ABOUT 32 SHELLS, SERVES 6 TO 8

Chef Linda: Like an old friend, this classic Italian casserole is casual, comforting, and compassionate. By using readily available products, like vegan sausages and mozzarella, and remaking favorite foods like ricotta cheese, these stuffed shells will taste just the way you remember. We used vegan sausage to make the filling extra-hearty, but leave it out of you prefer.

Allergens: Contains gluten and soy
Make Ahead: Tofu ricotta can be made 1 or 2 days in advance.
Tip: Use the same filling to make vegan lasagna.

Ingredients

Shells
Salt for pasta water
1 (12- to 16-ounce) box of jumbo pasta shells
1 Tbsp oil

Tofu Ricotta
1 (14- to 16-ounce) package of firm tofu
¼ cup nutritional yeast
2 Tbsps fresh lemon juice
2 tsps oil
2 tsps onion powder
1 tsp garlic powder
½ tsp salt

Filling
1 Tbsp oil
½ medium onion, finely chopped, about ½ cup
2 Italian-flavored vegan sausages, about ½ pound,
    finely chopped or crumbled
1 (10-ounce) package frozen, chopped spinach,
    thawed and squeezed to remove water
3 cloves of garlic, minced, about 1 Tbsp
1 tsps dried oregano
1 tsp dried basil
½ tsp crushed red pepper flakes
½ tsp salt
Ground black pepper, to taste
1 cup shredded vegan mozzarella, divided
1 (24-ounce) jar marinara sauce, or 3 cups homemade
Chopped basil, for garnish

Directions

1. Preheat oven to 375°F. Lightly oil a 9-inch by 13-inch casserole dish.
2. To make the shells, bring a large pot of salted water to a boil. Add the pasta shells and oil (to prevent sticking) and cook for 10 to 12 minutes, until al dente (slightly firm to the bite). Drain and rinse under cold water.
3. To make the tofu ricotta, finely crumble the tofu into a medium bowl. Mix in remaining ingredients.
4. To make the filling, heat the olive oil in a large pan over medium-high heat. Add the onion, stirring occasionally, until soft, 8 to 10 minutes. Add the sausage, stirring occasionally, until browned, about 5 minutes. Add the spinach, garlic, oregano, basil, crushed red pepper flakes, salt, and black pepper. Cook several more minutes until heated through. Remove from heat. Add the ricotta and ½ cup of mozzarella to the pan. Stir to combine.
5. Spread a few tablespoons of sauce on the bottom of the casserole dish. Use a spoon to generously fill the shells and arrange them, open side up, in the casserole dish. Spoon the remaining marinara sauce over the shells. Sprinkle with the remaining mozzarella. Cover with foil and bake for about 25 minutes, until the sauce bubbles around the edges. Remove foil and continue baking for another 10 minutes, or until the edges start to brown and crsip. Serve garnished with chopped basil.

Skillet Shepherd's Pie

SERVES 8 TO 10

Chef Linda: When the weather turns chilly and comfort food is top of mind, you'll turn to this recipe again and again. Traditionally, shepherd's pie is made with ground beef or lamb. We developed this dish for a Sanctuary cooking class on comfort food to demonstrate how using a kinder approach can still yield familiar tastes and textures. Lentils and mushrooms provide the rich, meaty flavor. You'll also find the other ingredients comfortably reassuring: potatoes, carrots, onions, celery, and peas. We love the ease of making and baking this dish in a cast iron skillet, but use a 9-inch square casserole dish if you don't have one. Enjoy it with your favorite people on a cold and cozy night.

Allergens: Contains ingredients that contain gluten and soy

Ingredients

Mashed Potato Topping

2½ pounds russet potatoes, about 6 large potatoes
1 Tbsp salt
1 cup vegetable broth
½ cup vegan cream cheese (optional)
3 Tbsps vegan butter, more for dotting
¼ tsp ground nutmeg

Filling

¾ cup dried green or brown lentils (or 2 cups cooked)
½ tsp salt
1 Tbsp olive oil
1 (10-ounce) package button mushrooms, very finely chopped, about 2 cups
1 medium onion, finely chopped, about 1 cup
3 medium carrots, chopped ¼-inch pieces, about 1½ cups
3 stalks celery, chopped ¼-inch pieces, about 1½ cups
3 large cloves garlic, minced, about 1 Tbsp
2 tsps dried thyme
1 tsp rubbed sage
1 tsp salt
Ground black pepper, to taste
2½ Tbsps cornstarch
2 Tbsps ketchup
2 Tbsps vegan Worcestershire sauce
2 cups vegetable broth, plus more to thin if necessary
1 cup frozen green peas, thawed

Directions

1. To make the mashed potato topping, cover potatoes with cold water in a large pot and add the salt. Bring to a low boil then reduce heat to keep potatoes at a low simmer until fork-tender. Drain potatoes and return them to the pot. Add vegetable broth, cream cheese, butter, and nutmeg. Using a potato masher or electric beater, slowly mix until potatoes are relatively smooth and creamy. Don't overmix or potatoes will be gluey. Some chunks are welcome.

2. To make the lentils for the filling, add them to a pot along with salt. Cover with at least 2 inches of water, about 2½ cups. Bring the water to a rapid simmer over medium-high heat, then reduce to medium-low and gently simmer for 15 to 20 minutes, or until lentils are tender but not mushy. Add more liquid if necessary. Strain any remaining water.

3. Preheat the oven to 375°F. While the lentils and potatoes are cooking, make the rest of the filling. Heat the oil in a large (12-inch) cast iron skillet or oven-proof pan over medium-high heat. Add the mushrooms, onion, carrots, celery, garlic, thyme, sage, salt, and black pepper. Cook, stirring occasionally, until most of the moisture from the mushrooms has cooked down and the vegetables are tender, about 15 minutes.

(continued on next page)

4. Sprinkle cornstarch over vegetables and stir. Add ketchup, Worcestershire sauce, broth and stir. Add the cooked lentils and peas to the pan and stir to combine. If the sauce is too thick, add a little water or broth to thin. There should be an ample amount of sauce with the filling; it should not be dry. Spread the mixture evenly in the pan.

5. Spoon dollops of potatoes over the filling and spread, leaving swoops and swirls, to cover. Bake until the filling bubbles around the sides and the topping starts to turn golden brown, about 30 minutes. Serve immediately. Alternatively, you can serve from the pan without baking.

Roasted Tempeh and Vegetable Piccata

SERVES 6 TO 8

Chef Linda: Those who say "hunger is the best sauce in the world" haven't had piccata sauce, because surely *this* is the best sauce in the world! Simple and pleasantly piquant, piccata hails from Italy and breathes life into everything it touches. Capers, garlic, and lemon juice are the classic elements in this sauce that will make your mouth pucker. We added mushrooms to make it extra hearty, but leave them out if you prefer. The sauce comes together without much fuss, which is hard to imagine given the elegant result. We have no doubt you'll use the sauce elsewhere—think mashed potatoes, rice, pasta, seitan . . . you get the idea!

Allergens: Contains soy and ingredients that may contain soy

Ingredients

1 (8-ounce) package tempeh, cut into ½-inch cubes
1½ cups water, enough to cover the tempeh
3 Tbsps tamari or soy sauce
1 pound of waxy potatoes (Yukon, yellow, or red), unpeeled and cut into 1-inch pieces
½ pound Brussels sprouts, trimmed and halved lengthwise
3 Tbsps olive oil
1 tsp salt

Piccata Sauce

2 Tbsps olive oil
½ medium onion, thinly sliced, about ½ cup
½ tsp salt
1 cup thinly sliced button mushrooms
3 cloves garlic, sliced very thinly or minced, about 1 Tbsp
2 Tbsps vegan butter
2 Tbsps cornstarch or arrowroot
2 cups vegetable broth
3 Tbsps fresh lemon juice
2 Tbsps capers, drained and rinsed
Ground black pepper, to taste
Chopped parsley, to garnish

Directions

1. Preheat oven to 400°F. Line a large baking tray with parchment.

2. In a small pot, cover the tempeh with the water and tamari. Bring to a boil, then reduce heat and simmer for about 10 minutes. Drain tempeh.

3. Arrange the seasoned tempeh, potatoes, and Brussels sprouts on the baking tray in a single layer. Drizzle with olive oil and sprinkle with salt. Use your hands to toss together and coat everything with oil. Roast in the oven for 25 to 30 minutes, or until potatoes and Brussels sprouts can be pierced easily with a sharp knife.

4. While tempeh and vegetables are roasting, make the piccata sauce. Heat oil in a large pan over medium heat. Add onion and salt. Cook, stirring occasionally, for 8 to 10 minutes, until onion is soft and translucent. Add the mushrooms, garlic, and butter. Continue to cook for about 8 minutes, until mushrooms have browned and cooked all the way through.

5. Make a slurry by stirring together in a small bowl the cornstarch and a couple of tablespoons of the broth until smooth; this prevents lumps in the sauce. Pour this into the pan and quickly add the remaining broth while stirring. Cook, stirring frequently, until the sauce thickens. Stir in lemon juice, capers, and black pepper. Transfer tempeh and vegetables from baking tray to pan. Stir to coat with sauce and remove from heat. Serve immediately, garnished with parsley.

Lentils with Pan-Fried Fennel and Celery Root

SERVES 6 TO 8

Chef Linda: We're in love with the combination of textures and flavors that create this earthy, wholesome dish. Celery root, or celeriac, is knobby and gnarly on the outside, but once peeled, you'll find its grassy, delicate celery flavor delightful in recipes like this one. Try it in cool-weather soups and stews as an alternative to potatoes. If you can't find celery root, parsnips make a fine substitute, as do carrots—just watch the cooking time and adjust to ensure proper doneness. Fennel adds a delicate sweet note here—whether sautéed, roasted, or raw, get to know this versatile vegetable, and you'll add interest to everyday dishes.

Allergens: Contains nuts

Tip: This dish is equally delicious as a salad. Chill and make the dressing in a separate bowl, then toss right before serving.

Ingredients

Dressing

⅓ cup extra virgin olive oil
⅓ cup fresh lemon juice, from about 3–4 lemons
1 Tbsp apple cider vinegar
1 Tbsp maple syrup
1 Tbsp yellow mustard
½ tsp salt, plus more to taste
Ground black pepper, to taste

Lentils

¾ cup dry green or brown lentils, or 2 cups cooked
½ teaspoon salt

Vegetables

2 Tbsps olive oil
1 pound celery root/celeriac, peeled with a sharp
    knife, cut in ½-inch pieces, about 2 cups
1 bulb fennel, fronds and stems trimmed, bulb halved
    and quartered very thinly sliced, about 2 cups
½ tsp salt
½ bunch of curly kale, chopped into bite-sized pieces,
    about 3 cups, packed
½ cup chopped walnuts
½ cup dried cranberries or dried cherries

Directions

1. To make the dressing, mix all the ingredients together in a large bowl. Taste and add more salt, if desired.

2. Pick over the lentils, discarding any withered ones or stones. Place them in a medium pot, cover generously with water, add salt, and bring to a boil. Lower the heat and simmer for 20 to 25 minutes, until just tender. Drain the lentils and empty into the bowl with the dressing. Avoid overcooking as lentils should be tender with a bit of a bite, not mushy.

3. To make the vegetables, heat the oil over medium-high heat in a large pan. Add celeriac and cook, stirring only occasionally allowing the sides to brown nicely, 10 to 12 minutes. Add fennel and salt. Continue to cook, stirring occasionally, for about 7 more minutes, until the fennel starts to soften and turn translucent. Add the kale and stir together. Cook for another 3 to 5 minutes until the kale is soft and bright green and the celeriac is fork-tender.

4. Add the vegetables to the bowl with the lentils and dressing. Add walnuts and dried cranberries and toss to combine. Serve immediately.

Swedish Meatballs and Gravy

MAKES 20 TO 24 MEATBALLS

Chef Linda: There are so many ways to make a delicious vegan meatball—with lentils, mushrooms, nuts, seitan, or tempeh. This compassionate version uses eggplant and white beans. The distinction between Italian-style and Swedish-style meatballs is mainly in the sauce. Italian meatballs are served in a tangy tomato sauce whereas Swedish meatballs are finished in a rich gravy made with sour cream or plain yogurt. The Swedish version is perfect to cozy up to on a cold winter's night. As the Swedes say, there's no bad weather, just bad clothes, so, as a nod to their origin, our Swedish meatballs have a heavy coat of breadcrumbs. We like the way it helps them stand up to the luscious gravy—and maybe it keeps them warm, too. Serve with classic pairings like mashed potatoes or noodles, or try a lighter approach and use spiralized zucchini (raw or quickly sautéed in a pan).

Allergens: Contains nuts, soy and ingredients that may contain gluten
Special Equipment: Food processor
Tip: If there are fewer mouths to feed, set aside extra meatballs *before* adding them to the pan with the gravy, and freeze them for up to 3 months. Extra gravy can also be frozen for up to 3 months.

Ingredients

Swedish Meatballs

4 Tbsps olive oil, divided
1 medium eggplant, about 1 pound, peeled and cut into 1-inch cubes
1 small onion, finely chopped, about ½ cup
1 tsp salt
3 large garlic cloves, minced, about 1 Tbsp
1 cup old-fashioned oats
2 cups plain or panko breadcrumbs, divided
½ cup walnuts
½ tsp salt
¼ tsp ground allspice
¼ tsp ground nutmeg
¼ tsp ground black pepper
1 (15.5-ounce) can white beans, drained and rinsed

Gravy

¼ cup vegan butter
¼ cup all-purpose flour
3 cups vegetable broth
⅓ cup nutritional yeast
2 Tbsps tamari or soy sauce
1 Tbsp vegan Worcestershire sauce
2 tsps Dijon or yellow mustard

½ tsp white pepper (or ground black pepper)
¼ tsp salt
1 cup unsweetened, plain nondairy yogurt

To Serve

Chopped parsley
Sautéed spiralized vegetables, like zucchini
Cooked noodles or mashed potatoes

Directions

1. To make the meatballs, heat 2 tablespoons of oil in a large skillet over medium heat. Add the eggplant, onion, and salt. Cook, stirring occasionally, for 15 to 20 minutes, until the eggplant is translucent and very soft. Add garlic in the last couple of minutes of cooking. Remove from heat and set aside.

2. Preheat the oven to 375°F. Line a baking tray with parchment. Depending on the size of your food processor, you may need to do the next step in two batches. In a food processor, pulse together the oats, 1 cup of breadcrumbs, walnuts, salt, allspice, nutmeg, and black pepper. Add the white beans and process until combined. Transfer the

(continued on next page)

eggplant to the food processor, scraping in any brown bits in the pan, and pulse until everything is combined. The mixture should be fairly well-blended but retain some texture. Set the pan aside for making the gravy.

3. Spread remaining 2 tablespoons of oil on the parchment. Place the remaining 1 cup of breadcrumbs in a small bowl. Using a tablespoon or portion scoop, shape the mixture into balls approximately 1½ inches in diameter. Place remaining breadcrumbs in a wide, shallow bowl. Roll each meatball in the breadcrumbs and arrange on the baking tray. Bake for about 30 minutes, until the meatballs are firm and crispy on the outside.

4. While the meatballs are baking, make the gravy. Melt the butter in the eggplant pan. Whisk in the flour and cook for 3 to 4 minutes. Whisk in the broth and stir until smooth and thickened. Stir in nutritional yeast, tamari, Worcestershire sauce, mustard, pepper, and salt. Gently simmer over medium-low heat until the gravy thickens, about 5 minutes. Stir in yogurt. Taste and add more salt if you like.

5. Transfer meatballs to the pan and spoon gravy over them. Cook gently for about 5 minutes. Transfer to a serving dish, sprinkle with parsley, and serve with spiralized vegetables or your favorite noodles or mashed potatoes.

Italian-Style Tempeh and Peppers

SERVES 4

Chef Linda: Sausage and peppers, with its classic aroma of sweet caramelized onions, oregano, basil, and fennel, is a classic comfort food. To prove we don't need animals to create our favorite dishes, we developed this recipe for a Compassionate Cuisine "Vegan 101" class using tempeh, a heart-healthy, high-protein food. A light, crisp salad will complete your meal. You just might want to double the recipe because the intoxicating aroma from your kitchen may attract friends you never knew you had.

Allergens: Contains soy and ingredients that may contain gluten

Ingredients

1 (8-ounce) package of tempeh, cut widthwise into
¼-inch wide strips
1½ cups water, enough to cover the tempeh
3 Tbsps tamari or soy sauce
5 Tbsps oil, divided
2 red bell peppers, cut into ¼-inch wide strips, about
2 cups
¼ tsp salt
2 large yellow onions, halved and thinly sliced along
the grain, about 3 cups
3 large garlic cloves, minced, about 1 Tbsp
2 tsps dried oregano
2 tsps dried basil
1 tsp ground fennel or fennel seeds
¼ to ½ tsp crushed red pepper flakes
Ground black pepper, to taste

To Serve

Cooked rice or sandwich rolls

Directions

1. In a small pot, cover the tempeh with water and tamari. Bring to a boil, then reduce heat and simmer for about 10 minutes. Drain tempeh, reserving about ¼ cup of cooking liquid.

2. Heat 2 tablespoons of oil in a large pan over medium-high heat. Working in batches, arrange slices of tempeh in a single layer in pan, adding another 1 tablespoon of oil, if necessary, as you go. Cook for 3 to 4 minutes on each side, until the tempeh starts to brown. Transfer tempeh to a paper towel–lined plate.

3. Use the same pan to make the vegetables. Heat 2 tablespoons of oil over medium-high heat. Add peppers and salt. Cook, stirring occasionally, for about 8 minutes, until peppers start to soften. Add onions, garlic, oregano, basil, fennel, crushed red pepper, and black pepper. Continue to cook for about 10 minutes, until the peppers and onions are very soft and have begun to turn brown around the edges.

4. Return the tempeh to the pan and gently stir to combine. Add reserved cooking liquid and cook several minutes more until flavors have mingled and some of the liquid has cooked down. Serve immediately over cooked rice or on rolls.

Thai Red Curry with Chickpeas, Sweet Potatoes, and Kale

SERVES 4

Chef Sara: This recipe has a sentimental backstory: it's one that I wrote for my cooking audition at the Sanctuary! Several years and many cooking classes later, it's still beloved for its great taste and ease of preparation. This fresh, simple take on Thai red curry features protein- and fiber-rich chickpeas, as well as two beloved nutritional powerhouses, sweet potatoes and kale. Serve this curry over your favorite cooked grain for an easy, satisfying meal any day of the week.

Allergens: Contains soy and ingredients that may contain gluten
Tip: Add more sriracha sauce if you like your curry with a kick, or omit it entirely for a milder flavor.

Ingredients

2 tsps coconut oil
1 medium red onion, chopped, about 1 cup
3–4 Tbsps Thai red curry paste
1 (13.5-ounce) can regular (not light) coconut milk
2 Tbsps tamari or soy sauce
2–3 tsps sriracha or hot sauce, to suit your level of desired spiciness (optional)
1 large sweet potato, peeled and cut into ½-inch cubes, approximately 2 cups
1 large bunch lacinato kale, stems removed, leaves cut into bite-sized pieces, about 4–5 cups
1 (15.5-ounce) can chickpeas, drained and rinsed, about 1½ cups
⅓ cup fresh Thai basil leaves, lightly packed, chopped (or Italian basil)
1 Tbsp fresh lime juice
Rice or grain of your choice
Fresh lime wedges

Directions

1. Heat the oil in a large saucepan over medium-high heat. Add the chopped onion and a pinch of salt. Cook, stirring frequently, until softened and translucent, 8 to 10 minutes. Add the curry paste and mix thoroughly, coating the onions with the paste to help prevent clumps of curry in the sauce. Cook for another 30 seconds or so, until fragrant.

2. Add the coconut milk, tamari, and sriracha sauce and mix well. Add the diced sweet potato. If the sweet potato isn't covered by the coconut milk mixture, add ¼ to ½ cup water so there is enough liquid to simmer evenly. Bring to a boil, reduce the heat to low, and cover. Simmer for 10 minutes, or until nearly tender. Add the kale and chickpeas, then cover again. Simmer gently for 8 to 10 minutes, until the kale is wilted and the sweet potato is fully cooked.

3. Stir in the chopped basil and lime juice. Serve with your choice of rice or grain and fresh lime wedges. Leftovers will keep in the refrigerator for three to five days.

Wild Mushroom Risotto

MAKES 6 SERVINGS

Chef Sara: Prepared during a popular Valentine's Day Compassionate Cuisine cooking class at the Sanctuary, our luscious risotto proves that even classic comfort foods can be made simply and deliciously vegan. For an umami boost, the mushrooms are roasted in the oven instead of sautéed. We used a local, artisan herbed cheese spread for extra creaminess, but any vegan cream cheese or your favorite soft cheese spread.

Allergens: Contains ingredient that contain nuts

Ingredients

Roasted Mushrooms

1 pound brown button mushrooms, thickly sliced, about 2–3 cups
4 ounces oyster mushrooms, pulled apart into individual "petals"
1 Tbsp olive oil
Salt, to taste
Ground black pepper, to taste

Risotto

6 cups vegetable broth
1 tsp salt, plus more to taste
Ground black pepper, to taste
2 Tbsps olive oil
2 large shallots, finely chopped, about ½ cup
3 cloves garlic, minced, about 1 Tbsp
1 Tbsp chopped fresh thyme, leaves only (or 1½ tsps dried thyme)
1½ cups uncooked Arborio rice
½ cup dry white wine (or 1 cup vegetable broth and 1 Tbsp mild vinegar)
¼ cup vegan cream cheese or herbed cheese spread (optional, but highly recommended)
Chopped parsley, for garnish

Directions

1. Preheat the oven to 425°F. Line a baking tray with parchment.

2. In a large bowl, toss the mushrooms with the oil, sprinkle with salt and pepper, then spread in a single layer on the prepared tray. Transfer to the oven and bake for approximately 20 minutes, until the mushrooms have shrunken and are starting to brown. Remove from the oven and allow to cool.

3. To make the risotto, while the mushrooms are roasting, heat the vegetable broth in a medium pot. Add the salt and black pepper. Taste the broth; it should taste a bit salty. Don't worry, this extra saltiness is necessary to properly flavor the rice. If the broth you used was low-sodium, add a pinch more salt. Keep the broth hot over low heat as you continue with the recipe.

4. Heat the oil in a wide, heavy-bottomed pan over medium heat. Add the shallots plus a pinch of salt, and cook, stirring frequently, until translucent, about 5 to 7 minutes. Add the garlic, thyme, and rice, and cook for an additional 2 to 3 minutes, until the rice starts to become translucent. Add the wine and allow to cook, stirring frequently, until the wine is mostly absorbed into the rice.

5. Add one or two ladles of hot broth to the rice and cook, stirring frequently, until the broth is almost absorbed by the rice. Adjust the heat as necessary so the risotto bubbles gently, but doesn't boil vigorously. Add another one or two ladles of broth, and repeat this process until you've used all but

(continued on next page)

one ladle of the broth. This will take 25 to 30 minutes. When finished, the rice will be tender all the way through but still al dente (slightly firm) in the center, surrounded by a creamy sauce. To make the stirring feel less tedious, recruit a loved one to help you out, or put on your favorite music or podcast.

6. Stir in the roasted mushrooms, remaining broth, and cheese. Cook briefly until heated through and bubbling. Serve immediately, garnished with parsley.

Easy Veggie Baked Ziti

SERVES 6 TO 8

Chef Linda: Comforting baked ziti has a place in everyone's heart. Made for family meals, this familiar favorite was remade, without dairy, for kids in our summer camp. Tofu makes a rich, ricotta-like cheese that's high in protein and only imperceptibly different from dairy-based ricotta. We add cauliflower to the pasta as it cooks to add texture and boost nutrition; it secretly melts into the softness of the dish and goes undetected. Substitute broccoli if you prefer, or use them both. It's a dish you'll look forward to every time.

Allergens: Contains soy
Make Ahead: Tofu ricotta can be made 1 or 2 days in advance.
Tip: If you have hearty appetites to handle, sauté some sliced vegan sausage and add when assembling the dish. This dish freezes well, so make a double batch and freeze before baking, then thaw in the refrigerator overnight and bake at 350°F for about 1 hour.

Ingredients

1 pound dried regular or gluten-free ziti or penne
2 cups fresh or frozen cauliflower florets

Tofu Ricotta

1 (14- to 16-ounce) package of firm tofu
¼ cup of unsweetened nondairy milk
¼ cup nutritional yeast
2 Tbsps fresh lemon juice
2 tsps olive oil
2 tsps onion powder
1 tsp garlic powder
½ tsp salt

Sauce

1 (32-ounce) jar marinara sauce, or 4 cups of
   homemade sauce, or more if you desire, divided
2 tsps dried oregano
2 tsps dried basil
½ tsp crushed red pepper flakes (optional)
1½ cups shredded vegan mozzarella cheese, divided
Chopped fresh basil or parsley, to garnish

Directions

1. Preheat the oven to 375°F. Bring a large pot of salted water to a boil. Add the ziti to the pot and cook according to package directions. With about 5 minutes left to cook, add the cauliflower, and bring to a gentle boil again. Continue cooking until pasta is al dente (soft with a little bite to it) and cauliflower is fork-tender. Note that the addition of vegetables will increase the stated cooking time of the pasta so check the pasta and cook accordingly. The key to success is to not overcook the pasta when boiling because it will cook again in the oven. Drain the pasta and cauliflower and return them to the pot.

2. While the pasta is cooking, make the tofu ricotta. Finely crumble the tofu into a medium bowl. Add milk, nutritional yeast, lemon juice, olive oil, onion powder, garlic powder, and salt. Mix until all ingredients are thoroughly combined.

3. To make the sauce, add about ⅔ of the marinara, oregano, basil, and crushed red pepper flakes to the pasta and stir to combine. Add the tofu ricotta and 1 cup of mozzarella. Stir gently. Empty the pasta into a large casserole dish and top with remaining sauce. Sprinkle with remaining mozzarella. Bake for about 20 minutes until heated through and the cheese is melted. Remove from oven, garnish with parsley, and serve immediately.

Stuffed Portobello Pizzas

SERVES 4 TO 6, DEPENDING ON THE SIZE OF PORTOBELLO

Chef Linda: Is it a stuffed mushroom or a pizza? It's both! This winning combination of meaty portobellos, creamy tofu ricotta, and tomato sauce has all the makings of an easy weeknight dinner that's sure to please all eaters. And there are lots of reasons why you want portobellos on your plate—they're good for you, easy to find, and provide valuable plant-based protein! Invite your friends to add pizzazz to these portobello pizzas by using their favorite toppings. And don't worry if you're spotted using a knife and fork to eat *this* pizza: it's so hearty and plump, there's really no other way.

> **Allergens:** Contains soy and ingredients that may contain gluten
> **Make Ahead:** Tofu ricotta can be made 1 or 2 days in advance.

Ingredients

Mushrooms
8–10 large portobello mushrooms, stems removed
2 Tbsps oil
Salt

Tofu Ricotta
1 (14- to 16-ounce) package of firm tofu
¼ cup nutritional yeast
2 Tbsps fresh lemon juice
2 tsps oil
2 tsp onion powder
1 tsp garlic powder
1 tsp salt

To Assemble
1 cup marinara sauce, jarred or homemade
1 cup vegan mozzarella, shredded

Topping Suggestions
Sliced black olives
Sliced hot cherry peppers
Cooked, chopped broccoli
Cooked, sliced or crumbled vegan sausage
Chopped basil, for garnish

Directions

1. Preheat oven to 400°F. Line a baking tray with parchment. Brush the tops of the mushrooms with oil and place them oiled-side down on the tray. Sprinkle with a little salt. Roast for about 15 minutes until water is released and mushrooms are dark brown. Drain or blot excess water from each mushroom.

2. While the mushrooms are roasting, make the tofu ricotta. Finely crumble the tofu into a medium bowl. Add nutritional yeast, lemon juice, olive oil, onion powder, garlic powder, and salt. Mix until all ingredients are thoroughly combined. After making pizzas, store any extra tofu ricotta in a covered container in the refrigerator for up to one week or in the freezer for up to three months.

3. Spread 1 to 2 tablespoons of marinara sauce on the mushroom. Top with 1 to 2 tablespoons of tofu ricotta. Drizzle another 1 tablespoon of marinara sauce on top. Sprinkle shredded mozzarella and finish with toppings.

4. Return the tray to the oven for about 10 minutes, or until the cheese has melted. Let mushrooms stand for a few minutes. Garnish with chopped basil before serving.

Sanctuary Story

FULL THROTTLE

I'd be lying if I said that our animal care crew cruises through winter unscathed, happily ignoring every insult that the season hurls their way. They don't. The challenges of a tough winter—below zero temperatures, snowstorms that dump two feet or more at a time, gale-force winds—test their grit and their heart, because no matter the weather, the work of caring well for three hundred charges must still get done. Animals must be blanketed, bedding in pig houses doubled or even tripled to ensure our porcine friends' safety and warmth, chicken wattles must be coated with Vaseline to prevent frostbite. On days like this, the animal care team is in full throttle, ensuring that even though *they* are struggling to stay warm, our animals are comfortable.

What does full-throttle actually *look* like? Well, rather than blanketing the three or four most compromised horses or goats, for instance, caretakers blanket

dozens of elderly animals. On the most treacherous days, our elderly and blind horses stay inside, so cleaning our twenty-stall main barn is far more difficult—there is exponentially more manure. Caretakers pile straw four feet high in the pig barn, and program overhead heaters to turn on during the bitterest hours of the long, cruel nights. Where it's safe to hang heat lamps, they do so, and where it isn't, chickens move into our heated offices, which adds many additional crates to the daily cleaning schedule.

And there's more to "full throttle" than the extra care the animals require. Locks and latches freeze shut and must be warmed or pried with gloveless hands, and sometimes fingers freeze to the metal itself. On days when two feet of snow has blanketed the ground overnight, Rich and Josh, our intrepid maintenance duo, alternate between snow blowing and snow plowing all day long so we have access to the thirty-five pastures and paddocks where our animals live, and Animal Care Director Kelly Mullins walks "equine alley" to determine whether it's too icy to risk turning out the horses. Our animal care team battles stress, worry, and exhaustion, on top of the sometimes subzero gale-force winds. Still, running on empty, they smile and grit their way through. Yes. Whatever it takes to ensure that *our animals are okay.* That's what "full throttle" looks like.

So it was this team, already worn weary by the season itself, that found Pliers, a thirty-five-year-old horse rescued from hopelessness with his mother fifteen months earlier, down in his paddock one early February morning, pinned awkwardly against the fence. This dangerous position is referred to as being "cast," and describes when a horse has either laid down or rolled so close to a wall or fence that he can't get his footing to stand. Judging by his appearance (described by Health Care Manager Kellie Myers as "beyond the shivering stage"), Pliers had been down for hours. He was as still as a stone.

Dr. Andrea Sotela of Rhinebeck Equine was called, and so was Kelly Mullins, Animal Care Director, who rushed in on her day off.

My phone rang at 8:15 a.m.

"Stevens," said Mullins. "Are you here?"

I wasn't. I was ninety minutes away.

"Pliers is down," she said. "We don't yet know what we're dealing with, but we've got an all-hands-on-deck situation."

"I'll take care of it," I said, easing my car off the thruway in order to make phone calls. "And I'll be there as soon as I can."

By the time I arrived, the barn was humming as staff and volunteers who'd dropped everything to come in on their day off cleaned stalls, filled hayracks and water buckets, and washed dishes. While the caretakers tried to save one precious life, the backup team managed the care of three hundred others.

I hurried down "equine alley" and from a distance saw seven people—two vets and five staff—clustered around a prone horse; even Rich, our buildings and grounds guy, was there in case we needed the tractor to lift Pliers or, more likely, to bury him.

I climbed over the gate. Another caretaker, Matt, was holding Ashley, Pliers' blind mother, in the run-in, away from her son. Still neurotically attached to him despite remarkable progress, she'd been sedated twice. Pliers was in the middle of the paddock, covered with a thermal blanket and additional ones. Caretaker Kate, encrusted in mud, held a bag of IV fluids, the umpteenth Pliers had received that morning.

Dr. Sotela ran down the scenario for me: the team had rolled Pliers over and away from the fence. They got him up. He fell. They got him up again. He fell again. He was too depleted, and the paddock, muddy from the rapid snow melt, was working against him. Dr. Sotela rattled off his body temperature (5 degrees below normal), a description of his gut sounds, the medications he'd received, the liters of fluids. And then the plan of action: more fluids, keep him settled as his body temperature rose and he recovered strength, and then three more attempts to help him stand. The first would be manual—just human strength and the will and reserves of a very old, very tired horse. If that failed, they'd attempt to lift him with heavy straps shoved under his belly. The final effort would utilize the tractor and tow straps to lift him into the air then gently lower him down, supporting him as he tried to bear his own weight.

"Mullins, are you on board with this?" I asked.

"Sure am," she said with conviction. "That's what we're gonna do."

Sanctuary work demands that we be *damned good* at assessing when it's time to let an animal go. To prolong the fight, and consequently the suffering, of an old, worn out animal is no more ethically justifiable than doing the same thing to one's own grandparent. One needs the wisdom to know not only *how possible* a good outcome is, but also what the animal would want, if he could speak. And then one needs the courage to honor that choice. We give these gut-wrenching moments our very best, but once we've done so, and we see that the fight in a precious life is gone, then our final act of love is to let go.

I looked at Pliers's face. I watched his labored breathing. I thought about his age, and about the years of neglect and the extent to which they'd taken their toll. And I felt certain that these were Pliers's final moments. But I *hadn't* been there for the previous three hours to see what had led up to right now. More important, I trusted the wisdom and the guts of our team to know when to say, "Enough." So while it was all I could do not to say, "I'm so sorry you disagree, but we're done here, guys," I didn't. Pliers, and the team, would continue to have their shot at the unlikeliest of happy endings.

I returned to the main barn, our hub. In the feed room, I organized the cleaning list: the sheep needed to be stripped; the piglets, ditto; Mario and Audrey's barn; the goats. The list grew. I transferred it to the cleaning board in the aisle, assigned staff to various tasks, then picked up my own tools—pitchfork, shovel, rake—and loaded them into the "Daisy Duke," our fluorescent yellow and orange work truck. I headed to one of the smaller pig barns, climbed the gate, and began cleaning. Shovel, lift, toss. Shovel, lift, toss. The barn emptied and the Daisy Duke filled, as Mario the pig kept me company.

"Are you having a good day?" I asked him. "Umph," he replied. "Umph. Umph." As I continued cleaning, he continued chatting.

I'd only been working for forty-five minutes but needed water, so I walked into the barn to discover Kelsey, our newest caretaker, putting way too many shavings in a stall.

"Hey, love, you can be a little less generous," I suggested.

"Mullins told me to put down extra shavings for the horses."

"What horses?" I asked.

"Ashley and Pliers."

My heart in my throat, I high-tailed it down equine alley to see ancient, blind Ashley being led from the pasture toward the main barn. And behind her, caked in mud from the tip of his ears to the bottom of his tail, came Pliers, steadied by Kate, the filthiest, happiest human I'd ever seen, taking one slow, tentative step toward the main barn. He was shaky, but very much alive.

Pliers hadn't had the energy to stand with human help, so in the end, tow straps and the long arms of the tractor bucket lifted him straight into the air and stood him on his feet. Limp when Rich had hoisted him, Pliers had the good sense to lean against the tractor for support when his feet touched the ground. There, still supported by the tow straps, he eagerly accepted hot mash and hay. Minutes passed as the crew stood surrounding him, surely as exhausted as our old boy. Eventually his shaking legs steadied. Once that happened, they removed the support straps, and then his walk to the barn began: a few steps. Rest. A few more. Rest again. His ordeal, it seemed, was over.

"It's a miracle," was the whispered refrain, because frankly, not one of us expected this ending. But a "miracle" is not what unfolded that February morning in a muddy paddock at Catskill Animal Sanctuary. Instead, the know-how of a good vet; the guts, grace, and grit of a bone-weary animal care team; and the trust of a horse not quite ready to pack it in coalesced to allow that old boy to live to see another day. Come to think of it, maybe that *is* a miracle.

That same night, I walked down to the barn and found Pliers snoozing in a warm barn stall, his body and psyche recovering from as much of a near-death situation as I've witnessed in my seventeen years of doing this work. Mama Ashley was in the stall next to him. A huge open window in the dividing wall allowed them to touch whenever they needed to. Down the aisle, Sister Mary Frances, our free-ranging potbelly pig, snored under a four-foot mound of straw and blankets. Hermione the goat called for me, and I headed down the aisle to say hello. All was well.

The crew that agreed to accept Ashley and Pliers to prevent them from being shot by their owner will face more winter days like this. But they will show up, on time and smiling, to give their very best, no matter what it takes. Because that's what they do. Just ask Pliers.

The crew that cares for the animals and the Sanctuary that protects them is the "special sauce" that makes us who we are. Without their undivided loyalty to our animal ambassadors, our work to educate and inspire would fall flat. Like our Caesar dressing (pg. 188), Artichoke-Cannellini Alfredo Sauce (pg. 187), and our Peanut Butter Miso Sauce (pg. 185), they work hard to add life, flavor, and vitality to this life-saving work.

Sauces and Dressings

And all at once, the meal comes to life with a drizzle or a splash—it's all in the sauce. There are whole books to be written on sauce, but here we offer just few of ours that have accompanied the dishes in this book. Sauces and dressings are like peacemakers or instigators; they gently unite disparate ingredients or incite a riot of flavors. Use these where you see fit. Contemplate their compassionate ingredients. Then create your own sauces, and don't keep them a secret.

Also pictured, Remoulade
Sauce (pg. 186)

Avocado-Scallion Sauce

MAKE ABOUT 2 CUPS

Chef Linda

Allergens: Contains nuts
Special Equipment: Food processor or blender

Ingredients

1 ripe avocado, peeled and pitted
½ cup raw cashews (not soaked)
½ jalapeño, seeded and roughly chopped
3 Tbsps fresh lime juice
2 scallions, roughly chopped, about ¼ cup
2 large cloves garlic, peeled
2 Tbsps cilantro leaves
½ tsp salt

Directions

1. Place all the ingredients in a blender or food processor and blend until smooth. Taste and adjust seasonings. To store extra sauce, empty into a small container. Place a piece of plastic wrap directly on top, touching the sauce, to prevent air exposure and browning. Cover with a lid and store in the refrigerator for two to three days.

Peanut Butter Miso Sauce

MAKES ABOUT ¾ CUP

Chef Linda

Allergens: Contains peanuts and soy

Ingredients

½ cup smooth, unsalted peanut butter (or ½ cup of your favorite nut butter, or replace half the nut butter with tahini)
3 Tbsps miso (white, yellow, or red—the darker the color, the stronger the taste)
1 Tbsp tamari or soy sauce
1 Tbsp toasted sesame oil
2 tsps maple syrup
1–2 tsps hot sauce (optional)
Up to ½ cup warm water

Directions

1. To make the sauce, stir together peanut butter, miso, tamari, toasted sesame oil, hot sauce, and syrup. Slowly add water and continue to whisk until a thick, pourable consistency is reached. Add more water by the tablespoon to thin to desired consistency.

Remoulade Sauce

MAKES ABOUT 1½ CUPS

Chef Linda

Allergens: Contains ingredients that may contain gluten and soy

Ingredients

1 cup vegan mayonnaise

¼ cup finely chopped shallots

2 Tbsps finely chopped fresh herbs (parsley, chives, chervil, or tarragon)

2 Tbsps chopped capers

2 Tbsps ketchup

2 tsps Dijon mustard

2 tsps fresh lemon juice

1 tsp vegan Worcestershire sauce

½ tsp paprika

1 large garlic clove, minced or grated, about ½ tsp

¼ tsp ground black pepper

⅛ tsp ground cayenne

Salt, to taste

Directions

1. Whisk together all the ingredients except the salt in a small bowl. Depending on the brand of vegan mayonnaise you use, you may or may not want to add a little salt. Taste first, then decide. Refrigerate until ready to serve.

The Only BBQ Sauce You'll Ever Need

MAKES ABOUT 1½ CUPS

Chef Linda

Allergens: Contains soy and ingredients that may contain gluten

Ingredients

1 (6-ounce) can tomato paste

¼ cup apple cider vinegar

3 Tbsps maple syrup, plus more to taste

2 Tbsps tamari or soy sauce

1 tsp hot sauce, plus more to taste

1 Tbsp yellow mustard

2 Tbsps vegan Worcestershire sauce

2 Tbsps molasses

2 Tbsps fresh lemon juice

1 Tbsp liquid smoke

2 tsps onion powder

½ tsp garlic powder

½ tsp ground white pepper, plus more to taste

Salt, to taste

Directions

1. Stir together all of the ingredients in a small bowl. Taste and adjust seasonings. Increase the heat with more hot sauce or white pepper or add more syrup to make it a bit sweeter.

Artichoke-Cannellini Alfredo Sauce

MAKES ABOUT 2½ CUPS

Chef Linda

Allergens: Contains nuts
Special Equipment: Blender

Ingredients

1 (15.5-ounce) can cannellini beans, drained and rinsed

1 cup marinated artichoke hearts, drained

½ cup raw cashews, soaked in water for 30 minutes, drained

⅓ cup nutritional yeast

2 large cloves garlic, peeled

2 Tbsps extra-virgin olive oil

2 Tbsps fresh lemon juice

¾ tsp salt

Ground black pepper, to taste

Directions

1. Place beans, artichokes, cashews, nutritional yeast, garlic, olive oil, lemon juice, salt, and pepper in a blender and purée until smooth, about 1 minute. Add water, by the tablespoon, to thin as desired. Serve immediately over hot pasta or store in a covered container and reheat, thinning with a little water if necessary, to serve.

Spinach Pesto

MAKES ABOUT 2 CUPS

Chef Linda

Allergens: Contains optional soy and nuts
Special Equipment: Food processor
Variations: Use kale or arugula in place of spinach. Include up to ½ cup peeled and chopped broccoli stems.

Ingredients

3 cups baby spinach, packed

¼ cup fresh herbs like sage, basil, or parsley

¼ cup walnuts (or pumpkin or hemp seeds for a nut-free version)

3 large cloves garlic, peeled

⅓ cup nutritional yeast

2 Tbsps fresh lemon juice, plus more to taste

1 Tbsp yellow miso (optional: if using miso, use ½ tsp salt instead of 1 tsp)

1 tsp salt, plus more to taste

½ cup extra virgin olive oil

Directions

1. Place ingredients except olive oil in the bowl of a food processor and pulse until finely chopped. With the processor on, drizzle in the olive oil through the top spout. Purée or leave a bit of texture, if you prefer. Taste and add more salt or lemon juice, if necessary. Use immediately or store in the refrigerator for up to a week. Pesto can be frozen for up to six months.

Cashew Caesar Salad Dressing

MAKES ABOUT 1¼ CUPS

Chef Linda

Allergens: Contains nuts and ingredients that contain gluten and soy
Special Equipment: Blender

Ingredients

1 cup raw cashews, soaked for 30 minutes, drained
¼ cup water
3 Tbsps lemon juice
2 Tbsps extra-virgin olive oil
2 Tbsps nutritional yeast
2 Tbsps capers, drained
1 Tbsp yellow miso
1 Tbsp vegan Worcestershire sauce
1 Tbsp Dijon mustard
3 large cloves garlic, peeled
¼ tsp ground black pepper
Salt, to taste

Directions

1. Place all of the ingredients except salt in a blender and blend until smooth and creamy. Add more water, a tablespoon at a time if necessary. Dressing should be strong and sharp as it will mellow with mixed with salad. The capers and miso add salt to this dressing, but taste and add a bit more if you choose.

Cashew Sour Cream

MAKES ABOUT 1½ CUPS

Chef Linda

Allergens: Contains nuts
Special Equipment: Blender

Ingredients

1 cup raw cashews, soaked for 30 minutes, drained
1 cup water
2 Tbsps fresh lemon juice, plus more to taste
¼ tsp salt, plus more to taste

Directions

1. Place the drained cashews in a blender. Add water, lemon juice, and salt. Blend on high speed until smooth and glossy, stopping to scrape down the sides as necessary. Add more water by the tablespoon if necessary. Taste and adjust flavor by adding more lemon juice or salt. Chill or serve immediately. The sour cream will thicken up after chilling. To thin it out, add 1 or 2 tablespoons of water to obtain the consistency you like.

Cashew Herb Cream

MAKES ABOUT 1½ CUPS

Chef Linda

Allergens: Contains nuts
Special Equipment: Blender

Ingredients

1 cup raw cashews, soaked for 30 minutes, drained
½ cup packed fresh parsley, cilantro, tarragon, or
basil leaves
2 large garlic cloves, peeled
¾ cup water
2 Tbsps fresh lime juice, plus more to taste
½ tsp salt, plus more to taste

Directions

1. Add drained cashews, herbs, garlic, water, lime juice, and salt to a blender. Blend on high speed for about 1 to 2 minutes, until smooth and creamy. Add more water, by the tablespoon, if necessary to help with blending. Taste and adjust flavors by adding more salt or lime juice.

Simple Golden Gravy

MAKES ABOUT 1½ CUPS

Chef Linda

Allergens: Contains soy and ingredients that may contain gluten

Ingredients

2 Tbsps olive oil or vegan butter
2 Tbsps all-purpose flour or gluten-free flour
1½ cups vegetable broth, plus more to thin if
necessary
½ cup nutritional yeast flakes
1 Tbsp tamari or soy sauce
2 tsps onion powder
1 tsp garlic powder
¼ tsp salt (optional)

Directions

1. Heat the oil in a small pot over medium heat. Add the flour and continuously whisk for 2 to 3 minutes. Slowly add in the broth and whisk until smooth. Add nutritional yeast, tamari, onion powder, and garlic powder. Continue to cook, whisking continuously, until mixture is thick and velvety. Taste and add salt if necessary. Thin to desired consistency with more broth. Store extra in a covered container for up to five days or freeze for up to three months. Gravy will thicken considerably when chilled. Microwave or heat on the stovetop, adding more broth to thin if necessary.

Sanctuary Story

I AM CHICKEN. LOOK THE HELL OUT.

Sanctuaries have known for a long time that far from being "bird-brained," chickens are bright, multifaceted individuals. After all, we engage with them 365 days a year, so we know them as well as you know the dog who pushes you to the corner of the bed at night or the cat who stretches across your keyboard. At Catskill, our free-range "Underfoot" chickens elicit wonder, laughter, respect, and delight from those of us lucky enough to move among them each day. Truly, truly: to know chickens is to love them.

Meet Sidra, for example. Sidra is a White Leghorn, the breed typically grown for its egg-laying capacity. A cheeky, active breed, Leghorns are crammed into wire cages and endure lives one wouldn't wish upon the vilest human. Sidra is one of the lucky ones. She is smart, as are most chickens, but that's just the start. Sidra is larger than life (all four pounds of her), living with abandon and keeping us on our toes every step of the way.

Curious and exceptionally confident, Sidra loves to explore both the "Welcome Hut" and "Peabody's Place," a temporary space that houses our cooking demos and educational programs. The hut is the place where guests check in, but it also doubles as our retail space. As visitors shop for T-shirts, books, cards, or other Catskill memorabilia, Sidra appears to shop, too, weaving between guests, inspecting items large and small while clearly hoping some are edible. With a grand sense of entitlement, she hops onto chairs in Peabody's Place, pecking at grains in

the whole foods exhibit or watching intently as Chef Sara demonstrates how to make chicken salad sans the animal. Sidra approves.

But it's at mealtime when Sidra's true daring emerges. She and her family—rooster Sebastian and

hen Pilar—make a mad dash to the pig barn when the feed truck leaves, because they know that it is the first stop, but also because pigs eat . . . well, they eat like pigs, chomping robustly, food flying in every direction from their mouths (what they lack in finesse they make up for in gusto). Unlike Sebastian and Pilar, who hang back until the pigs are finished, Sidra defies death each time she makes a mad dash into the barn and zips around between eight hungry pigs, any of whom could crush her with a quick jerk of the head, or worse, with a "GET THE HELL AWAY FROM MY BREAKFAST!" chomp on her tiny body. No mind. She is chicken. Look the hell out.

And look the hell out *especially* when it comes to Sidra's task of laying eggs. With literally thousands of places to choose from (she's a free-range bird on a 150-acre farm, for Lord's sake) Sidra insists on a single spot: in the barn kitchen, inside a half-bag of soft pine shavings placed under the kitchen table. Why she's so obsessively particular is curious to us, but we like to think she believes that one day, a tiny chick will emerge from one of those eggs, and what better place for a baby to be born than in a warm, soft, fluffy bed of shavings tucked under a table for protection, and in a heated kitchen, no less? We like to think, in other words, that Sidra's behavior is maternal instinct on steroids.

I was sitting in the long barn aisle, near the kitchen, my back against Callie the horse's stall wall, when I first observed the insanity. It was just me, Russell the potbelly pig, and chickens Sebastian, Pilar, and Sidra. Russell, Sebastian, Pilar and I were chillin'. Sidra, not so much. Sidra paced back and forth, back and forth in front of the kitchen door. She was *willing it* to open, and she was swearing her tiny head off.

Animal caretaker Crystal entered the barn.

"Why is she having a meltdown?" I asked, as Sidra continued pacing like a maniac.

"We've blocked the cat door from the other side so she can't come in," Crystal explained.

Catskill Animal Sanctuary's "kitchen" is located in the center of our main barn. It's a large, high-ceilinged room where we not only prepare individualized meals twice a day, but also store everything from grain to towels to some of our medical supplies. But the inappropriately named "kitchen" is also where some of our most vulnerable birds are housed at night in safe, cozy crates bedded generously with shavings. These birds—some with injuries, some with permanent disabilities—are allowed, if appropriate, to free range during the day. But housing them in "the kitchen" is the best way to keep a close eye on them.

Sidra is not one of the vulnerable, but with human traffic in and out of the kitchen all day long, she easily made it her daytime home and soon discovered the delight of laying her egg inside that bag of soft shavings intended for the crates of the other birds. She figured out in no time that if the human door was closed, then the cat door doubled as a fine chicken door, and she used it whenever she wanted to lay an egg or steal a grape from the produce containers.

If Sidra's behavior had been limited to laying eggs and pilfering produce, all would be well. But

NO. Free access to the kitchen proved problematic, for when other chickens dared to share the roomy space, she pecked them, chased them, and harassed them relentlessly. A generous spirit, she is not. Underscored. So Sidra has been booted out into the barn aisle during work hours.

To make matters worse, we humans foiled her Plan B.

Sidra learned in a nanosecond that if the front entrance to the maternity ward (Promised Land? What else?) was blocked, she could go to the back—by traveling down the long barn aisle, circling behind the barn, walking down a little path, hopping over the washroom door, and stealthily hiding until someone opened the back door to the kitchen.

But because she's a bully, we now make sure that the top half of the washroom door is locked. Permanently. No back door entry. No front door/cat door entry. She simply can't get in. Hence the meltdown.

You'd think that with all the other options available, Little Miss Thing would choose another protected area, another bed of soft shavings. Nope. Her determination to lay her egg *in the shavings . . . in the kitchen . . . under the table* is all-consuming. The other day, for instance, a new volunteer named Samantha thought she was walking past a small hen perched peacefully on a shelf just outside the kitchen door when suddenly she was dive bombed by a crazed white bird.

"I thought, 'Oh, how sweet . . . that chicken feels safe enough to rest right there with humans coming in and out all day,'" Samantha explained. "But the second I opened the kitchen door, she LOST HER MIND. She came right at my head. All I could see were wings flapping and legs flailing, and then she was over my shoulder, running through the kitchen and jumping into that shavings bag."

Samantha paused to recover, and had the composure to smile. "What was that about?" she asked.

I picture Sidra making her nest in the bed of shavings.

Mission accomplished.

It would seem Sidra's sassy side could use a little sweetening up. And do we have just the thing! An Apple Fritter Cake drizzled with sugar glaze (pg. 196). A Coconut Cream Pie sweet and silky enough to make you weep (pg. 203). And it's only fair to warn you about the cheesecake. *Oh, the cheesecake* (pg. 215). Sidra, we'd be crabby, too, if we couldn't eat these irresistible delights. Make them all, friends.

Sweets and Treats

What a tragedy life would be without the promise of something sweet. Whether it politely punctuates the end of a meal, barges into the middle of our day, or whispers to us late at night, there comes a time when we must succumb to a sweet treat. These recipes span the spectrum of humble to grand and affirm the extraordinary truth that we *can* indulge without animals. Cakes, cookies, tarts, or pies—they're all here, and they're all clamoring to be made.

Sweet Potato Cranberry Crisp

SERVES 8 TO 12

Chef Linda: Usually reserved for savory dishes, sweet potatoes have a wild side that thrives when paired with the sweeter things in life. In this recipe, we've given the familiar apple crisp a new twist by using these earthy, orange, beauties. To enhance their gentle, sweet flavor, we added fresh cranberries to lend a tart, bright accent and a bevy of health benefits. Impossibly scrumptious, healthy, and compassionate, this crisp is a hard act to follow. And it's delicious with a scoop of vegan ice cream or our Coconut Whipped Cream (pg. 223). Oh, how many ways can you say "yum"?

Allergens: Contains gluten and nuts

Tip: Use dried cranberries when fresh are out of season; just simmer the same quantity in ³/₄ cup orange juice to plump them up.

Ingredients

Filling

3 medium sweet potatoes, peeled and diced in ½-inch pieces, about 1 pound or 4 cups

1 cup fresh cranberries

¾ cup orange juice

¼ cup brown sugar, packed

2 tsps ground cinnamon

1 tsp ground nutmeg

1 tsp vanilla extract

Topping

½ cup old-fashioned oats

½ cup whole wheat flour

½ cup chopped pecans

¾ cup granulated sugar

1 tsp ground cinnamon

¼ tsp salt

¼ cup maple syrup

¼ cup coconut oil, melted

Directions

1. Preheat the oven to 350°F. In a large bowl, mix together the sweet potatoes, cranberries, orange juice, brown sugar, cinnamon, nutmeg, and vanilla. Empty into a 9-inch square casserole dish.

2. To make the topping, use the same bowl to mix the oats, flour, pecans, sugar, cinnamon, and salt. Add syrup and coconut oil and stir. Spoon the topping evenly over the sweet potato-cranberry filling and gently press down.

3. Bake covered with foil for 50 to 60 minutes until the sides are bubbling and the sweet potatoes are soft. Serve warm or at room temperature.

Apple Fritter Cake

MAKES ONE (9-INCH) PAN, 9 TO 12 PIECES

Chef Linda: Inspired by the old-fashioned taste of apple fritters, this cake is moist, studded with bits of apples, and drizzled with a sweet sugar glaze. We love serving it in the fall, when local apples are at their peak and the scent of the spices tempt our Homestead guests to rise and shine. Any firm, slightly tart apples will work, but don't let the search for the right ones keep you from making this cake. Just one bite proves that butter and eggs are not necessary to bake a decadent dessert.

Allergens: Contains gluten

Ingredients

Filling

1¼ pounds apples, about 4, chopped in ½-inch
    pieces, about 4 cups, like Honeycrisp or Gala
2 Tbsps brown sugar
1 tsp ground cinnamon
2 Tbsps water

Cake

1 cup unsweetened applesauce
½ cup apple or orange juice
½ cup granulated sugar
¼ cup oil
2 tsps vanilla extract
1 cup whole wheat flour
1 cup all-purpose flour
2 tsps baking powder
1 tsp baking soda
1 tsp salt
1 tsp ground cinnamon
½ tsp ground allspice
½ tsp ground ginger

Glaze

⅔ cup powdered sugar, sifted
3 tsps apple or orange juice

Directions

1. Preheat oven to 350°F. Lightly oil a 9-inch round or square baking dish.
2. To make the filling, place apples, sugar, cinnamon, and water in a pan over medium-high heat. Cook, stirring occasionally, for about 10 minutes or until apples and are fork-tender. Remove from heat.
3. To make the cake, mix applesauce, juice, sugar, oil, and vanilla together in a small bowl. In a large bowl, whisk together whole wheat and all-purpose flours, baking powder and soda, salt, cinnamon, allspice, and ginger. Add the wet ingredients to the dry and mix until just combined; the batter will be thick. Don't overmix or the cake will be tough and not tender.
4. Scoop about half of the batter into the prepared pan; spread to cover the bottom. Spoon ¾ of the apple filling evenly over cake batter. Scoop remaining batter on top and spread evenly. Distribute remaining apples on top. Bake for 55 to 65 minutes, or until the center of the cake is set. Remove from oven and set aside to cool while making the glaze.
5. To make the glaze, sift the powdered sugar into a small bowl. Add juice and stir until smooth. The glaze should be fairly thick or else it will soak into the cake. When the cake has cooled, drizzle the glaze over the top of cake. Let the glaze set for about 5 minutes before serving. Store the cake covered in the refrigerator for several days.

Blueberry Cobbler

SERVES 6

Chef Linda: The Betty, the grump, the slump, the dump, the buckle, or the sonker, a cobbler by any other name would taste just as sweet. A cobbler is a simple, rustic delight that highlights glorious fresh fruit, like summer's sweet blueberries, while giving you just enough tender, "cakey" topping to satisfy the torment of a spoiled sweet tooth. Swapping out dairy-based butter and milk for plant-based ingredients is all that's necessary to create a vegan version. Use frozen blueberries if you develop an out-of-season craving. Splendid for breakfast and sublime for dessert with a dollop of our Coconut Whipped Cream (pg. 223). Just what summer is all about.

Allergens: Contains gluten and ingredients that may contain soy

Ingredients

6 cups fresh blueberries, washed, dried and picked over
2 Tbsps cornstarch
1 Tbsp granulated sugar
1 Tbsp fresh lemon juice

Dough

2½ cups all-purpose flour
⅓ cup granulated sugar
1 Tbsp baking powder
1 tsp cinnamon
½ tsp salt
1½ sticks vegan butter, cut into small pieces
1 cup unsweetened nondairy milk
2 tsps vanilla

To Serve

Nondairy vanilla ice cream
Coconut Whipped Cream (pg. 223)
Fresh mint leaves, for garnish

Directions

1. Preheat oven to 400°F. In a 9-by-13-inch casserole dish, gently toss the blueberries with the cornstarch, sugar, and lemon juice.

2. In a medium bowl, whisk together the flour, sugar, baking powder, cinnamon, and salt. Add the butter pieces and rub together with your hands or cut with a pastry blender until it's the consistency of damp sand with some pea-sized pieces. Measure the milk and add the vanilla to the measuring cup, then pour it into the flour. Stir to combine, without overmixing. The dough should be thick and sticky. Plop clumps of batter on top of the blueberries, covering the most of the top but leaving some areas where the blueberries are visible.

3. Cover with foil and bake for 20 minutes. Remove foil and bake for another 15 to 20 minutes. Cobbler is ready when the blueberries are bubbling around the edges and the dough is mostly firm to the touch so check after 15 minutes. Remove from oven and let sit for about 15 minutes before serving.

Almond Raspberry Cake

MAKES 1 (9-INCH) ROUND CAKE, 8 TO 10 SLICES

Chef Linda: This is a cake for the ages. Exceptionally moist, it's truly something special. Our recipe proves once again that compassionate confections are made delicious with the simplest substitutions. Thank the almond paste for the density and elegance of this cake. Praise the delicate raspberries for the tart accent they contribute. Sigh over the gorgeous pink swirls. And acknowledge that it's not necessary to use eggs or dairy to achieve such greatness.

Allergens: Contains gluten, nuts, and ingredients that may contain soy

Special Equipment: Electric mixer (handheld or stand)

Ingredients

5 Tbsps vegan butter, softened, plus extra to butter cake pan

7 ounces almond paste (found in the baking aisle in a tube, can, or box)

½ cup granulated sugar

2 tsps vanilla extract

½ cup unsweetened nondairy milk

1 cup all-purpose flour

1 tsp baking powder

¼ tsp salt

1 heaping cup fresh raspberries (or frozen raspberries, thawed)

To Serve

Fresh raspberries

Vanilla ice cream

Coconut Whipped Cream (pg. 223)

Directions

1. Preheat oven to 350°F. Lightly butter a 9-inch round cake pan. Cut parchment to line the bottom of the pan.

2. With an electric mixer, cream together the butter and almond paste until smooth and creamy. Add sugar and vanilla and mix until no bumps are visible. Add milk and beat until glossy and completely smooth.

3. Add the flour to the mixture and sprinkle in the baking powder and salt. Mix until just combined. Using a spatula, gently fold in the raspberries. Pour batter into prepared cake pan. Bake for about 40 minutes, until the top of the cake is a dark, golden brown and puffed up. To ensure it's done, touch the center of the cake for firmness. It should not be mushy. If the cake looks very brown and the center is not done, loosely cover it with foil and bake for another 5 to 10 minutes.

4. Let the cake cool in the pan for about 30 minutes to an hour before serving. To serve, run a sharp knife around the edge of the pan. Hold a serving plate on top of the cake pan and invert to release the cake. Turn the plate back over and slice to serve. Top with a scoop of ice cream or coconut whipped cream and a few fresh berries.

Chocolate-Coconut Oatmeal Cookies

MAKES APPROXIMATELY 16 TO 20 COOKIES

Chef Sara: Sometimes the best things in life are the result of a happy accident—like these cookies! These cookies were made with some of the odds and ends in my pantry, and these scrumptious cookies were the result. The slightly chewy texture, gentle sweetness, and chocolatey goodness of these addictive little gems will make you plan ahead to have all the ingredients available on a snowy winter's day.

> **Allergens:** Contains nuts and ingredients that may contain soy
> **Tip:** For a subtle coconut flavor, use unrefined coconut oil. For a neutral flavor, use refined coconut oil.

Ingredients

1 Tbsp ground flaxseed
3 Tbsps warm water
½ cup coconut oil, melted
½ cup brown sugar
2 Tbsps maple syrup
1 tsp vanilla extract
½ cup almond flour or almond meal
½ cup oat flour
¾ tsp baking powder
½ tsp salt
½ tsp ground cinnamon
1 cup old-fashioned oats
¾ cup shredded unsweetened coconut
½ cup vegan chocolate chips

Directions

1. Preheat the oven to 375°F. Line two baking trays with parchment and set aside.
2. In a small bowl, whisk together the flaxseed with the water to make a "flax egg." Set aside to thicken for about 5 minutes.
3. In a large bowl, whisk together the melted coconut oil, brown sugar, maple syrup, and vanilla. Add the "flax egg" and whisk again until the mixture is smooth and slightly thickened.
4. In a medium bowl, stir together the almond flour, oat flour, baking powder, salt, and cinnamon. Add to the wet ingredients, using a spatula to stir everything together until no flour is visible. Add the oats, coconut, and chocolate chips, and stir until everything is well-incorporated. The dough will be a little sticky, but will hold its shape when scooped.
5. Use a portion scoop or two spoons to portion out approximate tablespoon measures of dough onto the prepared baking trays. The cookies should be about the same size. With wet hands, gently press each cookie down about halfway, flattening it slightly. Bake for 8 to 10 minutes, rotating the trays halfway through baking, until the cookies are golden brown around the edges. Remove from the oven and cool for a few minutes on the trays. Transfer the cookies to a wire rack to cool completely. Store in an airtight container at room temperature.

Deep, Dark Vegan Brownies

MAKES 24 (2-INCH SQUARE) BROWNIES

Chef Sara: These luscious brownies are dark, rich, and oh-so-chocolatey. They prove, again, that baking without eggs and dairy is delicious and easy. Using dark chocolate chips yield a less sweet result, which tastes especially wonderful when served warm with a scoop of your favorite vegan ice cream.

Allergens: Contains gluten, nuts, and ingredients that may contain soy
Tip: To make these brownies a little sweeter, use vegan semi-sweet chocolate chips instead of dark chocolate.

Ingredients

¼ cup ground flaxseed
¾ cup warm water
1 cup whole wheat pastry flour
¾ cup unsweetened cocoa powder
2 tsps baking powder
¼ tsp salt
½ cup melted refined coconut oil
1½ cups light brown sugar, packed
2 Tbsps smooth, unsalted almond butter
1½ tsps vanilla extract
1 cup vegan dark chocolate chips

Directions

1. Preheat the oven to 375°F. Lightly oil a 9-by-13-inch baking pan and set aside until needed.
2. In a small bowl, whisk together the ground flaxseed and water, and set aside for 10 minutes to thicken. This "flax egg" will help to bind the brownies as they bake.
3. Meanwhile, sift the flour, cocoa powder, baking soda, and salt into a large bowl. Whisk to mix thoroughly.
4. In medium bowl, add the "flax egg," melted coconut oil, brown sugar, almond butter, and vanilla. Whisk until the ingredients are completely incorporated and somewhat thickened. Pour the wet ingredients into the dry ingredients, and stir together with a spatula or wooden spoon until there's no trace of flour left. Stir in the chocolate chips.
5. Scrape the batter into the prepared baking pan and smooth out the top. Transfer to the preheated oven and bake for 25 to 30 minutes, until the edges are dry and pulling away from the pan, and the center is set, but still a bit soft. The brownies will firm up as they cool.
6. Remove from the oven and allow to cool for at least 15 minutes. Slice and serve warm or at room temperature.

Also pictured: Frozen Chocolate
Mousse Pie (pg. 205) and
Avocado Key Lime Pie (pg. 206)

Coconut Cream Pie

MAKES ONE (9-INCH) PIE, 8 TO 12 SERVINGS

Chef Sara: this decadent pie is a coconut lover's dream! Whenever we serve this at our staff lunches, it's gobbled up immediately. A homemade graham cracker and coconut crust encases a creamy coconut custard filling. Then it's topped with sweet coconut whipped cream and toasted shredded coconut. Agar flakes behave like a vegan gelatin, thickening the filling so the pie slices beautifully.

Allergens: Contains gluten and ingredients that may contain soy
Special Equipment: Food processor (to make graham cracker crumbs)
Make Ahead: Pie crust can be made a 1 or 2 days in advance.
Tip: Find agar online or in well-stocked natural food stores. Nabisco's regular graham crackers are vegan.

Ingredients

Pie Crust

1 cup vegan, graham cracker crumbs, from approximately 5–7 graham crackers, depending on the brand
½ cup unsweetened shredded coconut
2 Tbsps granulated sugar
4 Tbsps vegan butter, melted

Filling

1 Tbsp agar flakes
½ cup water
1 (13.5 ounce) can regular (not light) coconut milk
½ cup unsweetened nondairy milk
½ cup granulated sugar
Pinch of salt
¼ cup cornstarch
1 tsp vanilla extract
1 cup unsweetened shredded coconut
Coconut Whipped Cream (pg. 223)
Toasted shredded coconut, for garnish

Directions

1. To make the pie crust, preheat the oven to 325°F. Pulse graham crackers in a food processor until finely ground. In a medium bowl, combine graham cracker crumbs, coconut, sugar, and melted butter, and mix well until it barely holds together when pressed between your fingers.

2. Lightly grease a 9-inch pie plate, and spread the crust mixture evenly over the bottom and sides. Press it down evenly and firmly into the pie plate, using your fingers or the bottom of a measuring cup, covered with plastic wrap to prevent sticking. Be sure to press firmly, especially up the sides. This will ensure a stable crust. Prick the crust several times with a fork, including along the sides.

3. Bake at 325°F for 12 to 15 minutes, until golden brown. If the crust has puffed up a bit during baking, gently press it down with a spatula to compact it. Cool completely before filling.

4. To make the filling, combine agar flakes and water in a small pot and let sit for about 10 minutes to soften. Bring the mixture to a boil, cover, and simmer for about 10 minutes, until the agar is completely dissolved.

(continued on next page)

5. While the agar mixture is simmering, combine the coconut milk, nondairy milk, granulated sugar, and salt in a medium pot. Whisk in the cornstarch and bring to a boil over medium heat, whisking frequently to prevent sticking. After coming to a boil, the mixture will be the texture of a thin pudding. Stir in the vanilla extract, shredded coconut, and agar mixture. Mix well.

6. Pour the coconut custard into the prepared pie crust, smoothing out the top with the back of a spoon. Refrigerate for at least four hours, until set. To decorate the pie, spread or pipe coconut whipped cream over the pie surface and sprinkle with toasted coconut. To slice easily, dip a sharp knife in hot water, wipe with a clean cloth, and slice. Repeat for each slice for beautiful, clean slices.

Frozen Chocolate Mousse Pie

MAKES 1 (9-INCH) PIE

Chef Linda: Are there any words that bring more joy to the soul than *chocolate mousse*? Actually, yes: *Vegan chocolate mousse!* No eggs or milk in this compassionate version, and yet it's still impossibly rich, dark, and creamy. Our recipe, originally developed for a Sanctuary cooking class on no-bake desserts, uses heart-healthy avocados to create a silky filling. Don't be alarmed by the use of tamari and balsamic vinegar; good chocolate has complex flavors, and these two ingredients contribute to them. And oh, the crust! Dates, nuts, and chocolate chips work magic to create a simple gluten-free and healthy crust. You will need seconds, maybe even thirds.

Allergens: Contains nuts, soy, and ingredients that may contain gluten

Special Equipment: Food processor

Tip: Use raw cacao powder in place of cocoa powder for a dose of powerful antioxidants (forty times more than blueberries!).

Ingredients

Crust

1½ cups raw pecans
½ cup vegan chocolate chips
¼ tsp salt
1 cup pitted dates, about 10 to 12, roughly chopped and soaked in hot water for about 5 minutes

Chocolate Mousse

3 large avocados
¾ cup cocoa powder
½ cup + 1 Tbsp maple syrup
⅓ cup coconut cream
2 Tbsps tamari or soy sauce
1 Tbsp + 1 tsp balsamic vinegar
2 tsps vanilla extract

To Serve

Coconut Whipped Cream (pg. 223)

Directions

1. To make the crust, add the pecans, chocolate chips, and salt to a food processor and pulse until mixture is ground but still retains some medium chunks of chips and nuts. Drain the dates, squeezing out excess water, and add to the food processor. Pulse until everything is combined. Empty mixture into a 9-inch pie plate and press firmly up the sides and on the bottom. Finish by pressing firmly all the way around using the bottom of a metal measuring cup. Wash the food processor bowl.

2. To make the chocolate mousse, combine all the filling ingredients in the food processor and blend until creamy and smooth, scraping down the sides as necessary. Empty the filling into the prepared crust and spread evenly. Freeze for 2 to 3 hours. To serve, let pie sit out for about 15 to 20 minutes before slicing and serving alongside coconut whipped cream.

Avocado Key Lime Pie

MAKES 1 (9-INCH) PIE

Chef Linda: Sweet and tart key lime pie originated in the south where these small limes grow in abundance. Reminiscent of long and lazy summer days, this pie is a seasonal favorite. We gave this beloved dessert a compassionate makeover for our Sanctuary cooking class and kept the best parts—the creamy texture, lip-puckering taste, and crumbly crust. The unkind ingredients were easily replaced. It's just another example of how we can reinvent our favorite foods and never miss a beat. Make this simple pie when you need a little slice of heaven or when you want to share the joy of eating vegan with others.

Allergens: Contains gluten and ingredients that may contain soy
Special Equipment: Food processor
Make Ahead: Pie needs to chill for several hours before eating.

Ingredients

Crust
1½ cups vegan graham cracker crumbs, from about 9–13 graham crackers
8 Tbsps vegan butter, melted (or 8 Tbsps melted coconut oil and ⅛ tsp salt)

Filling
1 cup canned coconut cream
¼ cup cornstarch
2 avocados, pitted
½ cup + 1 Tbsp maple syrup
1 Tbsp lime zest, plus 1 tsp for garnish
½ cup fresh lime juice (from about 5–8 regular limes or 10–12 key limes, or use bottled key lime juice)
1 tsp vanilla extract
Pinch of salt

To serve
Coconut Whipped Cream (pg. 223)

Directions

1. To make the crust, break the graham crackers into the bowl of a food processor. Pulse to grind into fine crumbs. Add the melted butter and pulse until the mixture resembles wet sand. Empty crumbs into a 9-inch pie plate and press firmly up the sides and on the bottom. Finish by pressing firmly all the way around using the bottom of a metal measuring cup. Wash the food processor bowl.

2. To make the filling, place all the ingredients in a blender or food processor. Blend until completely smooth. Empty mixture into a small pot. Cook over low-medium heat, stirring constantly, until mixture thickens and begins to make big, gloppy bubbles, about 8 minutes.

3. Empty the filling into the prepared crust and spread evenly. Garnish with lime zest. Freeze for several hours and bring to room temperature 10 minutes before serving.

Nut-Crusted No-Bake Pumpkin Pie

MAKES 1 (9-INCH) PIE

Chef Linda: Spiced just right with aromatic cinnamon, ginger, and cloves, this pie is a healthy alternative to most holiday desserts and the only pumpkin pie recipe you'll ever need. The crust is a simple and nourishing blend of dried fruit and nuts, perfect for everyone, including your gluten-free guests. Without eggs, cornstarch is all you need to thicken the filling. A few minutes on the stovetop activates the starch and makes for a rich pie after it is chilled. We demonstrated this pie at our annual Thanksgiving event, and even the confirmed pumpkin-pie-haters asked for the recipe. With every bite, this pie will inspire compassionate eating at your holiday table.

Allergens: Contains nuts
Special Equipment: Food processor and blender
Make Ahead: Bake squash 1 or 2 days in advance for easy assembly. The entire pie can be made 1 day in advance.
Tip: We use kabocha squash (also called buttercup squash) instead of fresh pumpkin because of its low moisture content, gentle sweetness, and lack of stringiness.

Ingredients

Crust
1½ cups walnuts
1 heaping cup pitted, chopped dates, about 10 to 12
¼ cup dried cranberries
¼ cup dried, chopped figs
½ tsp vanilla extract
⅛ tsp salt

Filling
2 cups cooked kabocha/buttercup squash from a
    1½ pound squash (or canned pumpkin)
1½ cups regular canned coconut milk
⅓ cup maple syrup
2 Tbsps cornstarch
1 tsp vanilla extract
1½ tsps ground cinnamon
1 tsp ground ginger
½ tsp salt
¼ tsp ground cloves

To Serve
Coconut Whipped Cream (pg. 223)

Directions

1. To cook the squash, place the whole squash on a baking tray in an oven heated to 375°F. Bake for about 45 to 60 minutes, or until a sharp knife can be easily inserted. When the squash is cool, cut it in half. Scoop out and discard the seeds.

2. To make the crust, place all of the ingredients in a food processor. Pulse, stopping occasionally to scrape the sides, until the nuts are finely chopped, the ingredients are blended, and the mixture holds together when pinched. Empty into a 9-inch pie plate. Firmly press crust mixture onto the bottom and the sides of the pie plate. Use the bottom of a metal measuring cup to smooth.

3. To make the filling, place all the ingredients in a blender and blend until smooth. Pour the mixture into a medium pot and cook over medium-low heat, stirring continuously, until it starts to thicken. This should take 6 to 8 minutes. Remove from heat. Pour the filling into the crust. Carefully cover with plastic wrap without letting the wrap touch the filling. Refrigerate for several hours or overnight. Slice and serve with coconut whipped cream.

Classic Apple Pie

MAKES ONE 9-INCH PIE, ABOUT 8 TO 12 SERVINGS

Chef Sara: Apple pie, made from scratch and with love, is humble and heavenly, simple and sophisticated, classic and modern. It goes without saying that local, in-season apples make the best pie, but don't lose hope if apple season is over; buy what's available. One surefire way to ensure a delicious pie is to use several varieties of apples at once—Granny Smith, Macintosh, Empire, Jonathan, Cortland, and Golden Delicious. This classic recipe is adapted from a King Arthur Flour recipe.

Allergens: Contains gluten and ingredients that may contain soy

Ingredients

2 pie crusts, one fitted into 9-inch pie plate, the other rolled out and chilled (see our recipe on pg. 209 or purchase store-bought vegan crusts)

2 pounds apples, about 5–7 apples, preferably a mix of varieties, peeled, cored, and sliced, about 6 cups

2 Tbsps lemon juice

½–⅔ cup granulated sugar (use the larger quantity if your apples are tart)

2 Tbsps all-purpose flour

1 Tbsp cornstarch

½ tsp ground cinnamon

¼ tsp ground nutmeg

¼ tsp ground allspice

¼ cup apple cider or water

Nondairy milk for brushing crust

Turbinado or coarse sugar for sprinkling on the crust (optional)

Directions

1. Preheat the oven to 375°F. Place the pie plate fitted with the crust on a baking tray so you can easily transfer it to the oven.

2. In a large bowl, toss together the apples and lemon juice. Add the sugar, flour, cornstarch, cinnamon, nutmeg, and allspice, and gently mix until the fruit is evenly coated. Stir in the apple cider or water and transfer the filling to the prepared pie crust.

3. Cover the filling with the remaining crust, and cut five or six slits in the center of the dough to allow for airflow during baking. For a fun crust, cut out small shapes using a decorative cutter. Save the little cut outs and place them whimsically around the top of the crust. Crimp the edges together to seal. Alternatively, make a lattice crust. Using a pastry wheel, cut long strips of dough from the remaining pie crust and arrange in a lattice pattern. Trim the edges of the dough with scissors and crimp the two crusts together to seal. Brush the crust with a light, even coat of nondairy milk, and sprinkle with the optional turbinado sugar for a sweet and sparkly finish.

4. Place the baking tray in the oven and bake for 45 to 55 minutes, until the crust is golden-brown and the filling is thickened and bubbling. Remove, allow to cool on a wire rack, then serve.

Best-Ever Vegan Pie Crust

MAKES ONE (9-INCH) PIE CRUST

Chef Sara: Making pastry from scratch can feel intimidating, but it doesn't have to be! This recipe is an old favorite that yields a delicious pie crust that works perfectly for just about any pie. The tricks for achieving a tender, flaky crust include keeping your ingredients cold, using a light hand when mixing, and allowing the dough to rest.

Allergens: Contains gluten and ingredients that may contain soy
Special Equipment: Food processor, optional
Make Ahead: Dough needs to rest for at least 30 minutes before rolling. It can be made several days in advance.
Tip: If using this to make a savory crust, omit the sugar.

Ingredients

1½ cups all-purpose flour, plus more for rolling
1 Tbsp granulated sugar
¼ tsp salt (if using coconut oil instead of vegan butter, add an additional ¼ tsp salt)
½ cup (8 Tbsps) vegan butter or refined coconut oil, chilled
1 tsp apple cider vinegar
¼ cup + 2 Tbsps ice water, plus more as needed

Directions

1. In a medium-large bowl, combine the flour, sugar, and salt, and whisk together to mix. Use two knives or a pastry cutter to cut the cold vegan butter into ¼-inch cubes, add to the bowl, and place the bowl in the freezer to chill for 10 minutes. Alternatively, chill in the refrigerator for at least 30 minutes or up to several hours.

2. Using either a pastry cutter or two knives, cut the vegan butter into the flour mixture until the butter pieces are the size of small pebbles. Alternatively, use a food processor, pulsing a few times until the shortening pieces are the desired size. Be very careful not to allow the dough to gather up into a ball; overworking the dough will result in tough pastry. Mix together the apple cider vinegar and ice water in a small bowl, then pour over the crumbly dough, mixing together gently with a fork until the dough just holds together. Add in extra ice water as needed, 1 tablespoon at a time, if the dough is too dry.

3. Flour a work surface, gather the dough into a ball, and transfer to the floured surface. Pat the dough out into a rough circle approximately 5 to 6 inches across, then wrap the disc in plastic wrap, place in the refrigerator, and allow to chill for at least 1 hour or up to a few days. (The dough can also be frozen at this point, for later use.) Chilling the dough allows the gluten to relax, which will make the crust more tender.

4. When you're ready to roll the crust, flour a large piece of parchment, unwrap the chilled dough, and place the disc on the floured parchment. Sprinkle some more flour on top of the disc, then use a rolling pin to roll the dough out into a circle that's a several inches larger than your pie plate. Place the pie plate with the open surface flush against the rolled out crust, then, with one hand under the parchment and one securing the pie plate, flip everything over so the crust is sitting atop the pie plate. Gently peel off the parchment, press the crust down into the pie dish, and trim the edges. Decoratively crimp the edge however you like, or leave the edge plain if using a double or lattice crust later, and proceed with your recipe.

Summer Fruit Tart with Vanilla Custard and Pecan-Oat Crust

MAKES ONE (9- TO 10-INCH) TART, ABOUT 8 TO 10 SERVINGS

Chef Sara: This show-stopping summer dessert is all about the fruit. The riper and more succulent, the better! We love the combination of juicy white nectarines, plums, and strawberries. Have fun, get creative, and substitute any other gorgeous, ripe summer fruits such as peaches, blackberries, raspberries, blueberries, or petite red currants.

Allergens: Contains nuts
Special Equipment: 9- or 10-inch tart pan with removable bottom
Make Ahead: Custard and crust can be made 1 day in advance. The custard has to be chilled for at least 2 hours or overnight.

Ingredients

Crust

1½ cups old-fashioned oats
¾ cup pecans
¼ cup coconut oil, melted
3 Tbsps maple syrup
¼ tsp salt

Custard

1 (13.5-ounce) can full-fat coconut milk
¾ cup plain nondairy milk
⅔ cup granulated sugar
1 vanilla bean, seeds scraped out and reserved (or 1½ tsps vanilla extract)
¼ cup + 2 Tbsps cornstarch
Pinch of salt
Pinch of ground turmeric

Fruit Topping

2 pounds summer fruit of your choice, in whatever combination you like
¼ cup apricot or peach preserves, warmed in the microwave or on the stovetop (optional)

Directions

1. To make the crust, start by preheating the oven to 350°F. Lightly oil the tart pan and set aside until needed.

2. Place the oats in the bowl of a food processor and process for at least one or two minutes, until the oats have been ground into a flour. Add the pecans, and pulse a few times until the pecans are finely ground and incorporated, but not oily. Add the coconut oil, maple syrup, and salt, and pulse again until the mixture holds together. It will be bit sticky, but will hold together when pressed.

3. Transfer the mixture into the prepared tart pan, and use your fingers to spread it evenly across the bottom and sides of the pan, pressing firmly. Prick the crust evenly with a fork, then place in the preheated oven and bake for 10 to 15 minutes, until lightly browned. Set aside to cool.

4. To make the custard, combine the coconut milk, nondairy milk, sugar, vanilla bean seeds or extract, cornstarch, salt, and turmeric in a medium saucepan over medium-low heat, whisking to combine. Use a rubber spatula to stir the mixture slowly and evenly as it cooks to prevent

(continued on next page)

scorching. Cook until the custard is thick and bubbling, about 7 minutes. To keep the cornstarch from breaking down and thinning out the custard, remove from the heat as soon as the custard is thickened and bubbling. Pour the custard into a bowl, cover the surface of the custard with plastic wrap to prevent a film from forming, and chill until cold, at least two hours. Overnight is fine.

5. To assemble the fruit topping, begin by preparing your chosen fruit. For small berries, simply rinse, pat dry, and use them whole. Strawberries can be used whole if small, or sliced if larger. Nectarines and plums don't need to be peeled, just pitted and sliced. Because of their fuzzy skins, peaches are best peeled and then pitted and sliced. Regardless of which fruits you're using, prepare them before assembly and place them near your workstation.

6. Whisk the chilled custard to smooth it out, adding 1 tablespoon at a time of milk if the custard is too thick to spread. Spoon into the cooled crust and spread it evenly with a spatula. Arrange your prepared fruits across the top of the custard in whatever design you like. To give the tart a beautiful shine, use a pastry brush or crumpled paper towel to dab the warmed apricot or peach jam onto the top of the fruits, coating each piece.

7. For best results, serve within a few hours. Leftovers won't be as beautiful, but they will still taste delicious!

Old-Fashioned Pound Cake

MAKES THREE (5-INCH BY 3-INCH) LOAVES

Chef Linda: Pound cake received its name from very practical origins—the recipe called for a pound each of flour, butter, sugar, and eggs. And while this version tastes old fashioned—just the way it should—it uses no butter or eggs. We developed this recipe for a group of college students volunteering at the Sanctuary on their winter break to create a teaching moment about the tragic lives of dairy cows and egg-laying hens. Thankfully, everyone else who's enjoyed this cake over the years now knows that we can create our favorite foods without harming animals. This is a cake to savor: tender, comforting, and full of lovely vanilla flavor.

Allergens: Contains gluten and ingredients that may contain soy
Special Equipment: Electric mixer

Ingredients

Oil, for oiling pans
1½ cups unbleached all-purpose flour
2 tsps baking powder
½ tsp salt
½ pound vegan butter, softened
1½ cups granulated sugar
1 cup canned coconut milk, room temperature
2 tsps vanilla extract
1 tsp fresh lemon juice

To Serve

Fresh strawberries
Coconut Whipped Cream (pg. 223)

Directions

1. Preheat oven to 350°F. Lightly oil loaf pans.
2. Mix together flour, baking powder, and salt. Set aside. Cream together butter and sugar with an electric mixer on medium speed until fluffy. Mix in coconut milk, vanilla, and lemon juice.
3. With mixer on low speed, add in flour and mix just until incorporated. Spoon mixture into pans and lightly smooth the top. Place pans on a baking tray and bake on the center rack of the oven for 35 to 40 minutes until lightly browned around the edges.
4. Remove from oven and let cool completely before serving.

Cashew-Macadamia Cheesecake with Salted Caramel Sauce

MAKES 1 (9-INCH) CHEESECAKE, OR 12 TO 14 SERVINGS

Chef Linda: No one should have to do without cheesecake—ever! Smooth and rich, this cheesecake boasts compassion and nutrition as two of its main ingredients, something regular cheesecake can't do. Macadamia and cashews blend beautifully to create a creamy base. And is there anything a chickpea can't do? In this recipe, chickpeas create a dense texture and a complex taste than you wouldn't get with nuts alone. A simple graham cracker crust works beautifully (Nabisco's regular graham crackers are accidentally vegan), as does the gluten-free version that uses ground almonds and a little granulated sugar. The light, crumbly crust takes only minutes to make. The filling needs only a blender to create. And the salted caramel is optional, but more than worth it.

Allergens: Contains nuts and ingredients that may contain soy
Special Equipment: Blender, 9-inch springform pan

Ingredients

Graham Cracker Crust
1½ cups graham cracker crumbs, from about 9–13 crackers, depending on the brand
6 Tbsps vegan butter, melted (or 6 Tbsps melted coconut oil and ⅛ tsp salt), plus more for the pan)

Gluten-Free Almond Crust
1½ cups almond flour or almond meal
½ cup granulated sugar
¼ tsp salt
6 Tbsps vegan butter, melted, plus more for the pan

Filling
1 cup raw cashews, soaked for 2–3 hours in water, drained
1 cup unsalted macadamia nuts, soaked for 2–3 hours in water, drained
1 (15.5 ounce) can chickpeas, drained and rinsed
1 (15.5-ounce) can regular coconut milk
1 cup maple syrup
¼ cup fresh lemon juice
2 Tbsps apple cider vinegar
2 ½ Tbsps cornstarch
1 Tbsp tahini
2 tsps vanilla extract
¾ tsp salt

Salted Caramel Sauce
1 cup brown sugar, packed
6 Tbsps vegan butter, cut into chunks
½ cup canned coconut milk
2 tsps vanilla extract
¼ tsp coarse salt

To Serve
Flaked salt (optional)

Directions

1. Preheat oven to 325°F. Trace the bottom of the springform pan onto parchment and cut it out. Line the bottom of the pan with parchment circle and lightly oil the sides with butter. Line a baking tray with parchment and place the pan on top; this will make clean up easier.

2. To make the crust, break the graham crackers into a food processor and blend until finely ground. Add melted butter and pulse until the mixture resembles wet sand. Empty the crumbs into the springform pan and firmly press them evenly into the bottom and up the sides.

(continued on next page)

3. To make the filling, place all the ingredients in a high-speed blender. Blend, while scraping down sides occasionally, for about 2 minutes, or until completely smooth and creamy. There should be no gritty texture in the mixture.

4. To assemble the cake, pour the filling into the springform pan. Set the oven rack in the bottom position. Place the pan on a baking tray lined with parchment and put in the oven. Bake for about 50 minutes. If you notice the top is browning too much, place a piece of foil over the top of the pan without touching the filling.

5. To make the salted caramel sauce, place the sugar in a small, heavy-bottomed pot. Heat over medium-high heat, while stirring occasionally. As the sugar heats, it will begin to melt and darken. When that starts to happen, you'll need to stir it more frequently. Once the sugar is completely dissolved, remove the pot from heat and stir in the butter. When the butter is melted, place the pot back on the heat and stir in the milk. Cook, while stirring, until the mixture just starts to bubble. Keep cooking for about 1 minute after the initial boil, then remove from heat. Stir in vanilla and salt and set aside to cool.

6. The cake is done when it is mostly firm to the touch around the outer perimeter with a slightly less done center. It will firm up further when cooled completely. Remove the cake from oven and let cool on the counter before putting it into the refrigerator to chill for several hours or overnight.

7. To serve, cut slices and place on plates. Drizzle with salted caramel sauce and sprinkle with flaked salt. Extra caramel sauce can be stored in a sealed container for up to one month.

Strawberry-Pecan Thumbprint Cookies

MAKES APPROXIMATELY 2 DOZEN COOKIES

Chef Sara: This vegan spin on classic thumbprint cookies tastes much richer than the sum of its parts, thanks to the chopped pecans that toast in the oven as the cookies bake. Classic strawberry is our favorite filling here, but you can substitute your favorite sweet and sticky jam or jelly.

Allergens: Contains nuts
Special Equipment: Electric mixer
Tip: For a subtle coconut flavor, use unrefined coconut oil. For a neutral flavor, use refined coconut oil.

Ingredients

1 Tbsp ground flaxseed
3 Tbsps warm water
½ cup coconut oil, softened
½ cup coconut sugar or granulated sugar (coconut sugar adds a subtle caramel flavor)
1 tsp vanilla extract
1¼ cups gluten-free flour blend
¼ tsp salt
1½ cups finely chopped pecans
½ cup strawberry preserves or fruit spread

Directions

1. Preheat the oven to 350°F. Line two baking trays with parchment or silicone baking mats.

2. In a small bowl, mix together the ground flaxseed and warm water to make a "flax egg." Allow to sit for about 5 minutes to thicken.

3. Meanwhile, use an electric mixer to beat together the coconut oil and coconut sugar until light and fluffy. Add the vanilla and "flax egg" and beat again until well-combined. Add the flour and salt to the bowl, and mix on low speed until incorporated. Stay on low speed, or use a spatula and work by hand to mix in the chopped pecans. The dough will be slightly soft and sticky.

4. Use two spoons or a small portion scoop to portion out approximate tablespoon measures of dough. Gently roll each ball between your palms to smooth them, then place on the prepared baking trays, at least 1 inch apart. Use the palm of your hand to slightly flatten each dough ball, then use your thumb, a soup spoon, or a measuring spoon to make an indentation in the center of each cookie. If the spoon you're using is sticking, periodically dip it in warm water as you work to prevent sticking. Fill each indentation with a small amount of preserves. Try to keep the preserves level with the top of the indentation to prevent overflow.

5. Transfer to the oven and bake for 15 to 20 minutes, until the cookies are lightly browned and the pecans smell toasty. Cool briefly on the baking trays, then transfer to a cooling rack to cool completely.

Chewy Chocolate Gingerbread Cookies

MAKES 2 DOZEN COOKIES

Chef Sara: These chewy, slightly spicy, and just-sweet-enough cookies are adapted from a favorite recipe by Martha Stewart, and they're beloved by cooking class students and Sanctuary staff alike. In fact, after taking the photos for this recipe during our cookbook photo shoot, these cookies were gobbled up in record time! You'll love their crunchy sugary coating and warm, gingery bite of these special cookies.

Allergens: Contains gluten and ingredients that may contain soy
Special Equipment: Electric mixer recommended
Make Ahead: Dough can be made the day before, then shaped and baked.

Ingredients

1½ cups whole wheat pastry flour
1 Tbsp cocoa powder
1 Tbsp ground ginger
1½ tsps ground cinnamon
¼ tsp ground nutmeg
Pinch of ground cloves
8 Tbsps (1 stick) vegan butter (or solid, refined
    coconut oil and ½ tsp salt)
½ cup brown sugar, packed
¼ cup unsulfured molasses
2 Tbsps nondairy milk
1 tsp baking soda
⅔ cup vegan chocolate chips
¼ cup granulated sugar, for coating

Directions

1. Preheat the oven to 325°F. Line two baking trays with parchment.
2. In a medium bowl, whisk together the flour, cocoa, ginger, cinnamon, nutmeg, and cloves.
3. In another medium bowl, use an electric mixer to beat together the vegan butter and brown sugar until light and fluffy. Add the molasses and non-dairy milk to the butter and sugar, and beat until well incorporated. Dissolve the baking soda in 1 tablespoon hot water, then add to the bowl with the vegan butter and brown sugar and mix well.
4. Add half the dry ingredients to the wet and mix together on low speed until well incorporated. Add the remaining flour mixture, then use a spatula to mix the batter until there's no flour visible. Fold in the chocolate chips. The dough will be sticky, but not overly wet. Refrigerate the dough for at least 1 hour to make scooping and rolling easier.
5. Using a measuring spoon or a small scoop, portion out generous tablespoon-sized balls of dough, roll between your hands to smooth them, and then roll each ball of dough in the sugar. Place the sugar-coated cookies on the prepared baking sheets, leaving at least two inches between cookies, and flatten them slightly with your hands. Bake for 8 to 10 minutes, until barely set and lightly cracked on the surface. These cookies firm up when they cool, so aim for a slightly undercooked texture. Allow to cool for a few minutes on the baking tray, then transfer to a cooling rack to cool completely.

Chocolate Chip Cookie Dough Truffles

MAKES 18 TO 20 BITE-SIZED TRUFFLES

Chef Sara: Whether at a special event, staff lunch, or cooking class, these truffles have always been a crowd-pleasing and compassionate indulgence that are deceptively simple to make. They'll remind you of sneaking bites of raw cookie dough from the bowl as a kid, but because they're egg-free, they're completely safe to eat without any baking.

Allergens: Contains nuts and ingredients that may contain soy
Make Ahead: Truffle filling needs to chill for at least 30 minutes before dipping, or make it 1 day in advance.
Variation: To make coconut rum truffles, follow the same procedure but substitute ¼ cup coconut nectar for the maple syrup, 3 tablespoons coconut rum for the vanilla, and ½ cup + 2 tablespoons toasted unsweetened coconut for the mini chocolate chips. Garnish each coated truffle with a sprinkling of toasted coconut and chill until serving time.

Ingredients

Truffles
1½ cups almond meal
½ tsp salt
¼ cup maple syrup
¼ cup melted coconut oil
1½ tsps vanilla extract
⅓ cup vegan mini chocolate chips

Chocolate Coating
1 cup vegan dark chocolate chips
2 tsps coconut oil, melted

Directions

1. To make the truffles, mix together the almond meal, salt, and maple syrup until well incorporated. Add the melted coconut oil and vanilla extract and mix well to form a sticky dough. Add the chocolate chips and mix to incorporate.

2. Shape the dough into teaspoon-sized balls using a small scoop or two spoons and place on a parchment-lined plate or tray. Freeze for at least 30 minutes, until firm.

3. To make the chocolate coating, melt the dark chocolate chips and coconut oil together. Roll each truffle between your hands to smooth them, dip in the melted chocolate, using a fork to lift out each coated truffle. Place the coated truffles back on the parchment, and refrigerate until ready to serve. These will soften a bit at room temperature but are at their best served slightly chilled.

No-Bake Chocolate Peanut Butter Bars

MAKES ONE 9-INCH SQUARE PAN (16 TO 20 BARS)

Chef Sara: These fudgy, chocolate and peanut butter layered bars are irresistible! They come together quickly and require no baking. Children may prefer semi-sweet chocolate chips instead of dark chocolate, which yields a slightly sweeter result.

Allergens: Contains peanuts and ingredients that may contain soy

Ingredients

1½ sticks (¾ cup) vegan butter
½ cup brown sugar, firmly packed
1 tsp vanilla extract
3 cups quick oats
1 cup vegan dark chocolate chips
1 cup smooth, unsalted peanut butter
¼ tsp salt

Directions

1. Butter an 8-inch square baking pan, and set aside until needed.
2. Melt the butter in a large pot over medium heat. Stir in the brown sugar and the vanilla. Add the oats, reduce the heat to medium-low, and cook for 3 to 4 minutes, stirring frequently.
3. In another pot, place the chocolate chips, peanut butter, and salt and allow to melt over low heat, stirring frequently to prevent scorching. The mixture is ready when the chocolate is completely melted, with no visible chocolate pieces.
4. Spoon ⅔ of the oat mixture into the prepared baking pan, covering the bottom of the pan evenly. Use a spatula to firmly and evenly press the mixture into the pan. The more firmly the oats are pressed, the more stable the crust will be. Pour the chocolate–peanut butter mixture over the oat crust, smoothing it out with the back of a spoon. Finally, sprinkle the remaining oat mixture over the chocolate, pressing it gently into the chocolate.
5. Transfer to the refrigerator, and chill for at least three hours or overnight. Allow to sit at room temperature for 5 to 10 minutes before cutting and serving. Leftovers are best kept refrigerated, then brought out again when needed.

Coconut Whipped Cream

MAKES ABOUT 1 HEAPING CUP

Chef Linda: Let's be honest . . . isn't everything better with a little whipped cream? This simple recipe works just like using dairy-based heavy cream, but uses thick coconut cream instead. If you find a brand that works well for you, buy several cans so you'll always have a batch on hand for whenever you need a gentle touch of heavenly sweetness.

Make Ahead: Chill the coconut cream for several hours first. The finished whipped cream will firm as it chills, so it's ideal to make this recipe 1 hour before you need it.

Ingredients

1 (14-ounce) can coconut cream, chilled
½ cup powdered sugar
1 tsp vanilla
Pinch of salt

Directions

1. Scoop out chilled coconut cream into metal bowl. Sift in powdered sugar and add vanilla and salt. Using an electric mixer, whip the coconut cream until smooth. Serve immediately or chill before serving. Chilling the whipped cream will make it thicker. Extra cream will keep in the refrigerator for several days.

Real Deal Vegan Cannoli

MAKES 25 TO 30 CANNOLI

Chef Linda : "OMG!" "No way!" "These can't be vegan!" These comments are all from disbelieving participants in a Compassionate Cuisine Italian cooking class after tasting the grand finale: vegan cannoli that taste like the "real deal." Blistered and crunchy outer shells filled with creamy goodness, perfect cannoli are the stuff dreams are made of. To make them without a ricotta cheese filling—and without tofu—required a fair amount of trial and error before landing on a most unusual solution: baked potatoes. Fluffy, white, and mild, potatoes provide the right texture and neutral flavor to create the gently sweetened and imperceptibly tangy experience. You don't need a culinary degree to make these, just a little patience.

Allergens: Contains gluten, nuts, and ingredients that may contain soy
Special Equipment: Metal cannoli tubes, food thermometer (optional, but advised), food processor, rolling pin or pasta machine, and a 3-inch round cookie cutter
Make Ahead: Filling and dough for the shells can be made 1 day in advance.
Tip: If you're working without a food thermometer, it's been said that a 1-inch cube of bread dropped in the right temperature oil will take 60 seconds to brown. A 3-inch round, thin-rimmed glass will work in place of a cookie cutter.

Ingredients

Shells

2 cups all-purpose flour, plus more for rolling
3 Tbsps granulated sugar
2 tsps unsweetened cocoa powder
½ tsp ground cinnamon
½ tsp salt
½ cup apple juice
3 Tbsps mild-flavored oil
2 tsps apple cider vinegar
½ tsp almond extract
1 quart sunflower seed oil, for frying

Filling

2 large Russet/baking potatoes, about 1½ pounds, baked, still warm
1 Tbsp vegan butter
1 cup powdered sugar
1 heaping Tbsp canned coconut cream
¼ tsp salt
¼ cup mini semi-sweet vegan chocolate chips (optional)

To Decorate

1 cup finely chopped pistachios

½ cup semi-sweet vegan chocolate chips
Powdered sugar

Directions

1. To make the shells, start by making the dough. Mix the flour, sugar, cocoa powder, cinnamon, and salt in a medium bowl. Create a well in the middle and add apple juice, oil, vinegar, and almond extract. Stir to combine. When dough starts to come together, turn out onto a lightly floured surface and knead for several minutes until smooth and elastic. Wrap in plastic and let rest 30 minutes.

2. To make the filling, scoop the warm potato flesh from its skin into the bowl of a food processor. Add the butter, powdered sugar, coconut cream, and salt. Blend until the mixture is creamy and smooth. Add the chocolate chips and pulse once or twice to combine. Refrigerate for about 30 minutes.

3. To make the shells, heat the oil slowly to 375°F in a heavy bottomed pot. The oil should be about 4

(continued on next page)

inches deep. While the oil is heating, divide the dough into 4 pieces. Lightly flour the counter. Working with one piece and keeping the others wrapped in plastic, press dough into a flat rectangle, about ½ inch thick. Using a rolling pin, roll the dough until it is about the thickness of a dime. Alternatively, pass dough through the widest setting of a pasta machine, continuing to pass through narrower settings until desired thickness is achieved. Use a 3-inch cookie cutter to cut rounds from the dough.

4. Carefully wrap each round of dough around a cannoli mold. Use a little water on the edge to gently seal the edge shut and to assure it won't fall off during frying. With your finger, gently flare out the top and bottom edges ever-so-slightly from the mold. This will help you remove the dough from the tube after frying.

5. Use a pair of tongs to submerge the cannoli mold in the hot oil. Fry the shell in the oil until crispy, about 1½ minutes, turning it to ensure even browning. Remove from the oil with tongs and let the oil drip back into pot before setting it down on a paper towel–lined plate to cool.

6. When the cannoli tube has cooled enough to touch it, gently slide the cooked cannoli off and set aside on the paper towel to cool completely. It may take a little pressure to get the cannoli free from the tube, so push it down from the top rather than gripping the whole thing so as not to crush the bubbles in the fried dough. Wipe the cannoli tube to remove excess oil before using again for the next cannoli.

7. To decorate, line a baking tray with parchment. Place chopped pistachios in a small bowl. Melt the chocolate chips in a microwave or double boiler. Dip the ends of the cannoli shell, one side at a time, into the melted chocolate to coat the edges. Place the chocolate-dipped ends into the bowl of ground pistachios, then place them on a piece of parchment. Let the chocolate harden for about 10 minutes, then the cannoli will be ready to be filled. Note that to keep the shells crisp, it is best to fill them fairly close to serving time. You can also omit the melted chocolate and just sprinkle the chopped pistachios after filling them.

8. To fill the cannoli, scoop the chilled filling into a ziplock bag or a pastry bag with a ½-inch star or round tip. If using a ziplock baggie, fill with about ½ the filling. Snip off one corner so the opening is about ½-inch wide. Holding the cannoli shell in one hand, and the baggie or pastry bag in the other, squeeze gently and pipe the filling into one side of the shell, about halfway through. Switch sides and pipe filling into the other half so the entire shell is filled. Chill for 15 to 30 minutes and serve dusted with powdered sugar.

Authors

KATHY STEVENS

Kathy Stevens grew up on a large horse farm and has animals "in her DNA." She moved to Boston for graduate school in the 1980s; then, after a decade as a high school English teacher, was offered the opportunity to lead a new charter high school. Instead, she changed direction and, in 2001, cofounded Catskill Animal Sanctuary, where her love of teaching, her belief that education has the power to transform, and her love of animals come together. Today, Catskill is one of the world's best known and most beloved sanctuaries, having saved over four thousand farm animals through direct rescue, and exponentially more through ground-breaking programming that encourages humans to adopt veganism.

Kathy is the author of *Where the Blind Horse Sings* and *Animal Camp*, two critically and popularly-acclaimed books about the work of Catskill, and is a frequent contributor to books, podcasts, and articles on animal sentience, animal rights, and veganism. She takes her message of kindness to all beings and and the urgent imperative of veganism to conferences and colleges in the US and Canada. Kathy lives on the grounds of Catskill with her dogs Chumbley and Scout, and kisses many critters every day.

CHEF LINDA SOPER-KOLTON

Linda Soper-Kolton came to Catskill Animal Sanctuary in 2012 as a guest chef, intending to teach Compassionate Cuisine cooking classes for a season before returning to her vegetarian and vegan café in Fairfield, Connecticut. Lured by the magic of the sanctuary and the urgency of the mission, Linda stayed to lead and grow the culinary program, inspiring and educating with love, patience, and delicious food. More than seven years later, she continues to cook, teach, write, and kiss pigs.

Unlike many chefs, Linda did not grow up at the knee of a family matriarch in the kitchen. Instead, her early memories of mealtime included mashed potatoes made with milk powder and potato flakes, Friday's clean-out-the-fridge "spaghetti surprise," and a lot of liver. Linda learned to cook out of sheer necessity. In the humble kitchen of her first apartment, Linda spent nights baking, roasting, and simmering for roommates, coworkers, and anyone else she could find. With "food is love" as her mantra, cooking and feeding became her way of nurturing and connecting with others. In midlife, she fulfilled a lifelong dream of becoming a chef when she graduated from the Natural Gourmet Institute. Combining her chef's training with certification as a holistic health coach from the Institute for Integrative Nutrition, Linda is driven to love and influence others through compassionate, plant-based eating. Linda lives in Connecticut with her husband, Van; her son, Ethan; her dog, Jeter; her cat, Angel; and the many backyard critters who visit. When she's not in the kitchen creating, she's probably looking for her glasses.

CHEF SARA BOAN

Sara Boan has been a vegan chef and culinary instructor at Catskill Animal Sanctuary since 2016. Born and raised in the Appalachian foothills of southeastern Ohio, Sara learned to cook in the kitchens of her mother and grandmothers, where she was taught the importance of home-grown ingredients, time around the table with family and friends, and infusing every dish with love. She continues this legacy in her sold-out cooking classes and popular food demonstrations, where she showcases delicious vegan recipes with a side of compassion and kindness.

Sara holds degrees and certificates from Ohio University, The Natural Gourmet Institute for Health and Culinary Arts, and the Academy of Culinary Nutrition. Sharing her passion for delicious plant-based foods and living a compassionate vegan lifestyle are the great joys in her life. When she's not cooking, you can find her knitting and spinning, snuggling with her cats, and spending time with her partner.

Gratitude

To our photographer, Alexandra Shytsman, thank you for using your gifts to bring our food and dreams to life.

To Kristine Papa, volunteer photo shoot assistant your spirit and hard work were priceless. It was so much more than work. And we are so much more than grateful.

To Lisa Dawn Angerame, our recipe editor who volunteered many hours and many keystrokes to fix up, fiddle with, and finalize our recipes. What a miracle to have found you.

To Alison Ahern and her early and patient editing contributions.

To our intrepid Recipe Rockstars, the testers who have seen this book start, stop, and start again. At your own expense and on your own time, you've taken our creations and improved upon them with your honesty, scrutiny, and creativity. These recipes would not be what they are without you:

Adriane Raff Corwin, Adrienne Szamotula, Alex Fisher, Alicia Silvestri, Alisa Dyer, Alison and

Julia Ahrens, Amanda Stevens, Amberlee Baccari, Amy Callinan, Amy Johnson, Amy Stitt, Andrea Brosnan, Andrea Fowles Bracco, Andrea Lee Andrew Cruz, Ann Ault, Ann Jaffe, Ashley Nester, Barbara Motter, Barbara Magill, Becky Fairless, Betsey Noble, Carla Moore, Chelsea Hershey, Chelsea Schade, Cherie Erwin, Christen Wagner, Colleen Schropfer, Danielle DalCero, Dara Purvis, Darci Gemini, Dawn Hubbell, Dawn Lucas, Deana Speck, Deb Perry, Dee Henderson, Dian VanDerVolgen, Domenica Miller, Eileen Clark, Eileen Urbanic, Elizabeth Manning, Emily Elliott, Erin Madden, Felicia Greenfield, Gail Manz, Giovanna Gesmundo, Ifat Goldblat, Jacqueline Pisani Burke, Jane Welowszky, Jay English, Jeanne Friedman, Jeannine Anderson, Jen Brun, Jenny Donovan, Jessica Abraham, Jessica Sokol, Joshua Goldstein, Judie Mickelson, Judith Turkel, Judy Samoff, Juliane Arlt, Julie Squires, Kacie Mathison, Kaden Maguire, Kalyn Wetmore, Karen Mazich, Kathie Helm, Kaytee Lipari, Kirsten Doyle, Kristy Cross, Kyla Adams, Laura Goodnough Jones, Laura Kana, Lauren Barbieri, Lauren Gonzalez, Laurie Gold, Leah Oren, Leann Leake, Lesley Johnson and Matt Varley, Lindsey Oren, Lisa Canavan, Lisa Cole, Lisa Dawn Angerame, Liz Manning, Lizzy Snyder, Lois Samsel-Cronk, Lori Denson, M.T.Bruno (Sandra Hamzavi), Maria Granda, Marie Darci, Marsha Peters, Meghan Mahony, Melissa Butler, Melissa Sheik, Merri Rothman Parola, Mollie Didio and Michael Stolfi, Monica Gotz, Nancy Goldstein, Nicole Cennamo, Pamela Poli, Pamela Chassin, Patricia Garofano, Priya Arora, Randi Feuer, Rebecca Kassirer, Rebecca Konstantino, Rona Grossman, Sandra Angelella, Sarah Colford, Sarah Robles, Simone Rucolas, Sohini Patti Wellen, Stacey Clark, Stephanie Schlegel, Susan Armknecht, Susan Sullivan, Susan Woldenberg, Tamar Landau, Tamara Fontanes, Tanya Wolstenholme, Taylor Gilbert, Veronica Ciccarone-Kali, Veronica Finnegan, Yvonne Briggs.

To every person who has already made room for compassion on their plate and for those who are considering it; to the people who visit, who read, who ask, who try with hearts wide open—thank you. Our hope lies with each and every one of you.

And to the many who have—knowingly or unknowingly—inspired or contributed to this book. Trailblazers, activists, chefs, home cooks, bloggers, movie-makers, speakers, teachers, and authors. Strangers or friends, we are all one, longing, striving, and aching for peace.

Finally, to my husband, Van, for eating the good, the bad, and the ugly, and for all the key lime pies and for believing that this book should be written: There are no words. To my son Ethan, who inspires me to dig deep *every single day*. And always, to the One who makes everything possible. —Linda

We did it.

Conversion Charts

METRIC AND IMPERIAL CONVERSIONS

(These conversions are rounded for convenience)

Vegan Ingredient	Cups/Tablespoons/ Teaspoons	Ounces	Grams/Milliliters
Butter	1 cup/ 16 tablespoons/ 2 sticks	8 ounces	230 grams
Cheese, shredded	1 cup	4 ounces	110 grams
Cornstarch	1 tablespoon	0.3 ounce	8 grams
Cream cheese	1 tablespoon	0.5 ounce	14.5 grams
Flour, all-purpose	1 cup/1 tablespoon	4.5 ounces/0.3 ounce	125 grams/8 grams
Flour, whole wheat	1 cup	4 ounces	120 grams
Fruit, dried	1 cup	4 ounces	120 grams
Fruits or veggies, chopped	1 cup	5 to 7 ounces	145 to 200 grams
Fruits or veggies, puréed	1 cup	8.5 ounces	245 grams
Maple syrup or corn syrup	1 tablespoon	0.75 ounce	20 grams
Liquids: cream, milk, water, or juice	1 cup	8 fluid ounces	240 milliliters
Oats	1 cup	5.5 ounces	150 grams
Salt	1 teaspoon	0.2 ounces	6 grams
Spices: cinnamon, cloves, ginger, or nutmeg (ground)	1 teaspoon	0.2 ounce	5 milliliters
Sugar, brown, firmly packed	1 cup	7 ounces	200 grams
Sugar, white	1 cup/1 tablespoon	7 ounces/0.5 ounce	200 grams/12.5 grams
Vanilla extract	1 teaspoon	0.2 ounce	4 grams

OVEN TEMPERATURES

Fahrenheit	Celsius	Gas Mark
225°	110°	¼
250°	120°	½
275°	140°	1
300°	150°	2
325°	160°	3
350°	180°	4
375°	190°	5
400°	200°	6
425°	220°	7
450°	230°	8

Index